GIACOMO AGOSTINI

CHAMPION OF CHAMPIONS

MICK WALKER

DB PUBLISHING

First published in Great Britain in 2004 by
The Breedon Books Publishing Company Limited
Breedon House, 3 The Parker Centre,
Derby, DE21 4SZ.

This paperback edition published in Great Britain in 2013 by DB Publishing,
an imprint of JMD Media Ltd

Dedication

This book is dedicated to the rugged beauty and
peacefulness of Caithness in northern Scotland,
where I wrote the manuscript for *Giacomo
Agostini – Champion of Champions*.

ISBN 978-1-78091-217-2

Contents

Preface

THIS, THE second in a series intended to cover the careers of the world's greatest motorcycle racing champions, presents the man who has won the largest number of Grand Prix races and the most world titles, Giacomo Agostini.

The first in the series, *John Surtees: Motorcycle Maestro*, very much set the formula for the rest of the books to come. The second, *Giacomo Agostini: Champion of Champions*, is the biography of someone I have admired since I first raced against him at Mallory Park during the late 1960s. We were both born in the same year, 1942, but Giacomo is slightly my senior in the age stakes – and was much superior when it came to racing motorbikes!

Quite why no one has attempted to write a book on 'Ago' in the English language before is a great mystery to me. But I'm pleased they haven't as it gives me the chance to put matters right.

I was fortunate not only to have raced in the same era as Agostini, but also to have enjoyed contacts with many of the great Italian marques, not only MV Agusta, but also Ducati, Moto Guzzi and Cagiva; I acted for the latter three as their British representative at various times; I was also an MV dealer in the 1970s.

Compiling *Giacomo Agostini: Champion of Champions* was also made considerably easier by my many friends in the world of motorcycling and in this respect I would like to make special mention of Tommy Robb, Nobby Clark, the late Arthur Wheeler, Dan Shorey, John Surtees, Phil Read, the late Barry Sheene, Ian Welsh, George Paget and Bill Innoles.

The more one studies the achievements of Giacomo Agostini, the more one cannot fail to be impressed. As it was with John Surtees's unique bike and car world championship titles, so it is with Giacomo's incredible record-breaking number of GP wins and championships.

He began his racing career serving his apprenticeship aboard Moto Morini singles, then joined MV Agusta where he rode 350 and 500cc 3 and 4-cylinder models; then, in a move which surprised everyone, he joined Yamaha riding two-strokes for the first time. He stunned his critics when he immediately won his first race, no less an event than the Daytona 200. Even at the end of his career he managed to go out on a winning note, first with MV Agusta at the Nürburgring in 1976 (MVs last-ever GP appearance) and then a year later with a final victory on the Yamaha TZ 750 at Hockenheim.

I immensely enjoyed putting Giacomo Agostini's racing career on record, and hope you, the reader, will have as much enjoyment reading the finished work.

Mick Walker
Wisbech, Cambridgeshire

Chapter 1

Formative years

GIACOMO (pronounced Jack-o-mo) Agostini was born on 16 July 1942 at Brescia, a medium-sized town in northern Italy, but was brought up in the much smaller lakeside town of Lovere, near Bergamo. He then spent the remainder of his childhood years in Lovere, which is situated on the shores of Lake d'Iseo.

Giacomo was the oldest of four sons, the others being Gabriele, Mauro and the youngest Felice. Their parents, Amelio and Maria Vittoria, were well off and in many ways the Agostini family background was very similar to that other great champion of the same era, Mike Hailwood. But there was one big difference: whereas Stan Hailwood had always urged Mike on, Giacomo's parents did their best to persuade their eldest son not to go racing. But strangely, even though one father was deeply for and one was just as passionately against, both Hailwood and Agostini were to reach the very pinnacle of their chosen sport.

Early experiences

From an early age Giacomo was interested in motorcycles, if not always racing. He also learnt to ski – both on water and on snow – when he was

Giacomo Agostini was born on the 16 July 1942 at Brescia, a medium-sized town in northern Italy. Later his family moved to Lovere on the shores of Lake d'Iseo.

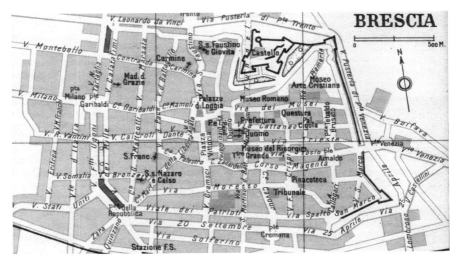

young. As far as motor vehicles are concerned, his first memories were of: 'a Vespa scooter that my father had as well as a car.' He goes on to recall: 'We lived in the country and, in those days, anyone could ride a 50cc machine on the roads in Italy – you didn't need a licence.' So when he was nine 'Mino', as his friends nicknamed him, was given a Bianchi moped. This was the Amalfi, with a 48cc two-stroke engine – actually it was virtually a conventional pedal-cycle with an engine!

A 1950s Vespa scooter similar to the one owned by Giacomo Agostini's father.

When he was 14 years old Giacomo was given a Parilla 125 motorcycle, but because this was not a moped he was not allowed to ride it on the public highway. Instead it was used off road. One day a school friend, Italo, persuaded the young Giacomo to enter a gymkhana event being organised locally in Lovere. But at first Giacomo refused, afraid 'that I would make a fool of myself.' However, after seeing a one-legged man signing on to take part in the competition, he said 'at least I can beat him and not finish last.'

When Giacomo reached 16, and was thus old enough to ride a motorcycle on public roads, his father Amelio bought him a Moto Guzzi Lodola. This was one of the original 175cc models that factory founder Carlo Guzzi had designed himself and used an overhead camshaft engine – later versions having a displacement of 235cc and pushrod operated valves.

It was this Guzzi which in many ways shaped Giacomo Agostini's subsequent racing career. On the 175cc Lodola, he learned many of his early riding skills on the road which bordered the lake and which went from Lovere to Costa Volpino. This stretch is cut out of solid rock, narrow and twisting in the extreme – a perfect place for the young Mino to race with his friends. But it is also a dangerous road and one day Giacomo nearly came to grief, as he was later to recall: 'I tried to overtake a lorry, but didn't have enough time and had to cut in between the lorry and its trailer.' However, it did teach him one important rule – never attempt the impossible.

The Parilla had also been retained and was by now being used in trials. Again, this early experience of off-road riding helped, as many other road racers have found down through the years, 'with my balance and appreciation of the various motorcycle controls and maintaining traction.'

Right from those first steps on the trail which would lead him, years later, to his record-breaking exploits, Giacomo Agostini always seemed to have an inner calmness. In fact Mike Hailwood was once to remark: 'He's the least Latin Italian you could ever meet. He never loses his head, never gets ruffled

Typical view of the mountainous country in northern Italy experienced by Giacomo as a youth. This photograph dates from 1954.

and never shouts and raves when things go wrong. His temperament is incredible; he takes everything good, or bad, in his stride and refuses to be moved to show any temper. I think that my attitudes were more "Italian" than his when we raced against each other. You can't help but like him.'

These qualities have played a vital role in Agostini's success, together with natural riding skills, a brain which plans with great precision and an ability to charm and not be overawed. Giacomo was, and still is, someone blessed with film-star good looks. Many such men are conceited; but not Giacomo Agostini. Even after he had become a many times world champion he was to remain much the same as he had been before he first came to the public's attention.

Of course, he is the first to admit that success is rewarding: 'I enjoy the fame. I enjoy the money and everything that goes with it.' But equally, when pressed, he says: 'But I also like peace and quiet. I like to be able to escape from time to time.' He was, and still is, someone who knows the importance of being able to relax.

Despite his calmness, Agostini was certainly not lacking in drive and ambition. When he was interviewed by journalist and racing enthusiast Ted Macauley in 1971 he said: 'All the time I feel I like to have an aim, something to be attracted to, something to master. I always wanted to race and when I finally achieved my ambition then I wanted to be a

Moto Guzzi 175 Lodola upon which Giacomo Agostini experienced much of his early riding at 16 years of age. On the Guzzi, he often rode from Lovere to Costa Volpino, near his home.

world champion. Now I have achieved that, I want to be the man who has been the champion the most number of times. Perhaps when I have passed the record I will have to change my job and set up another ambition.'

The mechanical side

When asked once if he was a good mechanic, Giacomo replied: 'Only average. When I raced the 175cc Morini I worked on the machine myself, helped by a friend who was a mechanic. I could do the normal routine jobs but he did the major overhauls.' Nevertheless, Giacomo did fully appreciate the importance of having his motorcycle set up properly so that he could give of his best. Legendary race mechanic and my friend, Nobby Clark, describes Giacomo Agostini as: 'totally professional in everything he does – second best is simply not good enough and this applies as much to the motorcycle as it did to his riding.'

Although his father was not keen for Giacomo to go racing, once he realised just how much his son wanted to do it – and what an excellent rider he was – the entire family closed ranks and gave him their blessing. In fact

Agostini's two boyhood racing heroes Carlo Ubbiali (3) and Tarquinio Provini (25). Both are seen here in 1959 aboard MV Agusta 250's. Little could Giacomo Agostini have realised that he would later score a record breaking 13 World Championship titles for the famous Italian marque.

Giacomo with his father Amelio and mother Maria Vittoria, together with his youngest brother Felice, circa late 1960s. By this time Giacomo's parents were fully supportive of his racing career.

the Agostini family has always been a close-knit affair. As an illustration of this, after becoming 500cc World Champion in 1966, Giacomo was interviewed by Mick Woollett for *Motor Cycling* at the end of that year. Not only revealing that he still lived with his parents in Lovere, but also in answer to the question: 'What will you do when you stop racing?' Giacomo replied: 'Well, I expect that I'll go into my father's business. He owns a transport [a lake ferry operation] and a road-building business and I worked for him for four or five years.'

In that same interview, another answer showed the then young Giacomo Agostini to be a thinking man's champion. Mick Woollett asked: 'what improvements would you like to see made to racing?' The reply was: 'I should like to see legislation aimed at eliminating oil from race circuits. Oil is the greatest hazard in racing and many riders have been killed because they skidded on lubricant dropped by another competitor. If you are really racing and happen to be the first one along after oil has been dropped you are almost certain to crash. At over 100mph you have little chance of seeing the oil and as soon as you hit it, you're off. I know because it happened to me at the East German GP when I was leading the 500cc race. I crashed at well over 100mph and am very lucky to be alive. Yet you still see machines on the starting line at World Championship races dripping oil. I would like to see a special official appointed to scrutineer bikes on the starting line. He should be empowered to ban any bike which he thinks is potentially dangerous. This would make racing safer for everyone – works men and private owners.'

As the following chapters reveal, Giacomo Agostini had all the right ingredients to be a great champion. Also, he was largely entirely able to handle the pressure that comes with the job. Later, as a team manager, he brought his skills to another important role in racing with both Yamaha and Cagiva. And finally, he has been an important link in the re-emergence of the legendary MV Agusta brand name, through the F4 Super Bike.

Chapter 2

Moto Morini

The Moto Morini Settebello (Seven of Diamonds) made its appearance back in 1955. And in 1961 it was the motorcycle which set Giacomo Agostini on his way in motorcycle sport – in hillclimbs rather than road racing.

LTHOUGH Giacomo Agostini's name will forever be associated with the magical marque of MV Agusta, with which 'Mino' was to win 13 of his record-breaking 15 World Championship titles, it was the tiny Moto Morini company which really set him on the road to success and glory. And of course today, with his world-wide fame, the reader might be forgiven for thinking everything had been planned and staged like some great military expedition. But of course the truth is somewhat different.

As revealed in the previous chapter the young Giacomo had learned to ride motorcycles near his home at Lovere on the shores of Lake d'Iseo in northern Italy. This is beautiful mountainous country with a maze of narrow twisting roads.

After witnessing his first motorcycle race meeting at Cesenatico in the summer of 1960, Giacomo Agostini was fired

In 1962 Giacomo Agostini took part in his first road race. He is seen here aboard a Moto Morini Settebello at the San Remo circuit on the Italian Riviera that year.

The 172cc (60 x 61mm) overhead valve Settebello engine with its steeply-inclined Dell'Orto SS1 carburettor.

with a great enthusiasm for the sport. However, his parents, and his father in particular, were against their eldest son taking up motorcycle sport. In fact, for his 18th birthday the present Giacomo would dearly have liked, a racing motorcycle, was a request his father flatly refused. But Giacomo was not to be denied, and he put down a deposit on a Moto Morini 175 Settebello with some savings he had. The Settebello was an ohv unit construction single, which was not only fast, but robust and simple to work on too.

Probably because of the mountainous terrain in the region where he lived, Giacomo Agostini's first truly competitive motorcycle event was a hill climb, and, using the 175 Settebello he had bought secretly, the youthful Giacomo surprised both spectators and his more experienced opponents by finishing

Moto Morini Settebello

The Moto Morini Settebello (seven of diamonds) was a series production machine intended for fast road work or junior (clubman's)-type racing events. It was derived from the 175 Turismo model which had made its debut on the company's stand at the international Milan Show in November 1952.

Both shared an overhead-valve single-cylinder engine with the 4-speed transmission and wet clutch in one neat unit. Primary drive was by gear. If the engine was well styled and well finished so was the frame, with a single front downtube and the engine forming a stressed member.

The near square bore and stroke dimensions of 60 x 61mm gave an exact displacement of 172.4cc. There were also enclosed Marzocchi-made telescopic front forks and rear shock absorbers from the same source.

However, in engine tune, carburettor size, brakes and weight, the Settebello was significantly different from its touring oriented brothers – and so was the performance. The cooking models were hard pushed to reach 70mph, whereas the Settebello could top 80mph in road guise and over 90mph with an open exhaust.

Introduced in time for the 1954 season, the Settebello proved an instant success both in production racing and sales charts. In standard 'over-the-counter' trim it came complete with clip-ons, high-lift camshaft, forged piston, larger valves, a Dell'Orto SS carburettor, conical brake hubs, alloy wheel rims, a bulbous 18-litre fuel tank, sprint saddle and lightweight spring steel mudguards. It came fully equipped for the street, but many served their time as racers rather than roadsters.

Besides Italy, the Settebello also proved very popular in France, where it won several titles over the years, well into the 1960s. But, of course, it was in its homeland that it had the most success, being ideally suited to Italian Formula Junior events, which included both road races and hillclimbs.

As described in the main text, Giacomo Agostini began his racing career with a Settebello in 1961, at first in hillclimbs and later in pure racing events. In many ways the little Moto Morini was an excellent bike for a racing novice, being both fast and reliable, its pushrod operated valves meaning it was also easier to work on and cheaper to maintain than a more complex and expensive overhead camshaft layout.

Formula 3 Aste Corte Settebello as used by Agostini in 1962 and part of 1963, with battery/coil ignition, Oldani brakes and Ceriani front forks.

Moto Morini

To trace the history of the Moto Morini marque, one has to go back to the period just prior to the outbreak of World War One in 1914. It was then that Alfonso Morini, after serving an apprenticeship with a local smithy, set up a tiny motorcycle repair workshop near his home in the central northern Italian town of Bologna.

Morini's workshop had already managed to create something of a reputation for good engineering work by the time he was called up for military service with the army in 1916. This, in turn, led directly to his gaining a posting to a car and motorcycle repair section at Padua.

The period in the service of the military provided Alfonso Morini with an excellent opportunity to widen his knowledge. When the cessation of hostilities came he was able to return to his Bologna workshop with sufficient experience to undertake a more ambitious business venture.

No longer satisfied by simply repairing machines, Morini realised that the time was ripe for manufacturing. To this end he enlisted Mario Mezzetti as a partner with very much the same enthusiasm and engineering skills as himself. The pair decided to pool their resources, and production of the first MM (Morini Mezzetti) began in 1924; this being powered by a 123cc single-cylinder two-stroke with a horizontal cylinder and 2-speed hand-change gearbox.

Soon the new machine was being entered in races, notably on the ultra-demanding Lario circuit near the Moto Guzzi works in Mandello del Lario on the shores of Lake Como. But without doubt, the victory that was to remain Morini's proudest moment came when he won his class in the 1927 Italian Grand Prix at Monza. After this triumph he left the riding to others.

During the early 1930s MM somehow survived during the awful years of the Depression, even finding the capital to finance their first four-stroke racer, a 174cc model with vertical cylinder and a single overhead camshaft, driven by an enclosed chain on the offside of the engine. This chain drive not only continued while the MM partnership lasted, but was a feature of Morini racing engine design right up to the 1950s. Among its many victories, the new 175 won the 1933 Italian GP – and also broke the world record for the flying kilo-

The Moto Morini factory in Bologna, very near the much bigger Ducati works.

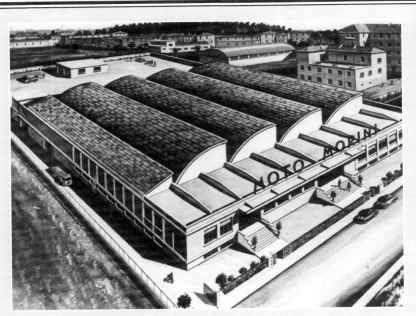

metre at over 100 mph. A 250cc version was also built, together with a larger 350cc model, on which Michele Mangione became 1938 Italian Senior Champion. However, this was the year that Morini broke away from the MM partnership.

Always something of an individualist, Alfonso Morini felt he needed to establish a factory of his own. However, his plan to build motorcycles had to wait until after World War Two. In fact, his company, Moto Morini, was one of the very first to put a new model on the market after the conflict. Going on sale in 1946, this was a robustly constructed 123.1cc (52 x 58mm) two-stroke single with piston port induction and a 3-speed unit construction engine with flywheel magneto ignition. A racing version soon followed.

One of the first riders to make a name for himself on the tiny Morini was novice Umberto Masetti, later to become a double 500cc world champion with Gilera. Another to enjoy early success on the Morini two-stroke was a young engineer by the name of Dante Lambertini. He was later to become head of the factory's race department, and the man largely responsible for the success achieved by the legendary 250cc dohc single raced by the likes of Tarquinio Provini and, of course, Giacomo Agostini.

Another achievement came when Moto Morini won the very first Italian Senior Championship (Masetti) for the 125cc class. However, with the arrival of the all-conquering FB Mondial twin-cam single in 1949, Morini soon switched to four-strokes. By the end of 1952 it appeared that Morini had everything worked out, as they beat rivals Mondial and MV in the final two rounds of the World Championship (in Italy and Spain). However, it was not to be, with the German NSU marque dominating the lightweight 125 and 250cc categories during 1953 and 1954.

For 1954 Moto Morini produced an enlarged 125, with which Emilio Mendogni won the 175cc Italian Senior title. Alfonso Morini then took the decision to switch his company's efforts from Grand Prix competition to production machine events. This led directly to the 175 ohv Settebello, the most sporting in a series of new models using the same basic engine. Described elsewhere in this chapter, the Settebello was responsible for setting Giacomo Agostini on the road to glory when he began his competitive motorcycling career in hill-climbing during 1961.

From the Settebello came the Rebello. However, the latter featured a chain-driven, sohc engine of particularly advanced design. Another feature was a 5-speed gearbox, which was exceedingly rare in those days, particularly for a sports model rather than a full GP bike.

The Rebello's engine (which shared the same 60 x 61mm bore and stroke dimensions as the Settebello) produced 22bhp and revved to over 9,000rpm; Morini claimed 105mph. A Rebello won the 1955 Milano-Taranto and Giro d'Italia (Tour of Italy) long distance road events, and also the latter in 1956. In fact, the machine proved itself such a fine all-round motorcycle that a larger (250cc) version with dohc was constructed for use in Grand Prix events. Again, this machine was to play a vital role in the progress of Giacomo Agostini's early career and is described in detail elsewhere in this chapter. The 250 Grand Prix dohc single ran for a decade, from 1957 through to 1967.

Alfonso Morini died in 1969, his place as head of the company being taken by his daughter Gabriella. From then on racing was to take a back seat, Moto Morini's main claim to fame in the 1970s being the arrival of the famous 3½ 350cc V-twin in touring and sport guises. In 1987 Moto Morini was acquired by the Castiglioni brothers who had entered the field of motorcycle manufacturers with Cagiva in 1978.

1963, and Giacomo Agostini aboard the Ducati 125 Formula 3 machine which supplemented his Moto Morini rides at the time.

second at Trento-Bondone, an event counting towards the Italian Hill Climb Championship series.

However, the results were published by both local and national newspapers – and when the Agostini family got to know the whole affair came out and that was Giacomo's only competitive event in 1961. In fact his wealthy father bought him an Alfa Romeo car – provided, as Giacomo says 'that I stopped.'

The next year, 1962, no one, not even his father, could prevent him pursuing what had now become a passion. Together with a couple of friends, who looked after the mechanical side, Giacomo began the season by winning hill climbs and at Bologna-San Luca he was spotted by no less than Alfonso Morini, boss of the famous Italian racing marque! So impressed was he with the Agostini style and verve that Morini offered him a factory-prepared 175 Settebello mount and so, after less than 10 events in total, Giacomo Agostini was a works rider.

In 1963 he tackled circuit racing for the first time. The result? Four races, four wins and the title of Italian Junior Champion on the Moto Morini 175. He also had the occasional outing on a Ducati 125 Formula 3 – on which he succeeded in having his first crash. In addition in the sport of hill climbing (popular at that time in northern Italy) Giacomo was virtually invincible, winning eight out of ten events and the national title.

Another machine which Giacomo rode during his early career was a Ducati 125 Formula 3. Together with the Moto Morini Settebello, the 125 (and 175cc) Ducati Formula 3's gave many Italian riders their first taste of competition during the late 1950s and early1960s.

Grand Prix debut

Towards the end of the 1963 season, as was the case every year at that time, came the Italian Grand Prix at Monza in early September. So Giacomo plucked up his courage and arranged an interview with the Morini boss at his office in Bologna – to ask for permission to ride one of the full GP models as used by works star Tarquinio Provini. The latter was then disputing that year's 250cc World Championship with Honda's Jim Redman. Alfonso Morini, after due consideration, said yes to Giacomo's request. The latter was so surprised that on his way out of the *Commandore's* office he knocked a typewriter off the desk!

At Monza, Giacomo immediately proved that his inclusion in the Moto Morini team for the event was fully justified, not only by showing up well during the qualifying period, but also on race day by leading the Grand Prix for three laps – in front of the world's top stars. Then, due to engine vibration, one of the footrests snapped and he was forced back, later to retire at the pits. But it had been an incredible display. How many other riders could boast that they had led their first ever GP? And when you study the first six riders to cross the finishing line of the 1963 Italian Grand Prix it is even more impressive:

1st	T. Provini (Moto Morini)
2nd	J. Redman (Honda)
3rd	L. Taveri (Honda)
4th	A. Shepherd (MZ)
5th	S. Malina (CZ)
6th	T. Robb (Honda)

Replacing Provini

The Monza performance had been enough to convince Alfonso Morini that not only was Giacomo Agostini a star of the future – but he was also an ideal man to replace Tarquinio Provini, who quit the Bologna team to join rivals Benelli at the end of 1963. So Giacomo was mounted on one of the fleet dohc Moto Morini singles for the 1964 season, to contest the Italian Senior Championship.

By mid-season Giacomo's performances had been so good that he was already beginning to attract the attention of motorcycle journalists not just from Italy, but from all around the world. The following news story from the British journal *Motor Cycle*, dated 30 July 1964, is typical:

Italy's old maestro and the new. Above is 31-year-old Tarquinio Provini, one of racing's most colourful and dashing riders ever. World 125cc champion in 1957 on an FB Mondial, he took the 250cc title the following year for MV Agusta. As a lone hand on the phenomenal Moto Morini single last year, he very nearly snatched the 250cc crown from Jim Redman's Honda four. No one expected Italy to throw up another star so bright, so soon. Yet she has. When Provini transferred to the Benelli four this season, 22-year-old Giacomo Agostini (below) took over the Moto Morini. Already he has ended Provini's three-year reign as Italian champion, breaking many of his lap records on the way. In his very first race on a pukka grand prix machine (rather than a sports racer) at Monza last September, Agostini

Alfonso Morini (right), the man who first spotted Giacomo Agostini's riding talents. He is seen here with the company's chief engineer, Dante Lambertini.

harassed Redman and Provini until forced to call at his pit at half distance. The recent West German Grand Prix was his first race outside Italy. He finished fourth in the shadow of Mike Duff's Yamaha, comfortably ahead of Provini. That's star class and no mistake.

There is no doubt that Giacomo Agostini's showing in the 1964 Italian 250 Senior Championship was truly impressive. Right from the off he was determined to stamp his authority on the event. The first round came at an international meeting at Modena, in late March. The 250cc event at Modena was, as the *Motor Cycle News* race report dated 25 March 1964 recalled, 'completely dominated' by the 'Old Morinis on which Provini won the race last year.' These bikes (ridden by Silvio Grassetti and Giacomo Agostini) featured the conventional 2-valve set-up, as the new 3-valve and twin carburettor layout was not ready in time. Even though Giacomo had suffered a practice crash, this did not affect his performance as he won at record speed and set a new lap record, which at 76.53mph was actually faster than that set by Mike Hailwood when winning the 500cc race on a four-cylinder MV Agusta!

A week later Giacomo repeated his Modena win in the second round of

Giacomo Agostini was signed by Alfonso Morini to contest the Italian Senior Championship series in 1963. He is seen here during the Shell Gold Cup at Imola in April that year aboard the DOHC Gran Premio single.

the Italian Senior Championship at Riccione. After this came another victory at a new 2.1-mile circuit at Cervia, near Ravena on the Italian Adriatic coast, in mid-April. This was the third round of the national championship. Yet again Giacomo Agostini came out on top. And again his winning speed of 73mph was faster than the 500cc race winner (Emilio Mendogni riding an MV four).

Imola Gold Cup

Some 50,000 spectators turned up at Imola for the annual international Gold Cup meeting. And, riding the latest 3-valve Moto Morini, Giacomo led the 250cc race from beginning to end. He was never seriously challenged, eventually winning the 23-lap, 71.7-mile race at a record speed of 89.133mph and setting a new lap record of 90.141mph. Besides second man Tarquinio Provini on the four-cylinder Benelli, Agostini lapped the entire field. The top six finishers were:

The old and the new. Tarquinio Provini (right) explaining some of the difficult points of racing at Monza to Morini new boy Giacomo Agostini on the eve of the Italian GP in September 1963.

1st	G. Agostini (Moto Morini)
2nd	T. Provini (Benelli)
3rd	R. Torras (Bultaco)
4th	R. Bryans (Honda)
5th	S. Malina (CZ)
6th	G. Milani (Aermacchi)

Again, it is worth noting that Giacomo's race average and fastest lap were quicker than the 350cc race winner (Jim Redman, Honda four).

Cesenatico on the Adriatic coast had, of course, been the venue for Giacomo Agostini's first view of motorcycle racing back in 1960 – and a

Moto Morini 250 Grand Prix

Giacomo Agostini's first experience of a full blown GP bike was with Alfonso Morini's two-fifty dohc single. Seen by many as one of the truly great motorcycle designs of all time, it had its origins in the early 175 Morinis, the Settebello (ohv) and Rebello (sohc).

The two-fifty's first race came at no less an event than the 1957 Italian Grand Prix. Ranged against a horde of pukka works entries from the likes of FB Mondial, MV Agusta and Moto Guzzi, Morini rider Emilio Mendogni lay third for some considerable time, before being finally forced out through a minor technical problem. Following this impressive showing, Alfonso Morini immediately authorised an extensive development programme which was to see the design emerge as a major contender for honours during the first half of the 1960s.

The original prototype two-fifty engine used by Mendogni featured dohc driven by chain (as on the 175 Rebello). However, tests soon proved that a system with spur pinion drive was superior in several respects. The actual displacement was identical in both engines: 246.667cc (69 x 66mm), with maximum power of 30bhp at 10,000rpm. Running on a compression ratio of 9.5:1, the engine featured a special steel connecting rod – the latter being heavily webbed at both the big and small-end eyes. The big-end bearing consisted of a series of hardened steel rollers retained within an aluminium cage. Large diameter valves employed hairpin springs. Carburetion was courtesy of a 30mm (1³⁄₁₆in) Dell'Orto SSI instrument with a remotely mounted float chamber, while engine lubrication was taken care of by a double-gear pump. The crankshaft featured internal circular flywheels and rotated on a trio of main bearings, one for the timing side, and two for the primary drive side. Both the primary drive gears and the multi-plate clutch were contained within an oil bath.

Two ignition systems were employed – one version of the machine was fitted with a magneto; the other had a dual contact breaker (on the off side), a battery and twin ignition coils. After extensive testing, the latter system proved superior. Both systems employed two sparking plugs.

Like that of the Rebello, the gearbox of the 250GP was 5-speed and a built-in unit with the engine. The frame and cycle parts also showed strong Rebello influence. However, the front brake had been updated, with a more powerful double-sided Amadoro-made assembly having been fitted in place of the original conical single-sided type. Dry weight at that stage of development was 113kg (249lb).

Intense work took place and, precisely 12 months to the day, Morini burst back on the international stage with a sensational victory in the 1958 250cc Italian Grand Prix.

The latest power unit, now producing 32bhp and with gear-driven dohc, featured a host of changes compared to the original engine – not least of which was a 6-speed transmission. Two entries were made at Monza in September 1958, with Mendogni being joined by Gianpiero Zubani. Mendogni led all the way and won comfortably, while teammate Zubani finally took the runner-up spot after a wheel-to-wheel race-long battle with MV's number one Carlo Ubbiali. During this hectic tussle, Zubani also set the fastest lap of the race at 106.30mph.

The following year, 1959, seemed full of promise for the Morini team, especially as it had also signed its first foreign rider, Englishman Derek Minter. However, although the Bologna factory pursued an active role in entering its riders in both international and national events throughout that year, successes were few and far between. This was because both MV Agusta and the East German MZ marque had new bikes with higher power outputs.

It was thus something of a shock therefore that Tarquinio Provini quit MV at the end of the year to join Morini – becoming their sole rider – as Mendogni, Zubani and Minter did not have their contracts renewed. This was largely for cost reasons – because of both the large amount (at least for such a small concern as Morini) being paid to Provini, and the need to concentrate resources on their new star rider.

Although Provini got a rostrum position (third) in the Isle of Man TT, his and Morini's activities in 1960 were largely confined to the Italian domestic scene.

The main reason for this was that a considerable test programme was being carried out. To provide the reader with a greater insight of how these tests were often conducted in the era, the following description is how one journalist reported the proceedings at the time:

> The Morini factory – situated very close to Ducati in Bologna – are working flat out to get their machines ready for the early Italian events. A few days ago one of our 'spies' spotted their race van on the approach road to the autostrada near Bologna. It was parked by the roadside and Provini was there with no fewer than four works machines, blasting up and down the road!

This period of intense burning of the midnight oil was to prove its worth over the following years, when the Moto Morini 250GP emerged as one of the truly great racing motorcycles. This was not so much because of its engine power, but because it was a complete package: reliability, speed, 'leech-like' handling (as Giacomo Agostini once described it), powerful brakes, wonderfully efficient streamlining and exceptionally low weight.

With Provini's great experience, the combination of man and machine was slowly moulded to form a dynamic partnership: in 1961 and 1962 Morini won the Senior Italian Championship and enjoyed several notable foreign successes. Alfonso Morini then authorised a bid to be made on the World Championship series in 1963. This has to be viewed in context: Morini was a man who had strongly stated that he was 'not interested in racing outside of the Italian borders'. But even though the boss was clearly of the opinion that his motorcycle now stood a chance, even he, in his wildest dreams, could not have imagined just how close the finish would be in the 10-round 1963 250cc World Championship.

After a full season of racing, a certain amount of bad luck (cancellation of the French round due to poor weather conditions; mechanical trouble in Holland; and the inability to obtain a visa for East Germany) and, fatally, the

In mid-July 1964 Giacomo Agostini achieved a long-standing ambition of racing abroad - in no lesser event than the West German Grand Prix at Solitude. He put up a tremendous showing, finally finishing fourth behind Jim Redman (Honda) and the Yamaha pairing of Phil Read and Mike Duff.

decision not to contest the Isle of Man TT, Tarquinio Provini still finished runner-up to the existing 250cc World Champion, Jim Redman, and his mighty four-cylinder Honda. Moreover, he lost the title by a mere two points! The vital difference was that Redman competed in the TT (which he won) and also the East German round.

However, Provini and Moto Morini had the enormous satisfaction of soundly beating the Honda man at Monza; over the tortuous Montjuich Park circuit in Barcelona; at the ultra-fast Hockenheim track in West Germany; and over the rough Buenos Aires Autodrome in Argentina, thus proving the great adaptability of the design. In addition, Provini took the Italian domestic title once more. Behind the scenes, however, something of a disagreement had developed between Provini and Moto Morini's chief engineer, Ing. Dante Lambertini. This was to result in Provini's decision to join Benelli at the end of that year.

Then it was the turn of the young Giacomo Agostini to become the Bologna factory's number one – and in the process win the 1964 Italian Championship title, beating Provini on the four-cylinder Benelli. Ago left to join MV Agusta, and Morini had a couple of years with only occasional participation in racing, with riders such as Bruno Spaggiari and Silvio Grassetti, before they returned to win the Italian title once more, with the up-and-coming Angelo Bergamonti in the saddle. This final success was a fitting tribute to Morini, as the man who had been instrumental in founding not one but two Italian marques (the other

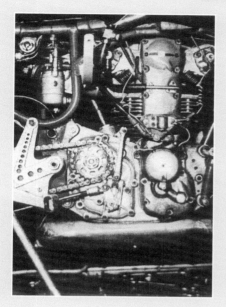

being the MM factory), died shortly thereafter in 1969.

The final development of the super-fast double overhead camshaft Moto Morini single, which Bergamonti rode to glory in 1967, had seen some 6bhp and 500rpm added since the original prototype had been ridden by Mendogni a decade before at Monza. During this time, the bore and stroke dimensions had been changed to 72 x 61mm, giving a new capacity of 248.36cc. Lambertini, assisted by fellow engineer Biavati (the latter having come from the FB Mondial race shop and specialising in cylinder-head work) had created a master-piece. In the process many things had been tested. For example, Biavati had constructed an experi-mental desmodromic valve system, which was ultimately rejected, as were both 3 and 4-valve cylinder heads. Actually, as is often the case, simplicity proved the best, and the engines which won championships for Provini, Agostini and finally Bergamonti were of the conventional 2-valve type.

What proved of the greatest value in Moto Morini's success was the atten-tion to detail and continuous testing, both on the bench and on the race circuit. It was this, above all else, which not only provided the extra horsepower, but gave the overall design its completeness and, of course, its superb reliability.

The fantastic two-fifty Moto Morini engine. At its peak it produced some 36bhp and could reach speeds of around 140mph.

The lifelike Protar model kit of the fabulous twin cam Moto Morini Grand Prix single, as raced by Provini and Giacomo Agostini.

Tarquinio Provini shaking hands with Giovanni Benelli after signing for the Pesaro factory in late 1963. However, his replacement at the Morini team Giacomo Agostini had the satisfaction of beating Provini to the Italian Senior Championship title in 1964.

mere four years later he made a triumphant return to win over the 2.5-mile circuit. The young Moto Morini rider was a clear winner – in fact the fight for second place was where the action came. Tarquinio Provini (Benelli) held second place for a while but was overtaken by Alan Shepherd (MZ) until both the Italian four and East German twin cried 'enough'. With Provini and Shepherd out of the race, second spot eventually went to Gilberto Milani (Aermacchi) after fighting off Ramon Torras (Bultaco) and Bruce Beale (Honda). For the record Giacomo Agostini's winning average speed was 81.95mph; and he also set a new lap record at 83.88mph.

Many of the top 250cc riders then quit the Italian scene to do battle in the first round of the 1964 Grand Prix season at Montjuich Park, Barcelona, Spain. With Provini winning on the Benelli four, Giacomo probably thought he should have been there. Instead he was forced to stay in Italy and concentrate on domestic racing. The fifth round of the Italian Senior Championship came at the end of May at the Vallelunga circuit, just north of Rome; the meeting was christened the Rome Grand Prix. The 250cc event became a duel between Giacomo's Moto Morini and the four-cylinder Honda of Jim Redman. But the local crowd's hopes that the Italian rider would repeat his victories of the first four rounds were shattered when the Moto Morini star fell at the halfway stage (caused by an engine seizure), when ahead of the World Champion. Luckily Giacomo was not injured, but he was out of the race and Redman went on to an easy win ahead of Aermacchi-mounted Gilberto Milani.

The Agostini/Moto Morini combination got back to winning ways in the sixth round of the Italian series at San Remo, with an easy victory over Luigi Taveri (Honda) and Milani (Aermacchi), with a race speed of 65.08mph and a fastest lap of 67.70mph.

Abroad for the first time

In mid-July 1964, Giacomo Agostini finally got his wish granted to take part in a meeting outside the Italian borders. This came at Solitude, in the seventh round of the 250cc World Championship series, the West German Grand Prix. The tree-lined circuit near Stuttgart was a particularly testing venue. Anxious to show up well at the highest level, Giacomo led the race for a while and eventually finished fourth. It was generally agreed by everyone fortunate enough to see the race that it was, as *Motor Cycle News* described, 'fabulous.' From half distance of the 11-lap, 78.036-mile race, Jim Redman and eventual winner Phil Read dominated. But as *MCN* went on to say:

> ... the battle between Phil and Jim completely overshadowed the blistering dicing that went on behind them. Giacomo Agostini, riding the incredibly fast single-cylinder Morini in a world classic for the first time this season, held third place for five laps but Mike Duff (Yamaha) was soon on his tail and then went ahead. But there was no shaking off the game Italian, who did everything he could to hold Mike on the faster machine. His cornering was fantastic – until he got into a king-size drift which nearly brought him down at the left-hander after the start.

But with the Moto Morini policy of not wishing to support GP racing, Giacomo was then forced to sit out the weeks from his appearance in Germany until almost two months later and the Italian Grand Prix at Monza. This was because the six-round Italian Senior Championship had already been concluded (with Ago walking away with the title, having won five out of the six races) – and in any case much of Italy comes to a halt for its annual holidays from mid-July until the end of August.

Monza

Monza 1964 was the venue for the debut of Honda's mighty RC164 six-

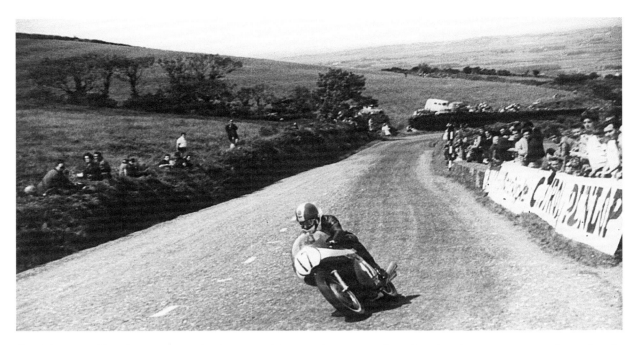

Provini approaching the
Gooseneck on the works
four-cylinder Benelli 250,
Lightweight TT, June 1964.

cylinder two-fifty. And it was also the decider in a season-long battle between Redman (Honda) and Read (Yamaha). The *Motor Cycle News* race report dated 16 September 1964 takes up the story:

> *Redman made a fantastic start. The acceleration of his six cylinder machine was terrific! Losing a few yards at the start Phil Read was hard after him with Giacomo Agostini, on the single cylinder Morini, third. In view of the multi-cylindered opposition, Agostini's ride was terrific, for at the finish 77.88 miles later, he was just 23.6 seconds down on the winner in fourth place.*

The top six finishers were:

1st	P. Read (Yamaha)
2nd	M. Duff (Yamaha)
3rd	J. Redman (Honda)
4th	G. Agostini (Moto Morini)
5th	A. Shepherd (MZ)
6th	L. Taveri (Honda)

After his performances during the 1964 season, there could be absolutely no doubt that in Giacomo Agostini Italy had its greatest potential rider for many a long year. Just how much potential there really was became clear

over the next few months. But the immediate decision that the gifted youngster had to make as 1964 came to a close was whether to stay with Moto
Morini, or to move on to a team with which he could display his undoubted
talents on the world stage. Really, there was only one answer.

Chapter 3

Signing for MV Agusta

GIACOMO AGOSTINI'S career received a major boost when it was revealed, towards the end of January 1964, that the highly promising former Moto Morini youngster had been signed up by Count Domenico Agusta, to join the MV racing team and partner the legendary Mike Hailwood. This news did not come as much of a surprise in Italy, as many observers had already marked Agostini out as someone who could go all the way to the top, after a string of outstanding performances during 1964.

So why had Giacomo decided to switch from the marque he had been involved with since the very beginning of his career, Moto Morini? One reason given at the time, notably by the Italian press corps, was, as Giacomo was heard to remark: 'that Morini is, once again, to concentrate its efforts entirely on Italian domestic meetings.' However, 'I [Agostini] am keen to have a crack at the World Championship – and I had started negotiations with other Italian factories interested in racing.'

Motor Cycling was able to report in its 6 February 1965 issue: 'MV have also signed Italy's reigning 250cc champion, brilliant 22-year-old Giacomo Agostini who shattered all opposition – including Tarquinio Provini – last year on a Morini.' The report went on to reveal that 'Agostini will contest both 350 and 500cc World Championships – in his first full GP season – which argues that MV are confident that their 350 is a match for Honda.' It was also reported that other MV teamsters for 1965 were Mike Hailwood (350/500cc) and Bruno Spaggiari (who was to ride the still experimental 125cc disc valve two-stroke single designed by German engineer Peter Durr).

By mid-February Giacomo was testing the five-hundred MV four at Modena (often used as a test circuit by the company since the mid-1950s). Hot on the heels of this news came the first photographs of a brand new

Count Domenico Agusta (left, sunglasses) with his new signing Giacomo Agostini.

MV introduced their new 3-cylinder machine in the 350cc class for the 1965 season. With four valves per cylinder the dohc engine displaced 349.2cc (55 x 49mm) and revved to over 12,000rpm and produced almost 60 bhp.

three-fifty 3-cylinder. The newcomer was appreciably lower and lighter than the already well-known 500 four. As the photographs revealed, two exhaust pipes were on the near (left) side, with the third pipe on the off (right) side. Actually in size and weight the new machine was much more akin to the now discarded 250 twin, rather than the heavyweight four.

A debut crash

While teammate Mike Hailwood jetted off to Daytona International Speedway, the home of the first round of the World Championships, where he won at a canter on his 500 MV (there was no 350 class), Giacomo Agostini stayed in Italy and made his race debut for MV at Modena. And as *Motor Cycling's* headline, from the 27 March 1965 issue, said: 'Last lap crash didn't stop Agostini.' The report continued 'In a race held in wet, torturous conditions, MVs new signing, despite a last lap spill which left his MV four with a grazed fairing and battered exhaust megaphones on the left side of the 500 MV, still made a winning start.'

Modena's circuit length was 2.47 miles to a lap – the race being 29 laps,

Mike Hailwood, seen here on one of the heavyweight MV 500 fours was Giacomo Agostini's team-mate in 1965. The two men remained great friends even after Mike joined Honda for the 1966 season.

a total of 68.48 miles. Giacomo was able to restart immediately after his crash, but it was something of an embarrassment for all concerned. The unfortunate incident occurred when he was overtaking a back marker through the chicane after the finishing straight and was forced onto the grass before crashing out.

Modena was the first round of the 1965 Italian Senior Championship series; with the poor weather no records were broken. The circuit, actually part of an army camp, had also had its surface damaged by tank drivers during the close season!

A week later, Giacomo more than made amends for his Modena crash, with *Motor Cycling's* headline reading 'Agostini beats Mike Hailwood', while *Motor Cycle News* said 'Mike the bike is beaten!' This was the first time for two years that Mike and his MV four had been vanquished in a 500cc race.

Both the MV works riders had cleared off from the rest of the field right from the start of the 34-lap, 68.9-mile race and steadily

Giacomo (right) with Mike Hailwood and, centre, MV team manager Nello Pagani; circa 1965. Mike and Giacomo shared a long and deep friendship.

The twin-cylinder Bianchi was still a challenger to the 350 and 500cc MV's in 1965, at least in Italy; even though the motorcycle division was about to close. This picture shows Remo Venturi on the larger Bianchi.

began to lap the entire field. Giacomo then found the right line through one bunch of back markers, whereas Hailwood was baulked and lost ground. Mike then put in a record lap of 74.69mph, in an attempt to catch his new teammate, but with a fading front brake the Englishman came home at the end of the race just over 11 seconds behind the Italian, the latter setting up a new race record of 72.52mph – beating the old figure set up by Remo Venturi (Bianchi) by 1.28mph.

A question mark

Prior to his victory over Mike at Riccione, many wondered if Giacomo Agostini would ever ride an MV again, after his debut crash at Modena. In fact, right up to the last minute a big question mark hung over his entry at Riccione – with a simple 'X' instead of his name in the race programme. In fact cynical commentators said that Hailwood had allowed him to win! However, this was incorrect – and as Mike was to comment later: 'Giacomo deserved his victory.'

MV Agusta, the history

Meccanica Verghera began trading in 1945, following an idea hatched by Count Domenico Agusta in late 1943 to design and build an ultra-lightweight 98cc two-stroke motorcycle, powered by a single-cylinder engine with piston-port induction. Initially equipped with 2-speeds, an extra ratio was added before production commenced. The newcomer was to have been called the 'Vespa' (wasp), but Piaggio got in first and registered the name for their new scooter, so Agusta's machine became simply an 'MV' when Domenico changed the name of the company to Meccanica Verghera (after the place where its production facilities were sited).

Interest in motorcycle sport in that area of northern Italy (a few kilometres west of Milan, and near the Monza autodrome) meant that a sports version of the 98cc model was soon built. With 6hp, it could reach a maximum speed of 56mph and it was often successful during the 1946 and 1947 seasons. In 1948, with 125cc racing becoming extremely popular in Italy and other European countries, MV brought out their own 125, a two-stroke with a heavily finned cylinder head and equipped with a 4-speed gearbox. Its introduction brought them into contact for the first time with two of the top names in the class, Moto Morini and FB Mondial. In that first year, however, MV's two rivals usually came out on top. However, at the Italian Grand Prix, held at Faenza because Monza was still to be repaired after war damage, the tables were turned and Franco Bertoni gave the Count his first ever race victory.

The Agusta family during the early 1950s: Countess Giuseppina Agusta with her four sons (left to right), Corrado (the youngest and only one still alive), Domenico, Vincenzo and Mario.

Another milestone was reached when MV built its first four-stroke – a 250cc ohv single with very British lines. Its long-stroke 63 x 80mm bore and stroke dimension assured that this was very much a touring, rather than a sporting, mount. But Count Agusta had set himself higher targets and during the close season of 1949–50 first Arturo Magni and then Ing. Piero Remor were persuaded to join MV from Gilera, Magni having been chief mechanic and

Remor chief designer at the famous Arcore factory. Remor had been the man behind Gilera's post-war 500 four-cylinder GP racer. And, helped by Magni, Remor built a new five-hundred four-cylinder racer for MV. But because it was virtually a carbon copy of the Gilera, Remor gave it three new features – shaft final drive, torsion bar suspension fore and aft, and gear-change pedals on either side. It was these new features which proved the design's failing and Remor soon left the company.

After Englishman Les Graham (the 1949 500cc World Champion riding an AJS) was signed at the end of 1950, a series of improvements were introduced. One of the first, at the beginning of 1951, was the fitment of a telescopic front fork, while conventional rear suspension legs replaced the torsion bars and conventional gear-change operation on one side of the machine only. However, the parallelogram (double) swinging arm was retained. Additionally, reliability proved a major problem.

These glitches saw the design extensively re-engineered for 1952 by Mario Montoli and Mario Rossi, with assistance from Arturo Magni. Most notably, the engine was extensively redesigned, being given 53 x 56.4mm bore and stroke dimensions (from the existing 125cc dohc single), compared to the outgoing square 54 x 54mm. Allied to other improvements, including four instead of two carburettors, power rose to 56bhp at 10,500rpm. Moreover, an entirely new crankcase featuring a 5-speed gearbox and chain instead of shaft final drive was a great improvement. There was also a new duplex frame, together with a single rear fork-type swinging. That year MV won their first world title (the 125cc) thanks to another Englishman, Cecil Sandford.

In 1953 number one rider Les Graham was killed instantly during the Senior TT. Just a couple of days earlier he had debuted a new 349.3cc (47.5 x 49.3mm) four in the Junior race. Count Agusta was so shocked and saddened by the death of Les Graham, that the four-cylinder models hardly made any appearances for the remainder of the year, although Carlo Bandirola gave the new three-fifty its first victory at a non-championship race at Schotten in Germany that summer.

But in reality it was not until 1956 that MV really came good in the bigger classes, with the signing of John Surtees. 'Big John', as he was known, went on to give MV seven world titles before his two-wheel retirement at the end of 1960. The other rider during the same era who enjoyed equal success on MVs was Carlo Ubbiali, who had the same number of MV world championship GP victories (37) as Surtees, but gained one more title; Ubbiali's successes all came in the 125 and 250cc classes.

A six-cylinder 500 debuted at the end of 1957, but was only raced once (by John Hartle) in 1958. Meanwhile, on the production front, MV, like the rest of the Italian motorcycle industry, found that sales nosedived as the 1950s turned into the 1960s. However, the company was not too badly affected by this downturn, thanks to Agusta's booming aviation division.

In racing after 1961, MV largely quit the smaller classes, thereafter concentrating on the 350 and 500cc machines, first with Gary Hocking, then Mike Hailwood and, from the beginning of the 1965 season, Giacomo Agostini. Fervently patriotic, Count Agusta achieved his greatest ambition when an Italian rider won the 350 and 500 World Championships on MV machines. With Mike Hailwood leaving to join the Japanese Honda marque for 1966, Giacomo took over as the number one – going on to win 13 titles with the Italian firm and two more with Yamaha. The MV Agusta racing record is an impressive one: 275 Grand Prix victories, 38 World rider titles, and 37 World manufacturers' titles.

Any remaining doubt over 'Ago' continuing as an MV teamster came to an end when both Mike Hailwood and Giacomo turned up to race in the third round of the Italian championships at Cervia on 10 April. The final placings in the 35-lap, 73.9-mile race were:

1st	M. Hailwood (MV Agusta)
2nd	G. Agostini (MV Agusta)
3rd	S. Grassetti (Bianchi)
4th	G. Mandolini (Moto Guzzi)
5th	R. Pasolini (Aermacchi)
6th	F. Stastny (Jawa)

Dashing straight to Italy after winning a 500cc race at Snetterton in Norfolk (riding a private Norton), Mike Hailwood then flew to Milan airport and drove the 200 miles to Imola, arriving just in time to climb aboard his works MV. Too late for practice, he was then forced to start at the back of the grid and in his eagerness to get through the pack and into the lead, which he did during the first lap, Hailwood overshot a bend and, although he did not come off, lost a good deal of ground.

This left teammate Giacomo Agostini, on his MV, to take the lead. Hailwood got back into the race and rode magnificently to overhaul the entire field yet again, and recapture the lead from Agostini during the 17th lap of a wet, dismal race. At the end Giacomo was six seconds behind the English World Champion.

Giacomo Agostini finishing runner-up behind Mike Hailwood at the 1965 Dutch TT. His machine is one of the heavyweight 500 fours, a motorcycle which Giacomo openly said he disliked; certainly compared to the three-cylinder model.

The highlight of the meeting, at least for Giacomo, was being able to take the new 350 triple out during practice, but it was not raced as there was no 350cc event.

Redman through hedge at Nürburgring

The 28 April 1965 issue of *Motor Cycle News* carried the headline: 'Redman through hedge at Nürburgring', going on to report 'The West German Grand Prix began dramatically when world champion Jim Redman and his 350 Honda four hurtled through a hedge while trying to catch Giacomo Agostini, on a new MV three, at the Nürburgring on Saturday.'

Agostini's victory was undoubtedly the highlight of the 28th international Eifel races, promoted to World Championship status for the first time. The only world-championship meeting to feature all six classes until the Isle of Man TT that year, the West German GP was staged on the shorter 4.8-mile southern 'loop' circuit in the Eifel mountains.

Bad weather, which was later to deteriorate into the worst-ever for a world title sidecar race, did not deter 120,000 spectators from watching the two-day meeting, with 125cc and 350cc races on Saturday, and the 50cc, 250cc, 500cc and sidecar races on Sunday.

In describing the 350cc race, Peter Howdle of *Motor Cycle News* had this to say:

> *Seldom has the appearance of a new machine proved so sensational. The MV 3 was on the front row, Agostini alongside Redman on his Honda. Practice times gave no clue; the MV was an unknown quantity. The fact that Hailwood's had blown up in the morning practice wasn't too encouraging. Mike wheeled out an old MV 4, starting from the back of a line-up of 48 riders. Redman made a scintillating start. But Agostini was right there with him, slipstreaming him at the end of the first lap, with Hailwood in third spot. First casualty was Russian Nicolai Sevastianov. He came off his Vostock 4 and rode back to the pits with a broken collarbone.*

The pace was hot at the front, with every one of the 120,000 spectators too busy watching the incredible duel between Redman and Agostini to take notice of anything else. For eight laps Redman led, with the young Italian and his untried triple looking as if he was glued to Redman's tail.

A scrap for fourth place between Jawa riders Franta Stastny and Gustav Havel ended when one of the former's pistons seized. By then the lap record had fallen time and time again, as the two leaders 'orbited the circuit lapping

The 500 four-cylinder MV was a large, heavy machine. And largely unchanged from the late 1950s except for a 6-speed gearbox.

riders left, right and centre in the struggle for supremacy' as reporter Howdle described the action.

On lap nine Giacomo took the lead and began pulling away, with Hailwood some two minutes behind Redman. Then, on lap 16, Redman reduced the gap – he was really trying. Then came drama: as the Honda star chased Agostini down to Mullenbach and then uphill through the forest, light rain began to fall. Suddenly Redman skidded. He took to the grass, hanging on desperately. But an accident was inevitable and he and his Honda parted company and crashed into a hedge.

And so it was that a piece of Grand Prix history was made, with Giacomo Agostini romping home to win a sensational race in which he lapped everyone save an oil-soaked Hailwood – and he was some three miles behind after the 20-lap, 96.2-mile event.

Agostini had won his first ever Grand Prix for the MV Agusta team; and the brand new 350 triple had won the first time out. What a day – and one which Giacomo Agostini still looks back on as one of the greatest and most satisfying victories of his entire career. The first six places were:

1st	G. Agostini (MV Agusta 3)
2nd	M. Hailwood (MV Agusta 4)
3rd	G. Havel (Jawa)
4th	R. Pasolini (Aermacchi)
5th	E. Klisa (Vostock)
6th	E. Driver (AJS)

Read's view

Phil Read (later to create much controversy when a teammate of Giacomo's,

Jim Redman, the 1965 350cc World Champion; but the Honda team captain only secured the title at the final round in Japan after Giacomo Agostini's bike went sick.

Jim Redman

Jim Redman quit Grand Prix racing after breaking his arm while racing one of the new Honda five-hundred four-cylinder models against Agostini's equally new larger three-cylinder model in torrential rain during the 1966 Belgian Grand Prix at Spa Francorchamps. Since the time he first joined Honda in 1960, Jim had proved a vital link in the company's growth to dominate much of Grand Prix racing during the early and mid-1960s.

Originally from England, but soon moving to Rhodesia (now Zimbabwe), Jim Redman, born on 8 November 1931, was in many ways the ultimate racing professional. Having first come to Europe during the late 1950s – with his own Ducati 125 Grand Prix dohc single and a brace of Manx Nortons – he was to display the cool, calculated approach which was to characterise his career. Crashes were infrequent, Jim believing that 'you have to finish a race to win it!' Certainly this is a formula needed to win season-long championship titles – finish every race in the highest possible position.

Honda needed just such a man, and the result was that Jim Redman became, in effect, the Honda Grand Prix team captain. His chance to join Honda as a full-time member of the team had come after the death of Australian Bob Brown at Solitude, the venue of the 1960 West German Grand Prix, although Redman had already ridden one of the Japanese 125 twins at Assen, Holland, finishing fourth. His debut on the larger 250 four came in August 1960 during the Ulster GP, Jim coming home third behind race winner Carlo Ubbiali (MV) and Honda teammate Tom Phillis. But that year (Honda's first full year in Europe) the Japanese marque were not the dominant force they were in later years, with Ubbiali and MV taking both the 125 and 250cc titles.

In 1961 Jim Redman's first GP victory came aboard one of the revised fours at the Belgian GP, followed later that year by another win, this time at the Italian round. He finished the season third in the 250cc class and fourth in the 125cc, already showing championship potential. During 1962 he won six of the 10 rounds counting towards the 250cc championship, thus winning the title; he also finished runner-up (behind Luigi Taveri) in the 125cc class. But the real surprise was his second title that year in the 350cc category on a larger four-cylinder model.

He repeated his title success in 1963, although in the 250cc series he was given a fight all year by Tarquinio Provini's dohc Moto Morini single. In 1964 his main challenge came from Phil Read (Yamaha), with the Englishman ultimately coming out on top, gaining five wins to Redman's three in the 11-round series. Redman scored his third 350cc crown, winning all eight rounds.

Then came 1965 and the arrival of new boy Agostini at MV. But even Ago and teammate Mike Hailwood could not stop Redman taking his sixth – and, as it happened – last world title on a combination of 349cc four-cylinder and the new 296cc six-cylinder Hondas.

At the beginning of 1966, Redman took the new four-cylinder Honda to victory in the first round of the 500cc World Championship at Hockenheim, with Agostini second. In the Isle of Man it was Hailwood first, Ago second. The third round at Assen saw Redman victorious with the Italian again runner-up. Then came that fateful day in Belgium, the crash and Jim Redman's subsequent retirement. He then returned home to Bulawayo – and became the Yamaha importer for Rhodesia. In recent years he has been a familiar figure, like many other stars of yesteryear, at historic events around the world.

while with MV in the mid-1970s) used to have a weekly column in *Motor Cycle News* entitled 'Read on...'. This is what Phil had to say in the 12 May 1965 issue after Ago's Nürburgring success:

> *What a great boost to GP racing is the new combination of Giacomo Agostini and the new MV 3. The young Italian is taking his racing very seriously, and I hear rumours that some weeks ago before the race, he had been at Nürburgring for a week learning the circuit. Also he has been to Assen and Francorchamps, and is now in the Isle of Man for weeks of pre-race practice. As I see it, this is the sensible thing to do, for to be runner-up to Mike Hailwood in the Senior race he has to lap at 103mph to beat some of the Nortons and Matchlesses. In the Junior, he will also have to lap at this speed if he intends to challenge Jim Redman on the slightly faster Honda 4.*

Mention is made of Giacomo being able to visit the Isle of Man for an extended period, and it is worth recalling that the third and fourth rounds of the 1965 World Championship were in Spain and France respectively and had no 350 or 500cc races.

Both Ago and Mike were back in Italy by mid-May to race at San Remo, although Hailwood's four blew up when it dropped a valve in the 500cc race, letting his teammate, who was hard on his heels, through to win; again there was no 350cc race.

TT practice

TT practice began on a Friday evening, *Motor Cycle News* reporting: 'it was

Fairing off view of the 500 MV four which Giacomo Agostini rode during the 1965 season.

miserably dismal with drizzly rain and fog for the first practicing session of this year's TT races'. The report went on:

> In view of the conditions it was enlightening that TT newcomer Giacomo Agostini, riding a 500 MV four, should have the distinction of leading the Senior class. Agostini showed that he means business, for he was the only rider to put in three laps.

Again demonstrating his keenness to learn this most difficult of circuits, the following morning's report carried the headline: 'Agostini slogs it out in heavy Saturday drizzle and fog.' The *Motor Cycle News* story continues:

> Disappointingly, the weather was still foul for the first early morning training period, on Saturday at 4.45am. Friday evening hadn't drawn many of the 478 total entries and on this occasion attracted even less. Forty-six was the sum total. But Giacomo Agostini was not for staying in bed and, determined to learn all he can of the TT circuit, led the 500s home.

As there were only four 500s – and one failed to complete a lap – this did not really give any pointers about what might happen on race day.

Celebrating his 23rd birthday in style

With an excellent rostrum position, coming third in his first ever TT race, Giacomo Agostini averaged 98.52mph for the 6-lap, 226.38-mile Junior race on Wednesday 16 June 1965; it was also his 23rd birthday. After all that distance the Italian finished only 3 minutes 1.2 seconds behind the race winner Jim Redman, with Phil Read (Yamaha) runner-up. This was even though 'The Kid from Bergamo', as one journalist nicknamed him, spent 1 minute 24 seconds in his pit with refuelling difficulties. But at least Giacomo finished, which was more than could be said for poor Mike Hailwood, who retired the other MV triple at just over half distance with a sick engine, after suffering oil leaks and a stretched final drive chain.

1st	J. Redman (Honda)
2nd	P. Read (Yamaha)
3rd	G. Agostini (MV Agusta 3)
4th	B. Beale (Honda)
5th	G. Jenkins (Norton)
6th	G. Milani (Aermacchi)

In the 23 June 1965 issue of *Motor Cycle News*, Charlie Rous, in his 'Paddock Gossip' column, wrote a piece entitled 'Myth Exploded'. He made the point that:

Giacomo Agostini has rather exploded the myth that it takes years to learn the TT course and that nobody can ever expect to do well in their first year. In the 350 race, in which he finished third, 3 minutes behind Jim Redman, the winner, at 98.52mph, his fastest lap was 99.98mph. This was the same time as that of Phil Read who finished second.

In the same issue of *MCN* Phil Read wrote:

I thought Agostini was riding very well and safely for his first time on the Island, although he used some strange lines on certain corners. In fact, I think he taught me a new line through the 32nd Milestone, which is three left-handed bends which are taken in one smooth sweep, going into the first wide and cutting the apex of the next two. Instead on the last lap (Phil and Giacomo were together for the final two laps of the race), when I was following him closely, he swept into the first left-hander on the inside. I prepared to shut

off the Yamaha and brake so as not to run over him but he kept the
MV on power and we came out of the last bend with me having lost
a few yards. Hmm!

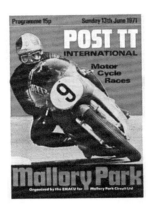

A gruelling Senior TT

The big news of the 1965 Senior TT was the appalling weather conditions – which saw both Mike Hailwood and Giacomo Agostini drop their MVs at the same spot. Although Mike remounted and went on to win his third consecutive Senior TT, it was at the slowest speed since Geoff Duke (Norton) won the 1950 race (which was held over 7 instead of 6 laps).

Yet Giacomo received a lot of good press for the way he handled his first TT races. Typical were Charlie Rous's comments: 'All eyes were on the young Italian, Agostini. He is a good rider, nobody denies that, but the way he went in those Mona conditions was terrific, as he battled to hold station behind Hailwood.' Another reporter simply said: 'The incredible Agostini.' But in the Senior race (with wet slippery roads) his undoing came at Sarah's Cottage. When winding up the all-powerful MV four around the turns away from Glen Helen and up Creg Willeys Hill he tweaked the throttle a bit too hard on the glistening tarmac and, as the *Motor Cycle News* race report commented, 'in a flurry of revs [he] was on his back – uninjured, but his machine too badly damaged to continue.'

Dutch TT

Next came the Dutch TT. The race was renowned for its good weather – almost 100,000 spectators turned out for the 40th anniversary of the Dutch classic. The 4.8-mile Assen circuit is a testing one and Giacomo Agostini decided to 'ride to finish' and learn the circuit. This he did, finishing third behind winner Redman (Honda) and teammate Hailwood in the 350cc event; while in the 500cc race he followed Mike around to finish runner-up. In fact, in practice, as *Motor Cycle News* commented: 'Agostini had not been much faster than the best of the single-banner runners and it seemed conceivable that here on the twists and turns of Assen was a chance to head an MV home.' But it didn't happen – thanks to the learning process – and some coaching from his teammate.

Eight days after Assen came the Belgian Grand Prix over the tremendously fast 8.76-mile Spa Francorchamps course. There was no 350cc class, only the 500cc race, held over 15 laps, or 131.42 miles, and contested by the MV pairing of Hailwood and Agostini. Mike won, averaging 120.59mph, Giacomo was runner-up with a speed of 117.88mph, and the next man home was Derek Minter (Norton), averaging 114.29mph.

Dull in East Germany

Except for his debut victory at the Nürburgring at the beginning of the season, Giacomo Agostini – and his teammate Mike Hailwood – seemed outpaced by the combination of Jim Redman and his Honda four. That was until the East German Grand Prix at the Sachsenring in mid-July. Even though the event was run in dull, wet conditions, it still attracted an amazing 200,000 spectators. The 21 July 1965 issue of *Motor Cycle News* reported what happened:

> *Who said that the MV 3 wasn't so hot? In Saturday's 350cc race Giacomo Agostini simply streaked away from Jim Redman's Honda 4 and gained around two seconds a lap. But the MVs didn't last. After lap 14 of the 18 laps, when he was leading Jim by over 20 seconds, Giacomo stopped with a suspected broken valve, half a mile from the start where Mike Hailwood on the other MV 3 had retired after only two laps. Both riders retired within 100 yards of each other, blowing up on a fast downhill sweep to the start and finish. 'It was nice of them to hand me the race on a plate,' Jim said afterwards. 'Agostini was really flying. Even if he was a bit wild, like taking to the grass near the Guthrie Memorial, he just shot ahead of me on the hills.'*

In the 500cc race it was a familiar story: Hailwood first, Agostini second, with average speeds of 93.62mph and 92.31mph respectively.

Even more spectators watched the Czech GP a week later – over 300,000 of them! The 350cc race over 11 laps and 95.3 miles proved extremely punishing, with only 15 of the 34 starters surviving to the finish. And yet again neither MV Agusta 3-cylinder model was among them. For three laps Redman was chased by Giacomo Agostini, but Ago fell while cranking his bike through a series of bends after the famous Farina curve, leaving Hailwood in second place on the other MV 3, some 25 seconds in arrears. Giacomo was unhurt. On the next lap Hailwood lost another 20 seconds. On the sixth lap, at just over half race distance, Hailwood's engine blew up in the village just past the start. 'I just caught it before the big bang' he commented after revealing a big-end had tightened. Although bothered by losing oil, Hailwood won the 500cc race and in doing so his fourth 500cc title in as many years – a new record. Again Giacomo finished runner-up, to gain yet more valuable track experience, which would prove so useful in future years. Hailwood's and Agostini's average speeds over the 13-lap, 112.5-mile 500cc Czech GP were 94.95mph and 93.15mph.

Redman's turn for bad luck in Ulster

Jim Redman crashed while holding a five-mile lead during the 350cc Ulster Grand Prix in early August. However, it was of no benefit to the MV duo of Hailwood and Agostini, because they were not there. The reason given to the organisers by MV Agusta for their non-appearance was that the factory 'needed the bikes back in Italy to prepare for the forthcoming Italian GP in early September.' In truth, Mike and Giacomo had already sealed first and second place in the 500cc championship, and in the 350cc division, Redman had all but sewn up the title with four victories. So why go all the way to Ulster when it was reported that the start and prize money would not even cover the team's travelling expenses? As it turned out, Redman's crash and the fact that MV Agusta did not go to Ulster were both of considerable significance to Giacomo Agostini, although he did not know it at the time.

A couple of weeks after the Ulster GP – and two weeks before Monza – came the Finnish round at Imatra. MV were on record as having said 'no racing before Monza', so it came as a shock when Giacomo Agostini turned up in Finland and was a double winner, taking the 350 and 500cc races with ease. Although it made no difference to the outcome of the 500cc championship – it having already been won by Hailwood – things now seemed slightly different in the 350cc class. With Redman out with a broken collarbone, in theory Giacomo could now win the championship – if he won in Italy and finished at least second in the final round at Suzuka, Japan.

Giacomo set two new class lap records in Finland – 85.70mph (350cc) and 87.67mph (500cc). But one person who was not pleased about MV going to Finland was Mike Hailwood – who told *Motor Cycle News* he was 'surprised, shocked and disappointed'. At the same time Mike did not blame his teammate, as he knew from experience how quickly Count Domenico Agusta could change his mind. And Giacomo Agostini was not in a position to argue in any case. With Redman still at home in South Africa nursing his broken collarbone a week prior to Monza, it was looked increasingly as if he would not be fit until the final round in Japan.

Monsoon at Monza

Rain lashed the circuit at Monza for most of race day. But the 350cc event – the first to be staged – escaped until the 24th of the 27 laps (race distance 96.47 miles). Redman was a non-starter so Giacomo looked favourite to take the win. There was no doubt that team orders came into the picture, and so it was Mike Hailwood's lot to hold second place while Giacomo Agostini took the lead. As *Motor Cycle News* recorded: 'This proved very easy for the MV pair. They darted into the lead and built up an ever-

Giacomo Agostini during the 1965 350cc Italian GP at Monza. He won the 27-lap, 96.47 mile event in 51 minutes 12.5 seconds, at an average speed of 113.03mph.

increasing gap from the first lap well ahead of Derek Woodman (251cc MZ) who was well ahead of the field.'

Unfortunately for Tarquinio Provini, who was having a first outing on the new full-size 350 Benelli four, he was slow to start, but after a couple of pit stops to change plugs he rode like a demon, coming through the field to take third place by the end of the race.

Towards the end of the 27th lap Hailwood, who had occasionally set the running to head the field before once again dropping back behind his team-mate, crashed. This happened just as the rain first came down. Braking for the Parabolica curve he suddenly went from dry to wet conditions – and down he went. Luckily he was uninjured and was able to race in the 500cc event later in the day. The final positions were:

1st	G. Agostini (MV Agusta)
2nd	S. Grassetti (Bianchi)
3rd	T. Provini (Benelli)
4th	F. Stastny (Jawa)
5th	D. Woodman (MZ)
6th	R. Pasolini (Aermacchi)

Silvio Grassetti raced a variety of machines over the years against Giacomo Agostini, including 350 and 500 Benelli fours and the Jawa V4 2-stroke. Grassetti is seen here with the ex-works Bianchi twin he rode in the 1965 350cc Dutch TT.

MVs go to Japan

After the Monza success it was officially announced that MV would be going to Japan – with both Giacomo Agostini and Mike Hailwood. Giacomo now had a definite chance to take the title from Jim Redman and Honda, but he couldn't do it alone. It was not sufficient for him to win the race – and in Japan that would be hard enough. He could only claim the title if he was to win and Jim Redman finish no higher than third.

Of the nine races in the 350cc series, the five best counted. And so far, Jim Redman had scored four wins (eight points each) and gained 32 points. Giacomo Agostini was not quite so well off. He had three wins and two third positions (four points each). Therefore, although with 32 his points score was equal to Redman's, it was stretched over five meetings. If Giacomo was able to win – and Mike Hailwood finish second – the title would go to MV Agusta.

The Japanese Grand Prix – the third staged – looked like being by far the best so far. Not only was the 350cc championship up for grabs, but the 50cc was being contested as well. The meeting was to be run over the 3.7-mile Suzuka circuit (owned by Honda, incidentally) on Sunday 2 October 1965.

As *Motor Cycling's* race report dated 27 October said:

Only the cruellest of luck robbed MV of success in both the individual and manufacturers categories of the 350cc World Championships. For Giacomo Agostini, who started the race tying on points with Honda captain Jim Redman, shot ahead from the start and had the race in his pocket when a contact breaker spring broke.

Motor Cycle News said 'The Italian rode magnificently, leading for eleven of the 25 laps, while Hailwood cleverly held off Redman. It was a masterly piece of tactical riding.' Eventually Giacomo limped home fifth, his chance of the championship gone.

Interestingly, back in mid-May that year Geoff Johnson of the Lucas competition department had demonstrated an electronic ignition system, as developed originally for MZ, to the MV factory at Gallarate. It was reported that 'the equipment was enthusiastically received and may replace the Bosch coil ignition, at present fitted to the MV 3.' I bet everyone connected wished MV had taken up the Lucas offer when the bike went sick. However, when being interviewed before leaving Japan, MVs race chief, Arturo Magni, said: 'electronic ignition, instead of the battery-coil system which failed and cost Agostini the world championship, was not considered desirable.' What he probably meant was that MV did not consider it sufficiently developed at that time. However, the main focus of the press speculation after Japan was whether Mike Hailwood would switch to Honda for 1966. Magni did not dismiss this possibility, only confirming that Mike 'remained under contract with MV until January'.

Even though he had lost the 350cc title, press and public praise for Giacomo's gallant attempt was widespread. The following is a typical extract from one newspaper at the time:

A big hand for MV and Giacomo Agostini. Their joint effort in so nearly beating Honda and Redman in the 350cc world championship was undoubtedly one of the highlights of the 1965 classic scene. Agostini, in his first year as an MV rider, put up a great fight on his MV three, raced for the first time when he won the West German GP. In case you've forgotten, Redman went through a Nürburgring hedge in his attempt to stay with Agostini.

Honda team captain Jim Redman and Giacomo Agostini battled down to the wire in the 1965 350cc World Championship series. Redman only winning after Ago's bike suffered a broken contact breaker spring at the final round in Japan.

The Honda 350 four of the type used by Jim Redman to win the 1965 350cc World Title.

Ago's performance at Suzuka merits the highest praise. To have lost such a big title through a little contact breaker spring was enough to make lesser men cry. To his eternal credit, Ago accepted defeat philosophically. Ironically, he had done 95 practice laps without a spot of bother.

By the end of November it was commonly known that Mike Hailwood would be switching to Honda for the following season. Less well known was the fact that Count Domenico Agusta did not intend to replace Mike with another rider – Giacomo Agostini would be MVs sole representative in the 1966 World Championship. Also not known at the time was that a larger version of the 7-speed triple was being developed for the 500cc class. This was in anticipation of the new machine Honda had promised Mike Hailwood to contest the blue riband class – the first time the Japanese company had ever raced in this, the premier class of Grand Prix racing.

As for Count Agusta, when attending the congress of an international power boat federation of which he was the president, in Brussels during December 1965, he said he was 'ready to counter the threat posed by Honda in the 500cc class.' Speaking to Guy Vanderbecken, head of the Martini competition department (who was closely connected with the promotion of

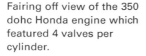

Fairing off view of the 350 dohc Honda engine which featured 4 valves per cylinder.

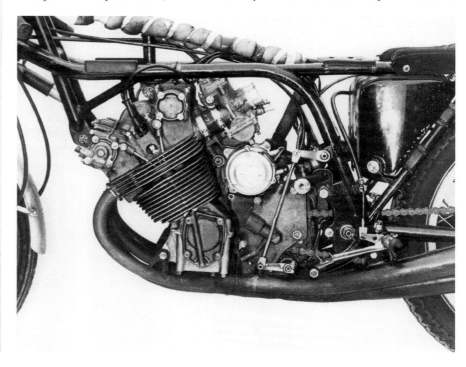

road races and other motorcycle events on the Continent, including the Belgian GP), the Count stated: 'This isn't the first time a 500cc racing Honda has been heralded but we're still waiting for it.' He went on to say: 'Far from frightening me, I await the presence of this machine with delight. It interests me, from a technical point of view.' And he acknowledged, 'Of course the presence of Mike Hailwood in the Honda team is a major setback. But despite that, we will face our rivals sportingly, and without fear, for we also have...'

Characteristically, the Count suddenly interrupted his flow of words. Then, after reflecting for a moment, he continued: 'But why should I yet reveal my surprise packet? Let us wait and see...' All this typical of a man who loved to keep everyone – including his riders – in the dark. Observers immediately began to speculate about what the Count meant by 'surprise packet'. *Motor Cycle News* thought he meant an updated version of the six-cylinder model raced only once, by John Hartle at Monza in 1958. Hartle was reported by *Motor Cycle News* in their 29 December 1965 issue as saying: 'the MV six was a beauty. It was the best handling bike I've ever ridden.' However, in contrast, in my book *John Surtees: Motorcycle Maestro*, John himself took a very different line, revealing that he considered

---

Count Domenico Agusta

Count Domenico Agusta was a man driven by the need to succeed in whatever he did. He ruled a business empire with a rod of iron. Few really knew him well and until his death in early 1971, the MV Agusta motorcycle marque generally flourished both in racing and from a commercial standpoint – although from the late 1950s the helicopter side of the business gradually assumed greater importance. There were no directors at MV, only the remainder of the family. And certainly the Count was autocratic in the extreme. There was no doubt in anybody's mind – rider, employee, journalist or rival manufacturer – that what the Count said, went at MV Agusta.

As Mike Hailwood was once to recall:

> It would be difficult to get five shillings out of the factory without his personal endorsement, he has his finger firmly on the pulse; nothing happens there that he doesn't know about. Every action, every move through the works has to have his personal signature before it is approved and accepted. Nobody dares make a decision without consulting him.

This unwillingness to delegate any responsibility was the reason why he – and the organisation he controlled – often fell behind the clock. John Surtees confirms this view: 'Often when I would visit the factory, probably after coming especially from England, I would be kept waiting, sometimes for hours on end'. And Mike Hailwood again: 'Once it was three days before I got to meet him.

I'm convinced that he was showing me who was the boss. Every move he made – everything about MV Agusta – seemed designed to give him this psychological advantage'.

Once described as a cross between actor Humphrey Bogart and a Mafia godfather, the Count was a short, stocky man, but, because of his manner, always gave the impression of being bigger than he actually was. He even had a special desk in his office, which was raised from the ground so that he could look down at those he was receiving. Because of his immense workload – he would usually arrive at 10.30 in the morning and not depart until the early hours of the next morning (except for a couple of hours at lunchtime) – he ensured that everything was designed to help smooth the running of the business. His home was a villa within the factory grounds, only a couple of minutes walk from his office. Mike Hailwood once said: 'He has a swivel chair at his desk so that he can spin round to get at the radio-telephone link he has with his helicopters, or to slide over to the battery of telephones that never seem to stop ringing.'

A little known fact was that the Count hated flying – even though Agusta was primarily an aviation concern both before and after World War Two. Instead he preferred to travel on his big yacht, his private train, or by any of his dozen or so chauffeur-driven cars. Because of this and his workaholic lifestyle he rarely watched his motorcycles in action, except at the local Monza circuit. He never visited the Isle of Man, even though he rated the event so highly that he commissioned full-size replicas of the silver trophies won by his riders over the world's longest and most difficult circuit.

Domenico, the eldest of four sons born to Giovanni and Giuseppina Agusta, was born in Palermo, Sicily, in 1907. He was a mere 21 years of age when his father died prematurely, aged 48. The young Domenico was thrown headlong into running the company his father had built up to become one of Italy's leading aviation concerns. When one considers that his father's untimely passing coincided with the most fearful industrial depression of the 20th century, the fact that the company weathered the storm suggests natural flair for the rigours of commercial life on the part of Domenico.

During the 1930s, with the rise of Fascism in Italy under its leader Benito Mussolini, Agusta, like many other industrial companies, decided to take military contracts rather than risk going out of business. When Italy finally joined the war on 10 June 1940, the Gallarate-based company was swept into the war effort and grew rapidly – massive production requiring a much larger workforce. But when the Allies landed in Sicily, before moving on to the southern tip of the Italian mainland during the autumn of 1943, the Count could clearly see the writing on the wall and began to prepare his business interests for the coming peace. He chose to develop powered two-wheelers – not just motorcycles, but scooters and mopeds too. At first the new company, MV (Meccanica Verghera), used two-stroke engines, but soon made the switch to the more sophisticated four-stroke, both for its series production roadsters and its competition machines, the latter including both road racers and off-road bikes at first.

Many commentators have said that the original reason why Count Domenico Agusta went racing was his love of the sport. This is incorrect, as during the late 1940s and early 1950s he went racing purely for publicity purposes, to promote his fledgling motorcycle firm. However, later, with more wealth at his disposal thanks to the rebirth of the aviation section of the Agusta empire, he saw racing as a way of expressing his own power. He ran his race team largely from his business offices, directing the proceedings as a general would do, many miles away from the scene of the battle. His loyal lieutenants, men like chief mechanic Arturo Magni and team manager Nello Pagani, would be at the circuit with the riders and other team personnel.

From the mid-1950s, thanks to a lucrative licence agreement from the American Bell helicopter firm, Agusta's business expanded greatly. However, the motorcycle arm (both the racing and roadster production) was not neglected and for many years provided a significant part of the group's annual turnover. By the end of the 1960s the Count was presiding over an industrial empire employing in excess of 5,000 workers. Then, on 2 February 1971, while visiting Milan on business, a few days short of his 64th birthday, Count Domenico Agusta suffered a fatal heart attack. And while it was announced that Corrado Agusta, the 47-year-old survivor of the family of four brothers, was to take over the reigns of what by then was the world's second-largest helicopter manufacturer and the most famous name in motorcycle racing, things would never be the same again. The real powerhouse and driving force of the Agusta legend had passed on.

the six the wrong way to go, saying: 'what was needed was a lighter version of the four cylinder.' Which is, of course, the way MV finally went after the early 1970s, before their ultimate demise at the end of 1976. But this is getting too far ahead of what was happening as Giacomo Agostini approached the 1966 season as MVs number one rider, now that Hailwood had switched camps to rivals Honda. The big question was, was he ready? Everyone awaited the answer, as 1965 became 1966.

Chapter 4

Ago v Mike

AFTER a year when Ago and Mike were teammates, in 1966 the ywere rivals on the track, with MV and Honda respectively. However, unlike many in a similar situation each respected the other, and they remained good friends. When interviewed in December 1966, Giacomo Agostini had this to say about this former teammate:

> *I learnt a lot from him when we were both in the MV team in 1965. I was the 'new boy' and in practice I used to follow Mike whenever I could. Before 1965 I had never ridden a 500cc machine. I had a lot to learn. Luckily for me, Mike used to go quite slowly during the first laps of practice which gave me a chance to tuck in behind him and watch exactly what he did, and when he did it. I improved and as the meetings passed I was able to hang on longer and longer.*

In addition, as Mike's father Stan said in June 1966, 'He [Agostini] is a brilliant, daring rider and one of the nicest guys to know. Mike and he are the biggest pals, let there be no mistake about that. No unfriendliness ever arose – just a natural spirit of keen rivalry.'

A lighter 500 MV

News of a new, lighter 500 MV – incorrectly rumoured to be a four – was published by the press in February 1966. Extensive testing was carried out by Giacomo in late February and early March, at both Modena and Monza.

The first meeting for MVs new number one came at Alicante, Spain, in mid-March. Then a week later, at Modena, the Italian season got under way. *Motor Cycling* was able to bring its readers the news, with a front-page headline: 'MV 350 Thrashes Gilera 500', going on to say:

> *Riding the latest three-cylinder 350cc MV Giacomo Agostini soundly thrashed the 500cc Gilera four when it made its first appearance since 1964 in the hands of Remo Venturi at Modena on*

Sunday; breaking race and lap records in the process, Agostini led from start to finish to win the first 500cc race of the 1966 Italian Championships by nearly half a mile. Third on a 500cc MV was Silvio Grassetti. But was Ago's bike actually fitted with a larger capacity?

Motor Cycle News simply called Ago's Modena performance 'sensational', saying:

Renzo Pasolini proved a thorn in Giacomo Agostini's side while riding four-cylinder Benelli machines during the late 1960s; certainly as regards the Italian street circuits. This shot is from Cesenatico in spring 1967.

Giacomo Agostini started the Italian season in sensational style at Modena on Sunday with a record breaking win on the MV 3 – in the 500cc class! He demoralised his challengers, by smashing Mike Hailwood's 1964 lap record, set up on an MV four, by almost a second.

Giacomo actually finished the race 24 seconds ahead of Venturi and more than 50 seconds in front of Grassetti. These three lapped the rest of the field, which included Renzo Pasolini, Giuseppe Mandolini, Gilberto Milani and Czech star Gustav Havel.

By the time the second round of the Italian Senior Championship was run at Riccione in early April, it was generally known that Giacomo Agostini was riding an experimental 'overbored' MV 3. But although the new engine suffered a blow-up, this came after Giacomo had already broken another Hailwood-held lap record and was comfortably leading the 500cc event, thus handing victory to Remo Venturi (Gilera).

Crashing out at Cervia

Motor Cycling dated 16 April 1966 carried the following headline 'Agostini injured: Imola threatened.' This related to a series of crashes which put Giacomo and Remo Venturi in hospital, killed a mechanic and injured a spectator and two policemen, at the third round of the Italian championships at the Cervia street circuit. Most of the accidents occurred in the 500cc race, held on a rain-soaked track made treacherous after a torrential downpour. Ago sustained arm and slight head injuries, and the race was subsequently halted – later the entire meeting was abandoned. Both Giacomo and Venturi came to grief while braking for a tight bend just after the start of the 2.1-mile course.

Fortunately the injuries sustained at Cervia didn't stop the MV star riding at the Imola *Coppa d'Oro* (Gold Cup) meeting a week later. 'Stars warm up for the World Classics in Italian Sunshine' said *Motor Cycle News* in their 20 April 1966 issue. But the big headline for the two-page report said: 'Agostini's Imola Double'.

Except for Luigi Taveri's victory on a Honda in the 125cc class, the remaining three races were all won by Italians on Italian bikes – the other being Tarquinio Provini who took his Benelli four to victory in the 250cc event. A crowd of over 40,000 spectators was overjoyed by these Italian successes, particularly as the field included several top foreign riders – among them Mike Hailwood and Jim Redman racing Honda fours in the 500 and 350cc classes respectively. There were also Bill Ivy and Phil Read (Yamahas) and Derek Minter, racing a Gilera for the first time for almost three years.

350cc Imola Gold Cup – 20 laps – 62.3 miles

1st	G. Agostini (MV Agusta 3)
2nd	T. Provini (Benelli)
3rd	M. Hailwood (Honda)
4th	G. Havel (Jawa)
5th	F. Stastny (Jawa)
6th	D. Minter (Seeley-AJS)

500cc Imola Gold Cup – 18 laps – 56.08 miles

1st	G. Agostini (MV Agusta 4)
2nd	D. Minter (Gilera)
3rd	J. Cooper (Norton)
4th	S. Graham (Matchless)
5th	J. Ahern (Norton)
6th	G. Milani (Aermacchi 350)

Disqualified

A helping hand from an MV mechanic who pushed the machine when the gearbox broke, caused Giacomo Agostini to lose third place in the 350cc race at Cesenatico, a week after Imola. This happened when, after gaining a 25-second lead, the illegal push-in occurred at the end of the final lap, leaving Tarquinio Provini to win from Mike Hailwood and John Cooper (Norton). In the 500cc race, Giacomo, again riding an MV four, won with ease from Renzo Pasolini (Aermacchi) and John Cooper (Norton). Derek Minter was again Gilera-mounted, but never challenging Ago, lost runner-up spot after the HT lead came off the magneto after 17 of the 23 laps of the race distance.

Giacomo talks to his mechanics prior to the start of the 1966 Senior TT in the Isle of Man.

Next, in mid-May, came what was the sixth round of the Italian Senior Championships, held over the twisting Ospedaletti circuit, near San Remo on the Italian Riviera. Giacomo won easily on the 500cc four-cylinder MV at a speed of 68.2mph. His fastest lap was 69.6mph. The Gilera threat never really materialised. First Benedicto Caldarella, the meteoric Argentinian who had challenged Mike Hailwood occasionally in 1964, crashed his Gilera in practice. In the race itself Remo Venturi got nowhere near Giacomo and was in fact strongly challenged by a number of Aermacchi 350 singles!

The first round of the 1966 championship season began in Spain – but as there were only classes for 50, 125 and 250cc, MV were not represented. And so Hockenheim was the first test. The *Motor Cycle News* headlines said it all: 'The mighty MV is beaten' and 'Honda flex their muscles'. In fact four out of the five solo classes went to the Japanese company at the West German GP – with only the 50cc race being won by another make (Suzuki).

In the 350cc race, after Ago's triple became a twin it was all over – and in the 500cc event Redman on the new Honda five-hundred four was simply too fast for the Italian who was still mounted on one of the old fours. What was Count Agusta going to do, observers asked?

Clermont-Ferrand

There was no 500cc race in the French Grand Prix at Clermont-Ferrand, only 250cc, sidecars, and the 350cc. After one lap of the near 5-mile circuit Mike Hailwood was 50 yards up on the three-cylinder MV of former team-mate Giacomo Agostini. Close behind came Tarquinio Provini on the Benelli four and Jim Redman on the second Honda four. For the first few laps, Hailwood piled on the coals, scraping the megaphones and wearing his rear tyre down to the last rib. Then he eased the pace slightly and Giacomo Agostini, 'riding truly brilliantly for a newcomer to the circuit' (*Motor Cycle News*, 1 June 1966) seemed to close the gap. Hailwood and Agostini then left Provini behind – and the latter eventually retired. Redman was troubled by one of his throttle cables breaking, while Aermacchi works riders Gilberto Milani and Renzo Pasolini finished fourth and fifth, just ahead of Bruce Beale (Honda 305cc CR77 twin).

Hailwood (who had also won the 250cc race earlier in the day) set the fastest lap, at 80.93mph, for the 20-lap, 100.04-mile race.

Next in the World Championship calendar should have come the Isle of Man TT, but 1966 was the year of the seaman's strike – so this was put back to the end of August (in the two weeks prior to the Manx Grand Prix).

'Out for the Count'

'Out for the Count' shouted the *Motor Cycle News* headline in the 29 June 1966 issue. This related to the fact that Mike Hailwood had crashed his 500cc Honda and that MV had hit back with a brand-new '500 three' at Assen, Holland. Actually the 'new' MV was something of a 'bitza', being described in *MV Agusta* (Mario Columbo and Roberto Patrignani) as: 'practically constructed on the battlefield during the practice sessions for the Dutch TT.' The cylinders of the three-fifty engine had been bored out from 48 to 55mm, giving a displacement of 377cc – but it was still well short of being a full '500'.

The *Motor Cycling* race report gave a vivid idea of the setting: 'Giacomo Agostini surprised Honda and the 100,000 crowd, by giving the Japanese works bikes a run for their money in the 500cc race.' However, following Mike Hailwood's crash, Jim Redman eventually caught and passed the MV to win by two seconds at record speed. But it was a pretty close-run affair after 20 laps and 95.74 miles. The race had begun with Redman streaking into the lead, followed by Giacomo on the new three (which he had chosen instead of the four). Hailwood's Honda was reluctant to fire and he was well back by the time he did get it going.

The *Motor Cycle News* race report takes up the story:

> In the twists of the first half lap, Agostini edged in front of Redman but on the swoops along the back straight Redman went past. Not for long, the red MV was back in front at the start. Suddenly, all eyes switched to Hailwood. His progress was meteoric. After two laps, he had Redman and Agostini in his sights. As they screamed along the back, he was 3½ seconds down. In a simply fantastic half lap – just over two miles – he gobbled up the distance and seared past the pair of them as they completed the third lap. His lap record of 3 min 11 sec set up last year on the MV, was made to look quite slow for Hailwood's new figure was 3 min 6.7 sec, 92.30mph. But it was not to last. Halfway round the fourth lap, he missed a gear entering a tight left hander and fell off.

Then came a fantastic duel, which eventually Giacomo seemed to have won, when he pulled out an eight-second lead. But then at the beginning of the 15th lap the Italian started having gear selection problems. This meant Redman was able to catch him up and eventually pass him, and the Honda man took victory. However, the race had proved that Giacomo was right to press for a bigger triple, rather than continue riding the more powerful, but much heavier and less manoeuvrable four-cylinder five-hundreds. MV race

In the World Championships it was men like Mike Hailwood and Jim Redman (the latter is seen here in Belgium during 1966) who were the main challengers to Ago and MV.

boss Arturo Magni commented: 'The four may well be used in high speed courses like Francorchamps, Monza and the TT.'

In the 350cc race Hailwood on the Honda four lapped everyone but Giacomo, whom he beat by over 40 seconds in the rain.

A thunderstorm in Belgium

Eight days after Assen came the Belgian Grand Prix. As was usual practice at Spa Francorchamps, there was no 350cc race. But the 8.76-mile circuit was, as *Motor Cycle News* so aptly put it, a 'washout for the big Honda'. Their report on the meeting began by saying 'The hitherto invincible Honda 500 was sunk with all hands in a torrential downpour which flooded out Sunday's Belgian Grand Prix. Jim Redman crashed, breaking an arm, and Mike Hailwood retired, suffering from exposure and gearbox trouble.'

This left Giacomo Agostini – riding the old four – to score 'a magnificent, if somewhat wet, victory'. This success meant that for the first time he was leading the 500cc World Championship.

500cc Belgian GP – 15 laps – 131.4 miles

1st	G. Agostini (MV Agusta 4)
2nd	S. Graham (Matchless)
3rd	J. Ahern (Norton)

Giacomo Agostini leads Jim Redman and Mike Hailwood (Hondas) during practice for the 1966 Belgian GP; it was destined to be Redman's last race meeting, as he retired after a crash in which he broke his wrist.

4th	G. Morsovszky (Matchless)
5th	J. Mawby (Norton)
6th	R. Chandler (Matchless)

Record-breaking in East Germany

The world title ambitions of Mr Honda took a severe knock as the Grand Prix circus went behind the Iron Curtain to contest the East German round at the famous Sachsenring circuit. *Motor Cycle News* said: 'Sensation of the meeting was Giacomo Agostini. He pulverised the lap record on his way to a win in the 350 class and did likewise in the 500 class – adding 4mph to Hailwood's MV record.' However, not everything went according to plan as Giacomo – after lapping the entire field in the 500cc race – crashed at 120mph, luckily escaping with nothing more than a badly skinned nose! The crash occurred while sweeping down the fast Heiterer Blick curve just before the Guthrie Memorial on the 5.3-mile Saxony circuit.

350cc East German GP – 18 laps – 96.2 miles

1st	G. Agostini (MV Agusta 3)
2nd	F. Stastny (Jawa)
3rd	G. Havel (Jawa)
4th	R. Pasolini (Aermacchi)
5th	A. Pagani (Aermacchi)
6th	J. Ahern (Norton)

By now the MV engineering team had increased the capacity of the larger triple to 420cc, while there had also been improvements to both the engine and the chassis. At last it was becoming competitive in a straight line compared to the old four, if not Honda's all-powerful bike. However, even

Ago pilots the new MV 500 three-cylinder during the Czech Grand Prix at Brno in 1966. The 491cc (60.5 x 57mm) triple shared gear driven dohc and four valves per cylinder with its smaller brother and produced 80bhp at 12,000rpm.

if the Japanese machine was quicker – as Hailwood was eventually to reveal – in the handling stakes, it was not in the same league as the Italian bike.

The Czech GP took place the following weekend at the Brno circuit. Looking slightly less handsome following his big crash at the Sachsenring, Giacomo sensibly resigned himself to a couple of runner-up positions in Czechoslovakia; thus consolidating his lead in the 500cc Championship. No one could have accused him of lacking courage, for with not only a very sore nose, but also a badly gashed right hand, he battled on in atrocious weather conditions. In fact, as an illustration of his determination and commitment to the job at hand, during the race all the stitches in his hand pulled apart!

With one 500 3 frame out of commission (from the East German crash) and the other not handling as it should, the team were forced to install the 420cc engine in one of the 350 frames. Unfortunately, the smaller engine frame accepted only a 3.00-section rear tyre instead of the 3.50 which the larger 420cc engine needed, so this was yet another handicap to overcome. All in all it was a brave showing.

King Mike deposed!
Mike Hailwood lost what was probably his last realistic chance of retaining the 500cc title he had held for the previous four years when, during the Finnish GP at Imatra, the Hailwood-Honda 500 combination was again humbled by Count Agusta's new challenger – Agostini and the 420cc MV 3. And, as *Motor Cycle News* said in the 10 August 1966 issue, 'Now MV and Giacomo Agostini, who is proving himself a truly great rider, look set to retain the championship for the Italian team.' Giacomo also set the fastest

MV Agusta 3-cylinder

The *Tre Cilindri* (3-cylinder) MV Agusta racers are firmly associated with Giacomo Agostini. In fact, as he once recalled, in comments made at the end of the 1966 season:

I like the three cylinder, it's 'my' motorcycle. I joined MV just as they were completing the first bike and I was the first ever to ride it. It's tailored to fit me, a small machine and very low. As I was used to the 250cc Moto Morini this suited me and I found it easier to ride than the bigger four cylinder machines.

The original idea behind the three-cylinder MV was the success garnered by Honda in 1962 by a larger displacement version of its 250cc four. This had an engine size of 285cc (47 x 41mm), thus allowing the Japanese marque to enter the 350cc class. Soon, a full-sized three-fifty – actually 339.4cc (49 x 45mm) – made its debut. As soon as it arrived on the GP scene it proved so superior to the ageing 349.3cc (47.5 x 49.3mm) MV four (which had made its debut back in 1953), that even with the brilliance of Mike Hailwood's riding ability the Italian bike was totally outclassed. In typical fashion, Count Domenico Agusta promptly decided to cut-and-run from the class rather than get beaten (as he had already done when the 250cc Honda four soundly trounced the MV twin with Gary Hocking aboard back in 1961). This only left the 500cc, with Hailwood taking the title in 1963, 1964, and again in 1965.

In that final year, an entirely new combination made its debut in the Grand Prix arena – Giacomo Agostini on the new three-fifty three-cylinder MV Agusta. As recounted elsewhere, this was just the tonic the autocratic Count needed – his dream having always been of an Italian rider capable of matching and beating the best in the larger (350 and 500cc) classes. In Ago the Count had just such a man, so he finally sanctioned the design and construction of a three-cylinder model, a concept which had been mooted at MV since as long ago as 1958.

The 343.9cc (48 x 46mm) across-the-frame triple had its air-cooled twin-cam cylinders inclined forward some 10 degrees from the vertical. Other features of the machine's impressive technical portfolio included a seven-speed gearbox, 18in wire wheels (with Borrani alloy rims), a 3.5-gallon (16-litre) fuel tank, and a quad-cam 240mm (9.44in) drum front brake of immense size and power.

The 343.8cc (48 x 46mm) across-the-frame three-cylinder engine with its air-cooled cylinders, which were inclined forward by 10 degrees from vertical.

The trio of Dell 'Orto SS1 28 A carburettors as used on the 350 and 500cc MV triples; two 'Matchbox'-type float chambers were used.

SSI 28 A

campione del mondo

350-500cc. m.v. agusta 3c.

With over 62.5bhp at 13,500 rpm available, the new MV could at last challenge the Japanese dominance in the class. This, allied to a maximum speed of 150mph, made it not only as rapid as its larger five-hundred four-cylinder brother; but because of its lighter weight and more compact size gave it a much superior power-to-weight ratio; all-in-all it was a more superior racing motorcycle than its predecessor had ever been. The dry weight was 116kg (256lb). Running on a compression ratio of 11:1, the 1965 MV three-fifty three was equipped with a trio of Dell'Orto SS28B carburettors with remotely mounted float chambers.

After emerging victorious from the 1965 350cc championship title race, MV's engineering team then set about the task of constructing a larger triple. At first the displacement was increased to 377cc (by boring the cylinders out to 55mm), then 420cc, next came 476cc, and finally, in 1967, 497.9cc (62 x 55.3mm). The engine, compared to the 350, sported a larger oil sump at the base of the engine (lengthened at the front).

Actually all the 500 class MV threes featured engines

Drawing of the 1969 MV Agusta 500 three-cylinder Grand Prix machine, with fairing cut away to show engine, carburettors and exhaust system.

which were virtually identical to the smaller 350 unit, with features such as the inclined cylinders, horizontally-split crankcases and dry multi-plate clutches. The carburettors were Dell'Orto SSI 28 A assemblies.

Even though the triples were eventually superseded by new versions of the four-cylinder theme, it was none the less the MV triple that did much to cement Giacomo Agostini's career as the world's most successful road racer – a position he has continued to hold to the present day.

lap at 87.13mph. In the 350cc race the Italian pairing went out because of stripped primary drive gears.

Even though Giacomo Agostini finished runner-up behind Mike Hailwood in both the 350 and 500cc races over the 7½-mile Dundrod road circuit in Northern Ireland – the scene of the Ulster Grand Prix – the young Italian was still crowned 1966 500cc World Champion. Little did he know it at the time, but this was to be the first of a record breaking 15 titles in all. It was Ago's first ever visit to the Ulster circuit, but even though he had no hope of keeping close to his former teammate and friend, Giacomo still lapped the entire field in both his races on his 350 and 420cc MV Agusta triples.

TT practice

With many riders still recovering from Saturday's Ulster GP and the voyage to the Isle of Man (Giacomo, together with Luigi Taveri, Mike Hailwood and Jim Redman, flew in by a Cambrian Airways De Havilland Viscount turboprop airliner), the following Monday's opening practice, for the postponed races, did not present a pleasant picture – the weather being cold and the track still damp in places. Giacomo followed his keenness of the previous year by turning out regardless. He also had the distinction of setting the fastest lap of the session at 92.91mph.

The same evening, in what *Motor Cycle News* described as 'almost perfect conditions', the MV rider took out both his 350 and 420cc threes – lapping at 97.96mph on the smaller model and an impressive 102.32mph on the 420cc bike, making him the fastest in both classes.

Although Jim Redman was present in the Isle of Man with the rest of the Honda team, the Rhodesian star was about to announce his retirement from Grand Prix racing following his big crash in the 500cc Belgian GP in early July.

Glorious weather during the remainder of the TT practice had everyone hoping it would be a repeat performance for the following race week – which it was. Interestingly, *Motor Cycle News* had a speed trap installed between Creg-Ny-Baa and Brandish. The results were:

350cc	G. Agostini (MV 3)	144.6mph
	M. Hailwood (Honda)	141.2mph
500cc	G. Agostini (MV 3)	151.9mph
	M. Hailwood (Honda)	151.9mph

The honours were shared between Ago and Mike, with the Italian winning the Junior TT on his 350 3. Any chance Mike Hailwood had was lost 10 minutes after he started when his Honda four dropped four of its eight valves into the two right (off-side) cylinders, wrecking the engine. After the race it was found that these new valves, sent from Japan by air especially for the race, were all faulty. The others, when tested, snapped like carrots when hit with a hammer in a vice. Giacomo thus became the first non-British rider ever to win the Junior TT. He also set new race and lap records for the class at 100.87mph and 103.09mph. And he led from start to finish.

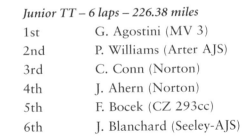

Junior TT – 6 laps – 226.38 miles

1st	G. Agostini (MV 3)
2nd	P. Williams (Arter AJS)
3rd	C. Conn (Norton)
4th	J. Ahern (Norton)
5th	F. Bocek (CZ 293cc)
6th	J. Blanchard (Seeley-AJS)

'That was the hairiest ever' exclaimed Mike Hailwood after hauling himself wearily out of the saddle of his Honda 500 four after winning the Senior TT and smashing the lap record with a new speed of 107.07mph. It was his ninth TT victory, but as he was the first to admit 'one of my hardest' as Giacomo Agostini astounded spectators – and Mike – by also breaking the old lap record. He took his three-cylinder MV round at 106.68mph – a few seconds faster than Hailwood's old record (set in 1963) on the MV four of 106.41mph. Although the sun was shining in Douglas, the conditions elsewhere caused a dramatic drop in speeds towards the end of the 6-lap race.

A masterly performance at Monza

The final round of the 500cc championship took place at Monza just over a week after the Senior TT. But even though Mike Hailwood retired from the 35-lap, 125-mile race after only 10 minutes (the same time span as in the Junior TT) with broken exhaust valves on his Honda, Giacomo still delivered a masterly performance.

Isle of Man TT

When asked about what was his favourite circuit was, Giacomo Agostini replied:

Well, that depends. If it's just from the point of view of riding motor-cycles, then my favourite circuit is the Isle of Man – it has everything. You go uphill, downhill, over bridges, under trees, through villages, round first-gear hairpins, and 200kph corners: for me, it's the best. You climb a high mountain, then come down near the beach, and in between, the sun might shine or the rain might fall. Nothing else in motorcycle racing can compare to this.

But there was a proviso – a big proviso. And it was the reason why Agostini quit the magic Island after the 1972 TT – the dangerous nature of the most demanding of all road race circuits. Giacomo explained:

I am talking of only the riding, without any other considerations at all. I tried not to admit it even to myself in those days, because when you are young you don't think of the danger; you just want to ride the bikes. But if you have any concern for security, any thoughts of danger, you must forget the Isle of Man.

It's impossible to protect such a long circuit adequately, though the people there always tried their best, and the helicopter was an important safety factor other shorter circuits should have copied more quickly! I loved racing there, better even than Monza, but after my friend Gilberto Parlotti was killed there (on a Morbidelli 125 in 1972) I said, enough.

Giacomo went on to recall:

Because we got so much pleasure from the Isle of Man, it was diffi-cult to see the dangers and respond to them. But after many years you see so many riders die in the TT [Parlotti being the 99th competitor to be killed on the world famous circuit] and you wonder why it is necessary to race there. OK – the satisfaction is very good, the atmosphere is fantastic, but why go on racing there when each year there's another friend who leaves you forever because of that wonderful, terrible circuit.

As one who has raced over that same circuit (during the Ago era, Manx GP, 1966, 1967, 1970 and 1971) I can understand his feelings entirely. I too in many ways love the Isle of Man, but now can see the downsides. And certainly, although the circuit has been smoothed out compared to the 1960s and 1970s, quite simply today's racing motorcycles are *too* fast for that particularly diffi-cult course. If I was a young man again I would probably be prepared to race on an RS125 Honda there, but a Yamaha R1 or Suzuki GSX-R1000 – no way!

Because of its unique history and magnetism the Isle of Man TT and Manx GP races continue to the present day. Now they are even more a social gath-ering of like-minded enthusiasts from every part of the globe; personally I prefer the Manx to the TT – it's less crowded. But how did the Isle of Man TT get to become the legend it is today? To find the answer one has to go back to Tuesday 28 May 1907, when 18 single-cylinder and seven twin-cylinder machines lined up for the start of the first TT. In those days engine size and weight were unrestricted, but it was obligatory to carry tools, petrol consumption was limited, and the machines had to be fitted with pedals – for emergencies!

The first course was considerably shorter and did not include the now famous Mountain section – since these gradients were too much to ask from the flimsy and low-powered motorcycles of the time. But following World War One, the now famous 37.73-mile circuit became the yardstick by which motorcycle design and riding ability was judged – and remained so until the Grand Prix riders followed Agostini's lead and quit en masse after 1972. The fact remains that a motorcycle engine, chassis and other components such as brakes, tyres and suspension have no greater testing ground.

The Motor Cycle Racing Guide 1974 summed up the TT in the following way – and also gave a good insight into how things were seen at that time:

> A rider who finishes in the top third of the field in a TT race has made a name for himself. On the other hand, a world champion who has never carried off the TT is hardly a real world champion at all. By modern standards the TT course is too dangerous. Firstly, the track is really bumpy and the surface changes constantly. Secondly, the entire circuit is flanked by walls, trees, telegraph poles, pavements, etc.; so that any rider coming off is extremely lucky if he does not land in hospital. For this reason 'full out' riding is unknown. Riders give their machines as much 'stick' as they can, but they always have a safety margin in reserve. Record lap times prove this very clearly. In 1967, when Mike Hailwood came up against Agostini, a competitor of almost equal brilliance, he set up a record lap speed – still unbeaten today – of 108.77mph. In 1972 Agostini won by the proverbial 'mile', yet his fastest lap was only 105.39mph!

Whatever anyone may say, one thing is sure – as long as the TT exists there will always be riders who cannot resist the challenge of the Mountain Circuit, despite the fact that the financial rewards are small, while the maintenance costs and travel expenses are high.

As *Motor Cycle News* said in their 14 September 1966 issue: 'He did not have to finish (with Hailwood already out he had won the championship). But what a race he rode, riding an MV three he lapped the entire field twice to win at 118.87mph.'

But Mike Hailwood also received a tremendous reception. There was a standing ovation from the crowd as he pushed into the pits and the first to shake his hand in sympathy was Count Domenico Agusta, who would undoubtedly have preferred to have seen the contest between these two great riders go the full distance.

At the end Giacomo was carried shoulder high by adoring fans, having just become the first Italian to win the 500cc title since Gilera-mounted Libero Liberati back in 1957.

When asked to choose the most satisfying moment in his entire career,

Giacomo points to that day at Monza, saying: 'When I won my first world title: for me it was the most important. All my life, I wait for this moment, I dream of being the champion, and it is at Monza it comes true.'

In the 350cc race Mike Hailwood was a non-starter. Even so Giacomo still broke the race and lap records at 115.57mph and 119.32mph respectively, proving what a determined, professional competitor he had become.

350cc Italian GP – 27 laps – 96.47 miles

1st	G. Agostini (MV 3)
2nd	R. Pasolini (Aermacchi)
3rd	A. Pagani (Aermacchi)
4th	S. Grassetti (Bianchi)
5th	F. Stastny (Jawa)
6th	G. Havel (Jawa)

500cc Italian GP – 35 laps – 125 miles

1st	G. Agostini (MV 3)
2nd	P. Williams (Arter Matchless)
3rd	J. Findlay (McIntyre Matchless)
4th	F. Stevens (Hannah Paton)
5th	W. Scheimann (Norton)
6th	E. Lenz (Matchless)

A first-ever mainland British appearance

Giacomo Agostini was the star billing in his first ever British mainland (discounting Northern Ireland) appearance at Mallory Park for the big 'Race of the Year' meeting, two weeks after Monza. And Giacomo had a brilliant, if lucky, debut, winning all five races he contested. The 'lucky' part of it concerned his victory in the main race of the day, the 30-lap 1000 Guineas, when Mike Hailwood was forced out through a puncture in his rear tyre while he was in the lead. One newspaper reported:

Race fans at Mallory on Sunday took to Agostini so much that, after winning the big race, he needed a police escort to take him from the race office to his van. Fans gave him a pop group's reception. Some of the girls literally screamed as he signed autographs.

'Ago idol of Brands' said the front-page headlines in the 12 October 1966 issue of *Motor Cycle News*: 'Giacomo Agostini came, saw and conquered at

Giacomo Agostini in winning form at Brands Hatch in October 1966. His film star looks and terrific riding skills endeared him to the British public.

Brands Hatch on Sunday. Not only did he thrash the opposition, but he conquered the hearts of 25,000 spectators who acclaimed him as the most popular rider ever to visit Britain.' *MCN* continued 'On his first visit to the "scratchers" circuit for the *Evening News* "Race of the South", the world champion staggered everyone with a breathtaking performance which brought him three clear-cut wins.' So what happened to Mike Hailwood? Well, his challenge lasted fully 50 yards before the engine of the six-cylinder Honda disintegrated. A con rod broke and smashed its way through the crankcase, showering the track with oil.

After his victories Giacomo spoke over the circuit's PA system to the British crowd in Italian (which was translated) 'I would like to thank the English public for having supported me as they have done and I hope to come again next year and do as well.' When interviewed after his Mallory and Brands performances Giacomo was asked: 'What do you think of the racing?'. His reply came back: 'I was surprised there were so many events. At Mallory there was hardly five minutes between races. In fact on one occasion I didn't even have time to take my helmet off before I was due to race again! In Italy it takes a day to run three races, here you run seven or eight.'

After Mallory Park and Brands Hatch came a final racing event back in Italy at Vallelunga, north of Rome, during late October, the seventh and final round of the Italian Senior Championship. But after a bad start and after setting a record lap of 71.224mph, Giacomo crashed while trying to catch Renzo Pasolini on a new 16-valve 350 Benelli four. Although reportedly uninjured, this was incorrect – as he had in fact suffered a broken bone in his foot. So a planned return visit to England 'to help learn the language' was delayed and then shortened due to having to make an early return to Italy to 'get the plaster off'.

His original intention had been to stay in England for two months, but actually this turned out to be only three weeks. This included taking in the London Earls Court Show in November 1966. Giacomo said: 'I like London and enjoyed my stay. In fact my only complaint is the weather – it changes so quickly. In Italy we have bad weather but when it's bad it's bad for two or three days and then fine for two or three days. Here it can change in minutes.'

Man of the Year

The 16 November 1966 issue of *Motor Cycle News* reported that the new 500cc World Champion had made a surprise appearance at the Earls Court Show and not only that, but he would be presented with the 'Man of the Year' trophy – the first foreign rider ever to receive the award. The top six positions in the Man of the Year competition, as voted for by readers of *Motor Cycle News*, were:

1st	Giacomo Agostini	17.9%
2nd	Mike Hailwood	16.7%
3rd	Barry Briggs	10.6%
4th	Peter Williams	9.8%
5th	Bill Ivy	7.1%
6th	Dave Bickers	6.5%

As the *Motor Cycle News* copy revealed, 'To British race followers he is no longer a foreigner, but a favourite among champions.'

Past winners:

1965	Bill Ivy
1964	Jeff Smith
1963	Mike Hailwood
1962	Derek Minter
1961	Mike Hailwood
1960	Dave Bickers
1959	John Surtees
1958	John Surtees

Early 1967 and Giacomo Agostini (MV 350 three-cylinder) leads Renzo Pasolini's Benelli four at Cesenatico on the Adriatic coast. This venue was one of the most popular of the Italian street circuits during the era.

Renzo Pasolini ('Paso' to his fans and friends) was a notoriously hard rider. On his day he could beat virtually anyone, but to win championships one had to be consistent over a whole season.

When he received his award, Giacomo said in broken English: 'I would like to thank all the readers of *Motor Cycle News* for the honour they have done me in making me Man of the Year. Now I must race well enough next season to catch up with Mike Hailwood and get the *MCN* title twice.'

A new season begins

A new season got under way in March 1967. Even though the rumour machine had been in full swing, Giacomo Agostini began the next year, as he had ended the previous one, MVs one and only rider.

The first race of the Italian calendar was the international Modena meeting in mid-March. But Giacomo was out of luck because after setting the fastest practice lap, he was forced to make three pit stops in quick succession in a bid to trace a persistent misfire; eventually found to be a faulty carburettor. By the time it had been identified he was three laps down, but regained a lap to eventually finish ninth, in a race won by Benelli's Renzo Pasolini. However, Ago did have the satisfaction of setting the fastest lap of the race, at 79.91mph.

Then, at Riccione a couple of weeks later, Mike Hailwood beat Giacomo by less than a second in what everyone who witnessed it agreed it was one of the most exciting races seen in Italy for many years. This was in the 350cc event. Mike was riding a new six-cylinder 297cc Honda, Giacomo the latest MV 3. At the start Hailwood took the lead. Then Giacomo caught Mike, and the two champions duelled for the lead for several laps, the advantage changing hands

many times during the 26-lap, 52.7-mile race.

In the 500cc race Ago beat Renzo Pasolini on the new five-hundred Benelli four.

Giacomo got his own back on Mike when the two met the following week at Cervia, with Hailwood's three-fifty never matching the MV in the 500cc race (there was no 350cc class). The final result was:

Cervia 500cc – 24 laps – 58.16 miles
1st	G. Agostini (MV 3)
2nd	R. Pasolini (Benelli)
3rd	A. Bergamonti (Paton)
4th	J. Findlay (McIntyre Matchless)
5th	R. Gallina (Ducati)
6th	K. Carruthers (Aermacchi)

A snow storm hit Imola just before its annual Gold Cup meeting, *Motor Cycling* reported in their 29 April 1967 issue: 'A five-inch fall on Friday night completely covered the circuit when competitors arrived for practice on Saturday.' With cold winds sweeping across the north Italian plain the snow refused to melt and after a special meeting, the organisers decided to

The combination of Mike Hailwood and the 297cc six-cylinder Honda proved a hard nut to crack for Giacomo Agostini in 1967.

'Mike-the-Bike' Hailwood

Seen by many as their number one motorcycle racing star of all time, S.M.B. (Stanley Michael Bailey) Hailwood was born in Oxford on 2 April 1940, the son of a self-made millionaire motorcycle dealer. His father, Stan, had competed pre-war on two, three and four wheels, before going on to build up the largest grouping of dealerships seen up to that time in Great Britain.

Mike began his racing career aboard an MV Agusta 125 Competizione sohc production racer loaned to him by family friend Bill Webster (a close friend of Count Domenico Agusta). This debut came at Oulton Park, Cheshire, under the watchful eyes of both his father and Bill Webster; Mike was then 17 years of age.

There is no doubt that Stan Hailwood went about buying success, with the best bikes, the best tuners, and a huge media machine. However, Mike did not really need this vast support, as he had talent in abundance. An example of Stan Hailwood's 'methods' is shown by a story concerning the NSU Sportmax Mike rode during the early part of his career. In 1955 John Surtees had raced the then new German bike thanks to his employers Vincent (who were the British NSU distributors). John was given a bike plus a spare engine. Then, towards the end of 1957, John received a phone call from Stan asking: 'Can we borrow the NSU for Mike to use in South Africa this winter?' John agreed and the machine went to the Hailwood équipe. A few weeks later John got another call from Stan: 'Can we borrow the spare engine?' Again John Surtees agreed. Now Stan had both bike and engine – and John was never to see either again. Because Stan conveniently became an NSU dealer – the 'deal' with the new London-based importers meaning that Kings of Oxford would only become

Mike Hailwood was Giacomo Agostini's team-mate at MV during 1965. The Englishman is seen here winning the 500cc Dutch TT that year.

With new teammate Jim Redman (left) at the beginning of the 1966 season.

agents if Stan could keep the racer and the engine – even though it had been given to John Surtees...

In many ways Mike Hailwood was embarrassed by his father's wheeler dealings, and as soon as he could he became self sufficient – his race results giving him freedom from his father's overpowering attention. In fact Mike nicknamed his father 'Stan the Wallet'. But this was not before Stan had bought bikes such as a 125 Paton, a 125 Grand Prix Ducati, various Desmo Ducati twins and singles for the 125, 250 and 350cc classes, an ex-works FB Mondial 250 single, a squadron of Manx Nortons and an AJS 7R. In 1958 Mike was able to score a trio of British Championships (125, 250 and 350cc).

Mike's first Grand Prix victory came aboard a 125 Ducati Desmo single during the 1959 Ulster GP – the man he beat that day was none other than his future teammate at MV, Gary Hocking (riding a works MZ). That year he also won all four British Championships – a feat he repeated the following year and one which no man before or since has equalled.

For 1961 Mike rode 125 and 250cc works Hondas, plus a 350cc AJS 7R and a 500cc Manx Norton. He gained his first world title, the 250cc, on the four-cylinder Honda, took the 125 and 250cc Isle of Man TTs and the Senior race on his Norton. On the latter machine (tuned by Bill Lacey) he averaged over 100mph for the 6-lap, 226-mile race.

At the end of 1961 he signed for MV Agusta – going on to win the 500cc world title four years in a row (1962–5). In 1965 this meant that Mike was a teammate of Giacomo Agostini. And as this book reveals the time together and the following two seasons (with Honda), when the two rivals were in rival camps, were probably both competitors' hardest years. As Giacomo Agostini reveals, he admired Mike Hailwood more than any other rider and openly admits that during 1965 he learnt an awful lot from Mike, which stood him in good stead for the remainder of his career. Not only that but they remained good friends until Mike's untimely death in a car accident in 1982.

After rejoining Honda for the 1966 season, Mike won both the 250 and

350cc classes on the new six-cylinder models, equalling this feat the following year before switching his attention to four wheels. But even he could not tame the wayward five-hundred four-cylinder Honda (nicknamed the 'camel').

For more than a decade he largely stayed away from bikes (except for a couple of outings on BSA and Yamaha machines) before making a historic comeback TT victory on a Ducati v-twin in 1978. The following year, 1979, he rode a Suzuki to a final TT victory. Then he retired once more, becoming a partner in the Hailwood & Gould business (with fellow World Champion Rod Gould). By a twist of fate the premises they used had formerly been the home of the Birmingham branch of Kings of Oxford (part of father Stan's former dealership chain).

Mike died tragically (with his young daughter Michelle) while driving home in his Rover SDI car after collecting a fish and chip supper on 14 March 1982.

postpone practice until Monday and to run the racing on Tuesday. And thanks to Imola's communist mayor, Amedeo Ruggi, who had battled with the authorities in Rome, there were now several improvements to facilities at the circuit, including a grandstand, concrete pits and a timekeepers' and press tower, while more improvements, including an hotel, were promised for 1968.

Watched by some 40,000 spectators, Giacomo Agostini got Imola off to a flying start by leading his great rival Mike Hailwood in the first race of the day, the 350cc event, followed by Renzo Pasolini on the works four-cylinder Benelli. But Pasolini passed Hailwood next time, and, a lap later, Mike

Developed from the smaller 250cc version, the 297cc Honda six was a fabulous machine. The noise it made caused the hair to stand up on the backs of the necks of competitors and spectators alike.

retired with a broken brake lever, leaving Giacomo to win with ease – and set a new class lap record of 99.998mph for the 23-lap, 71.7-mile race. Actually, when winning the 500cc race later in the day, the MV rider's fastest lap at 96.41mph was slower than the 350cc event, despite the increased engine size.

The Honda RC 174 297cc (41 × 37.5mm) six-cylinder engine; it put out 65bhp at 17,000rpm.

The start of a great GP year

1967 was to witness a titanic struggle between Giacomo and Mike in the 500cc World Championship – one which was to go right down to the wire in the 10-round series.

Hockenheim in West Germany got the season started. Here the MV three (now 497.9cc, 62 × 55mm) came out on top after the crankshaft of Hailwood's Honda broke. The MV rider also set the fastest lap (a new record) at 117.19mph. Earlier the 180,000-strong crowd had seen Mike on the new 297cc six-cylinder Honda beat Giacomo in the 350cc event.

As there were no 350 or 500cc bikes at the French GP at Clermont-Ferrand, the next tussle between the two men came in the Isle of Man TT.

At that stage few could have guessed just how dramatic and exciting the outcome was to be.

Giacomo Agostini had five MVs to choose from in the Isle of Man – three 500ccs and a pair of 350s. One of the larger models was the latest of the four-cylinder heavyweights. Giacomo had used this to win the recent non-championship Austrian GP, and he turned out on this same bike for the first TT practice period. He reeled off three laps, the fastest at over 100mph. However, he openly admitted preferring the three-cylinder models. 'The four is too big for me. The three is much easier to control over the bumps' he said, going on to reveal 'during the first practice I nearly lost control of the four, over the bumps near Ballaspur my feet slipped off the footrests and I was left hanging on with my legs trailing behind me.' MV had a trio of mechanics at the TT, plus team manager Arturo Magni and a brand new Fiat transporter bearing the proud logo *Reparto Corse MV*. Another reason why Giacomo preferred the smaller, lighter three-cylinder was because he was of relatively small stature, although with a powerful upper body.

A 'fantastic' ride by Mike Hailwood made the 1967 Junior TT a real record breaker. From a standing start, Mike just missed becoming the first man ever to beat the 21-minute lap barrier for the fearsome Mountain Circuit. But he did lap at 21 min 0.8 sec, a speed of 107.73mph. And that beat Giacomo's 1966 lap record by over 4mph and was a new absolute motorcycle record for the 37.73-mile Mountain course, over half a mile an hour faster than Mike's own 500cc figure set on a Honda the previous year.

Although he still came out the winner of the Senior TT, two days after the Junior, the contest between Mike and Giacomo turned out to be one of the truly great races in motorcycling history – even though the two men who made it so hardly saw each other during their long battle. Right from the start Giacomo, who was celebrating his 25th birthday, was ahead of Mike on corrected time. And, starting 30 seconds behind Hailwood, he kept ahead on time for nearly five laps, in the process becoming the first rider to lap the Mountain course in under 21 minutes, with a standing start speed of 108.36mph!

Allowing for the starting interval, there were never more than some 12 seconds between the two men. And, after hoisting the lap record to 108.77mph, Hailwood was only one second in arrears at the end of the third lap. Then, in 45 seconds of pit lane drama, Mike dropped back as he attempted to fix a loose twistgrip. But finally, when Giacomo was two seconds ahead – and looked to be heading for victory – the MVs Regina chain broke and the 500cc World Champion retired, while Hailwood, hampered by the loose twistgrip, came home to his 12th TT victory –

breaking the record held by pre-war star Stanley Woods. Like all the other solo events in his Diamond Jubilee TT, the race was plagued by retirements and of the 91 starters, only 37 completed the 226.38 miles.

When interviewed by Alan Cathcart for *Classic Racer* in the summer 1986 issue, Giacomo had this to say of that 1967 Senior TT:

> *I shall never forget my fiercest race with Mike – yet we hardly saw each other for more than two hours, while we were locked in such a bitter duel. I am leading sometimes on the Mountain by ten seconds, but by five only at Ballaugh Bridge, then he is in front again, then me. But we never see each other till the fuel stop. When we are in the pits together for a little while before we resume our lonely paths, still – how do you say? – neck and neck. On the last lap we are still together on the clock and I think, 'I will now win' – but then I stop on the Mountain with a broken chain. I cry all night,*

Giacomo seen here astride a veteran Douglas flat-twin; TT week, Isle of Man, June 1967.

Ago's MV 500 triple prior to the titanic duel between the Italian and Mike Hailwood (Honda), Senior TT, June 1967. MV team manager and chief spanner-man Arturo Magni is on the left of the picture.

I am so disappointed because to me the Isle of Man is the most important race for a rider to win, and to beat Mike Hailwood is not easy.

Motor Cycling's speed trap recorded Mike's Honda at 154.5mph,

Giacomo Agostini during the 1967 Senior TT at Brandish, some 35½ miles out. He shattered the lap record from a standing start at 108.58mph. Ago was later forced to retire with less than half a lap to go, with a broken final drive chain.

Mike Hailwood about to restart during the 1967 Senior TT; in front is Giacomo Agostini and his MV. As Ago was later to recall, this, one of the greatest races ever, was fought out with neither rider seeing each other except at this pit stop.

The 1967 Honda 500 four-cylinder. Nicknamed the 'Camel' by Hailwood, it was tremendously powerful, but the handling and roadholding left much to be desired.

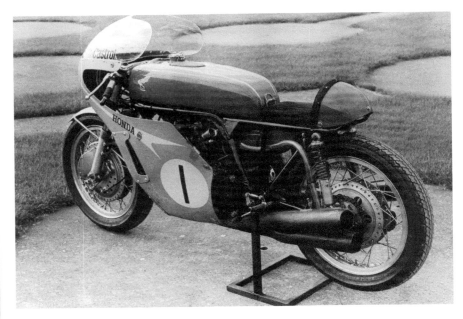

whereas Giacomo's MV 3 went through the electronic eye at 152.5mph. After the race Mike made no secret of the fact that he thought that Giacomo would have won had he kept going.

Agostini 'Master of Mallory'

Just two days after his Senior TT disappointment, Giacomo Agostini won the two major events at Mallory Park's post-TT meeting. But the near-record crowd which lined the 1.35-mile Leicestershire circuit must have despaired at ever seeing Mike Hailwood and Giacomo meet in a fair duel. The previous year, a puncture put Mike out, whereas in June 1967, riding a 'hack' four-cylinder, Hailwood never looked capable of catching Agostini and retired on lap six with bent valves while down in fifth spot.

Then came a resumption of the Ago v Mike battle for the 500cc World Championship. At the Dutch TT Mike won, then eight days later Giacomo took the flag at Spa Francorchamps, the scene of the Belgian GP. Next, in East Germany, at the Sachsenring, Mike posted a retirement, leaving victory to Giacomo. But the Englishman was back to winning form in the Czech Grand Prix at Brno a week later. However, a crash at the next round at Imatra, Finland, was to swing the title pendulum back towards Agostini and MV. Aquaplaning on a streaming-wet corner during a torrential downpour, Hailwood's 500cc Honda hurtled off the circuit and wrapped itself round one of the many trackside trees which lined the Finnish circuit. This fourth-lap crash came when Mike was trying to make up a 22-second deficit on Giacomo's flying MV.

500cc Finnish GP – 23 laps – 86.2 miles

1st	G. Agostini (MV 3)
2nd	J. Hartle (Matchless)
3rd	B. Nelson (Norton)
4th	B. Granath (Matchless-Metisse)
5th	F. Stevens (Hannah Paton)
6th	M. Hawthorne (Norton)

Mechanical trouble

Needing just one more win to virtually clinch the 500cc title for a second year, Giacomo then had the misfortune to suffer a mechanical failure on the start-line of the Ulster GP, when his clutch burnt out! Realising what had happened, Giacomo stopped and pushed back to his pit. There his mechanics stripped the clutch, rebuilt it with new plates and sent him on his way – nearly four laps behind his title challenger. The record 80,000 crowd, enjoying the first fine-weather Ulster GP for many years, gave the Italian tremendous encouragement. And it said a lot for Giacomo's sportsmanship that he kept going and completed the race, to finish in 20th position.

Strangely, it was in Ulster that he had his one and only race victory in the 350cc class that year. But his task was made easier by the absence of Mike, who, having already made sure of the championship, concentrated on the 250 and 500cc classes.

Giacomo splashes through truly awful flooded conditions to win the 1967 500cc Finnish Grand Prix at Imatra. His average speed for the 23-lap, 86.2 mile race was 73.70mph.

350cc Ulster GP – 15 laps – 112 miles

1st	G. Agostini (MV 3)
2nd	R. Bryans (297cc Honda 6)
3rd	H. Rosner (251cc MZ)
4th	K. Carruthers (Aermacchi-Metisse)
5th	B. Steenson (Aermacchi)
6th	I. McGregor (Norton)

Back on home ground at Monza in early September, Giacomo made virtually sure of retaining the 500cc title for a second year with victory in the 35-lap, 124.95-mile race. But Mike Hailwood looked to be the winner for the majority of the race, until slowed by gearbox trouble a couple of laps from the end. In fact it was the Englishman who posted the fastest lap (a new record) at 126.85mph. In the 350cc race, after battling with Renzo Pasolini's four-cylinder Benelli, Giacomo retired in a race won by Honda-

Receiving the victor's laurels after winning the Race of the Year at Mallory Park, Leicestershire, September 1967.

mounted Ralph Bryans.

Although he won the 1000cc final at Mallory Park on Sunday 17 September 1967 on a 420cc MV 3, Giacomo had to accept second best to Mike Hailwood riding a 297cc Honda six in the main 30-lap, 40.5-mile 'Race of the Year'.

Then, riding a cautious, tactical race, Giacomo followed Mike Hailwood home to finish second in the 500cc Canadian Grand Prix at Mosport Park, Ontario, to retain the world championship. Then the next day at Brands Hatch, after a jet-flight across the Atlantic, he 'threw caution to the winds' as the 4 October 1967 issue of the *Motor Cycle* reported, and crashed his three-cylinder MV at the notorious Paddock Hill Bend at Brands. The MV was pretty badly battered, but Giacomo got away unscathed.

Brands Hatch on an October day in 1967. Giacomo awaits the fall of the starter's flag in sombre mood.

In retrospect, retaining the 500cc world crown was the number one priority – which was ultimately achieved. This was certainly a championship which critics could not say was anything other than one of the hardest won in the series since the FIM instigated the World Series back in 1949. But it did mean other championships that year were neglected, notably the 350cc (won by Hailwood) and the 500cc Italian Senior title (won by Angelo Bergamonti, Hannah Paton). And unlike the previous year, Giacomo

The mighty 500 four-cylinder Honda in action with Mike Hailwood aboard. But this combination was unable to beat Ago and the MV triple in the blue riband GP class in both 1966 and 1967; then Honda announced its retirement.

Silvio Grassetti finishing runner-up in the 350cc Italian GP at Monza in September 1967. Grassetti often raced against Agostini, but they were destined never to be teammates.

Agostini did not contest the final round of the 350cc World Championships in Japan.

While visiting England in November, Giacomo attempted to purchase a new 441cc BSA Victor scrambler when he toured the BSA factory in Birmingham, but failed. 'All existing machines have been sold' said a BSA spokesman. A bit of a PR disaster for BSA – surely a bike could have been found? Back in Italy, on his father's estate at Lovere near Bergamo in northern Italy, Giacomo was a keen off-road motorcyclist and already had a 250cc Greeves Challenger. He visited BSA on his way to the Coleraine Club's annual dinner in Northern Ireland. Giacomo also spent a considerable time (as in the previous year) in London. In two years he had picked up enough English to have a reasonable (but not perfect!) command of the language.

And so 1967 drew to a close; at that time neither Giacomo Agostini nor Mike Hailwood realised that they would not be doing battle together the following year, to defend their respective world titles.

Chapter 5

Dominating the World

AS 1968 arrived reports from Japan suggested that Honda was about to unveil a series of new racers – a six-cylinder 125, a 250cc V8 and a 500cc six. Meanwhile Mike Hailwood, who had become a South African citizen, had lapped every rider and shattered every record at the Roy Hesketh Circuit, Pietermaritzburg, on Boxing Day 1967, with a 'fantastic show' (*Motor Cycle*) to win the Dickie Dale Memorial Trophy, which was run concurrently for 250, 350 and 500cc machines.

Then, in the first race meeting of the new season in Europe, Phil Read riding a four-cylinder 250cc Yamaha beat Giacomo Agostini to win the 350cc class on a road circuit, overlooking the Spanish resort of Alicante. The two aces were never more than a few yards apart. But the big surprise of the Alicante meeting was the speed of the new 250 and 350cc Desmo Ducati singles ridden by Bruno Spaggiari. Only the works Yamahas of Read and Bill Ivy and Giacomo's MV were quicker.

350cc Alicante – 20 laps – 78.91 miles

1st	P. Read (252cc Yamaha)
2nd	G. Agostini (MV 3)
3rd	B. Spaggiari (Ducati)
4th	A. Bergamonti (Paton)
5th	J. Findlay (Aermacchi)
6th	G. Milani (Aermacchi)

It was also at Alicante that Honda teamster Ralph Bryans was contacted by his wife, who informed him that a cable had arrived from Honda, summoning him to Japan. Mike Hailwood was also being pursued in a similar way. The following week the world knew why – Honda was to quit Grand Prix events. Development work on new bikes had been suspended.

Although both Bryans and Hailwood were supplied with bikes for 1968 – it was on strict instructions that they were not to be used to contest any of the races counting towards the World Championship series. The Honda GP challenge had hit the buffers.

So why did Honda quit? One reason was that even a company as large and profitable as the Japanese marque could no longer justify the huge expense of building ever more complex multi-cylinder specials to combat their rivals. In a way the Japanese had reached exactly the same conclusions as the Italians a decade earlier, when FB Mondial, Moto Guzzi and Gilera had all retired at the end of the 1957 season.

In addition a proposal had already been put to the FIM's technical committee, concerning a new rule to limit motorcycles up to and including 250cc to a maximum of two cylinders and six gears from 1970 onwards – this was later to be adopted. Motorcycles above that engine size would also not be permitted more than six gears.

How would the Count react?

The big question now being asked was how would Count Domenico Agusta react? Actually he was probably smiling – if not laughing – as he learnt of the Honda withdrawal. For the perceptive Italian industrialist had told Giacomo Agostini that the 500cc MV triple had been fast enough to score again in 1968 – and that he didn't intend to spend a lot of money building a new bike.

So in the end, the wily Count had the last laugh. For with Hailwood out of the way, Giacomo Agostini would have a clear run on the big MV – with the only challenge likely to come from Benelli. It also meant that the 350cc class would be a happy hunting ground for MV Agusta once again.

Competition

So who would provide the competition in the 500cc class, now that Honda had left the scene? Well, on paper at least, there were several possible challengers in the spring of 1968. First Benelli, who have already been mentioned. Then there was the three-man team of Billie Nelson, Angelo Bergamonti and Bill Smith on Paton dohc twins funded by the Scot Bill Hannah, who was then based in Liverpool.

The Westlake twin, the Fontana-designed Cardani three and the twin-cylinder Linto (the latter essentially a pair of Aermacchi 250cc ohv cylinders in a common crankcase), were also in the frame. But in practice, except for the Benelli, and to a smaller degree, the Paton, these challengers were largely unsuccessful, leaving MV unopposed, as after the Italian withdrawal at the end of 1957. However, as John Surtees proved, a good rider can still set new race and lap records to show his true class in the face of minimal opposition. In early March the traditional Italian season opener, the international Modena meeting, had been postponed – in fact it was not run that year. The reason? The track surface had broken up and the insurers would not cover the meeting until repairs were made. But this did not stop practice at the venue, which had been in great demand as Fiat had the exclusive use of Monza throughout February 1968 and in March the latter circuit closed for repairs.

Hailwood springs a surprise

Out for the first time on a new, privately funded Reynolds-framed 500cc Honda, Mike Hailwood appeared to have Giacomo beaten at Rimini, in Italy, at the end of March. However, that was until Mike tweaked the throttle a shade too hard and slid off. That mistake cost him half a minute, and thereafter the Englishman had to settle for runner-up spot.

The Benelli star Renzo Pasolini was one of the very few who could sometimes give Giacomo Agostini (seen here at the left of the picture with his back to the camera) challenge the MV world champion at this time.

But, in truth, it was the World Championships which really counted, both for Giacomo Agostini and MV Agusta – and of course Mike Hailwood had been effectively removed from the 1968 series thanks to Mr Honda.

The press always homed in on the chance to report on the Ago v Mike duels. Round two of this conflict in the early season Italian meetings went decidedly Giacomo's way when Hailwood lost out in a rain-soaked race. Then to compound matters the Honda rider fell while pursuing Benelli-mounted Renzo Pasolini. The latter then became the first man to beat Hailwood and the 297cc six-cylinder Honda since it had made its debut at the West German GP a year before.

A week later Hailwood turned the tables to win another rain-lashed meeting, coming out on top in a 500cc duel with Ago. However, he again crashed in the 350cc event, which again went to Pasolini.

A forest fire

It took a forest fire to stop Giacomo on the bigger of his two three-cylinder MVs at the West German GP at the Nürburgring. But even then it could not stop him eventually winning both the 500cc and 350cc races. Sweeping through the tinder-dry pine woods which cloak the Eifel Mountains, the fire reached the very edge of the 4.8-mile South Loop course during the 500cc event. Billowing smoke cut visibility to a few yards, and, rushing to the

Angelo Bergamonti was Giacomo Agostini's teammate at MV Agusta during part of 1970 and early 1971. He is seen here scoring a double victory at the Spanish GP over the weekend of 26/27 September 1970. Sadly, he was to be fatally injured in a crash at the Riccione street circuit on 4 April 1971.

Angelo Bergamonti

Prior to joining MV Agusta as Giacomo Agostini's teammate for the Italian Grand Prix at Monza on 13 September 1970, Angelo Bergamonti had already made a name for himself as a works rider for Aermacchi, Moto Morini and Paton. In 1967 he won Morini's final Italian Championship title (on a type of machine formally used by Provini and Agostini) and had also taken the 500cc domestic crown the same year with the Paton. He also won the National 125cc title in 1970 riding a single-cylinder two-stroke Aermacchi. These performances underlined his versatility aboard a range of different sizes and engine types of motorcycle.

Born in the northern province of Cremona on 18 March 1939, Angelo Bergamonti has often been compared to the famous Norton star Ray Amm (who suffered a fatal accident while making his MV debut aboard a 350 four at Imola in April 1955). Like Amm, Bergamonti was recklessly brave, and one who did not understand the word 'defeat'.

Known to his friends and fans simply as 'Berga', he probably found it extremely difficult to join Agostini as the junior partner – the 'back-up' man. But during his debut outing at Monza he did just that, coming home second behind Ago in both the 350 and 500cc races.

He repeated these performances a week later at Imola and again at Ospedaletti shortly thereafter. Then, at the final round of the 1970 World Championship series, he won both races on the MV triples (and set new lap records) at Montjuich Park, Barcelona – having been sent alone to Spain, without Agostini.

During the close season of 1970–1 Bergamonti appeared to buckle down to his role in the MV team. Instead of his desperate 'all-out' riding there appeared, at least on the surface, a new maturity – resisting the temptation to try to be number one regardless of the danger.

At the beginning of the new 1971 season, when Bergamonti beat Agostini in the 350cc race at Modena and in the 500cc event at Rimini, he displayed a cool, collected resolve which seemed to mark him out as a potential challenger to Ago that year.

However, then came a celebrated duel between master and pupil at the Riccione street circuit on 4 April 1971, where heavy rain had left the road surface in a dangerous state due to flooding. A few laps after a poor start in the 350cc race, Bergamonti was within striking distance of his teammate – in fact he was rapidly overtaking him – when his machine aquaplaned, sending the unfortunate Bergamonti 'flying head first' as one report stated, into a granite curb at the roadside. Thus, tragically, this forceful rider died, taking with him the dreams of glory that many thought were on the very point of coming true.

danger area, officials stopped the race. So, having led all the way, Agostini was flagged off after completing 19 of the scheduled 26 laps. He had already lapped the entire field and broken the 500cc lap record set by Mike Hailwood on the MV 4 in 1965. Earlier Giacomo had seen off a challenge from Pasolini (Benelli) in the 350cc race, and had lapped nearly 1mph faster, notching up a fantastic record lap at 92.83mph.

Back in Italy at Cervia a week after his Nürburgring double, Giacomo Agostini easily beat Mike Hailwood (297 Honda 6) in the 350cc race – and also set the fastest lap at 81.90mph. But in the 500cc he lost second gear and was forced to retire, leaving victory to Mike, from Bergamonti (Paton) in second place.

In early May Giacomo scored a double victory at a big international meeting held over the German Hockenheim circuit. The main 500cc race, which he won from Billie Nelson (Paton) and Rob Fitton (Norton), was over 30 laps, or 126.16 miles.

Junior–Senior TT double

As the *Motor Cycle* 'TT Report' said on its front page dated 19 June 1968:

He came; he competed; he conquered. Two years ago Italy's Giacomo Agostini scored the first Junior TT victory by a foreign rider. Last week he became the first non-Briton to do the Junior-Senior double. He did it by slicing 7 seconds off Mike Hailwood's 1967 record 350cc average on Wednesday and by cruising to a leisurely 8½ minute Friday win. He finished elated, thirsty, overwhelmed – and the toast of thousands of sun-drenched spectators. Viva Agostini!

Junior TT – 6 laps – 226.38 miles

1st	G. Agostini (MV 3)
2nd	R. Pasolini (Benelli)
3rd	B. Smith (305cc Honda)
4th	D. Woodman (Aermacchi)
5th	J. Cooper (Seeley)
6th	J. Findlay (Aermacchi)

After the TT, Giacomo Agostini and his old sparring partner Mike Hailwood locked horns again. Mike won the 350 and 1000cc races (on the 297cc Honda 6), while Giacomo took a popular victory in the 500cc race on his three-cylinder MV. And waiting for the popular Italian as he crossed the finishing line after his victory were not only the winner's laurels, but also a 26th birthday cake and a bottle of champagne – which he promptly shared with the pair who had featured in an exciting dice for second spot, Alan Barnett (Kirby Metisse) and John Cooper (Seeley).

Two easy wins

The 1968 Dutch TT brought two easy wins for Giacomo on his three-cylinder MV Agustas, while the lightweight classes were dominated by works Yamahas. However, if it sounds dull, it certainly was not, with the huge crowd witnessing one of the 'best world championship meetings for a long time' (*Motor Cycling*). For behind the works riders and, sometimes, even up with them, the privateers waged tremendous battles around the twists and turns of the testing 4.8-mile Assen circuit.

In no class was the struggle for places keener than in the 500cc class, in which that truly cosmopolitan personality Jack Findlay (born in Australia, living in Italy and racing under a French licence), snatched runner-up spot by getting the front wheel of his McIntyre-Matchless G50 home just ahead of John Cooper (Seeley) and Peter Williams (Arter Matchless). Billie Nelson had been with this group all the way, but his Hannah-Paton ran out of oil and seized a mile from the finish. Billie came off in the incident, but he still pushed in, although he arrived at the finish line too late to qualify as a finisher. There's determination for you!

For the first six laps of the 500cc race, Giacomo had been content to keep the revs down and stay just in front of a group of five riders: Findlay, Cooper, Williams and Silvio Grassetti (ex-works Bianchi). Then the World Champion decided that he would use maximum perfor-

From 1968 until 1971, Giacomo Agostini reigned supreme, with nobody being able to effectively challenge him or his three-cylinder MV Agustas.

mance and simply disappeared into the distance. In the 350cc race Ago's victory was even more emphatic and by the finish he had lapped the entire field at least once during the 20-lap, 95.75-mile race.

A new Belgian lap record
Giacomo Agostini and his MV triple set a new lap record of 129.58mph in winning the 1968 500cc Belgian Grand Prix. From Giacomo's gearing MV team manager Arturo Magni worked out that the machine's speed down the Masta straight was no less than 172mph! This was the World Champion's fifth 500cc GP victory in succession and it virtually clinched the title for him – for the third year running.

At the beginning of the 15-lap, 131.41-mile race, Giacomo had got off to a poor start. At the end of the first lap Alberto Pagani on the new Linto twin led, with the MV star second and Jack Findlay on his trusty McIntyre-Matchless third. However, after pulling away from the singles, the Linto quit on lap three, leaving Giacomo to go in search of a new lap record.

The next stopping point in the 1968 GP circus came behind the Iron Curtain in communist East Germany, where, in winning both his races, Giacomo Agostini made sure of retaining his 500cc crown – and virtually sealed the 350cc title to boot. Even though he was never pressed in either race, he still displayed his class by breaking the lap record in the 500cc race, setting a new speed of 109.86mph.

350cc East German GP – 18 laps – 96.39 miles
1st	G. Agostini (MV 3)
2nd	H. Rosner (MZ)
3rd	K. Carruthers (Aermacchi-Drixton)
4th	W. Molloy (Bultaco)
5th	D. Woodman (Aermacchi-Metisse)
6th	B. Nelson (Norton)

500cc East German GP – 20 laps – 107.06 miles
1st	G. Agostini (MV3)
2nd	A. Pagani (Linto)
3rd	J. Findlay (McIntyre-Matchless)
4th	J. Cooper (Seeley)
5th	B. Nelson (Hannah Paton)
6th	G. Nash (Norton)

Double champion

For the first time in his career, Giacomo Agostini clinched the 350 and 500cc world championship double. His achievement came at the Czech Grand Prix, held over the 8.66-mile Brno road circuit, which was made treacherous by bad weather conditions. The course at Brno was a real road circuit. It weaved its way through villages, across open land, and up and down among pine forests, actually swooping into a suburb of the city itself at one point. The poor weather meant that no records were broken and the greasy surface caught out many riders – but not Giacomo. In commenting on his performance, *Motor Cycle* said:

> *This was not so easy, for heavy showers transformed the circuit into a skating rink that reduced speeds by half. The tarry surface was so slippery when wet that Agostini could not use full throttle even on the straights without wheel-spin sending the bike slithering, motocross style across the road – and everyone else was in much the same boat.*

Another victory came at the Finnish GP, where over the 3.7-mile tree-lined Imatra circuit Giacomo set a new 500cc lap record of 93.33mph – compared to the old speed of 87.68mph which he had put up in 1965. The race speed was also a record. There was no 350cc event.

Yet another double came at the next round, held over the 7.4-mile Dundrod circuit overlooking the city of Belfast, home of the Ulster Grand Prix. Giacomo also had the satisfaction of breaking the 350cc lap record, going round at 106.37mph. But there was no record breaking in the 500cc event, as the race began in pouring rain. In fact, whereas he had averaged 102.74mph in the 350cc class, the MV rider's average speed for the bigger engine size was down to 94.89mph.

Hailwood returns

The big news in the days leading up to the 1968 Italian GP at Monza was that Mike Hailwood had been offered works MV Agustas for the event – and he had accepted. However, when the practicing sessions came around Mike refused to accept Count Agusta's instructions to finish second to Giacomo – and so he turned down the 350 and 500cc three-cylinder racers offered. Instead he chose to ride a four-cylinder 500cc Benelli. But the former Honda teamster's only GP ride of the year ended on the third lap of the rain-soaked race when he crashed while braking for a corner just behind Giacomo Agostini. Mike suffered a cut wrist and, unable to restart the machine, retired. 1968 was the first year, since his first international season, that Mike Hailwood had ended the year without a single world championship point to his name.

Overnight rain – and more wet weather on race day – left the high-speed 3.5-mile Monza track treacherously slippery and there were several crashes to add to Hailwood's. But all this wet weather didn't seem to affect the MV double world champion. *Motor Cycle* described the start of the 350cc race:

Although a downpour saturated the track and soaked riders assembled on the grid for the 350cc race, it did nothing to dampen Giacomo Agostini's enthusiasm as he catapulted his MV into the lead ahead of the Benelli fours of Renzo Pasolini and Silvio Grassetti.

350cc Italian GP – 27 laps – 96.47 miles

1st	G. Agostini (MV 3)
2nd	R. Pasolini (Benelli)
3rd	S. Grassetti (Benelli)
4th	B. Stasa (CZ)
5th	B. Spaggiari (Ducati)
6th	F. Stastny (Jawa 4)

500cc Italian GP – 35 laps – 124.95 miles

1st	G. Agostini (MV 3)
2nd	R. Pasolini (Benelli)
3rd	A. Bergamonti (Paton)
4th	A. Pagani (Linto)
5th	S. Bertarelli (Paton)
6th	K. Carruthers (Norton)

So the 1968 Grand Prix season came to an end – marking the beginning of a period where, except for the odd crash or mechanical breakdown, Giacomo Agostini and MV would dominate the world of motorcycle Grand Prix racing, in a similar way to John Surtees a decade earlier – but for a longer period.

Mike Hailwood showed Giacomo the way home at Mallory Park's 'Race of the Year', winning on his 297cc six-cylinder Honda, ahead of the Italian five-hundred MV three. But a shower at the beginning of the main race rather spoilt the spectacle that a near-record crowd had come to see, as it provided a slippery circuit, meaning Ago's power advantage was, as the

Motor Cycle race report of 25 September 1968 put it: 'down the drain'. Giacomo's only consolation at Mallory came with a victory in the 1000cc race. Mike Hailwood later repeated his victory over Giacomo Agostini at Brands Hatch the following month.

A foretaste of things to come

In a foretaste of what was to come when they were MV teamsters several years later, the two 1968 double world champions, Giacomo Agostini and Phil Read, the latter having his first ride on a Benelli four, fought out a great race when they clashed at Vallelunga, a few kilometres north of Rome, on a Sunday in late October. Read led the 500cc race for the first three laps, with Benelli teammate Renzo Pasolini effectively getting in Agostini's way. Then the MV star got past Pasolini and got to grips with Read. Thereafter a fierce exchange of positions took place between the two champions, before finally, after breaking the lap record, Giacomo went on to win the 30-lap, 58.16-mile race, averaging 76.43mph.

At the end of 1968 the book *Hailwood* by Ted Macauley was published. In it Mike paid tribute to his former MV teammate, saying: 'For my money, Agostini is the finest Italian rider since Carlo Ubbiali; he's a quick learner, he has plenty of courage and he's brimming with skill. After I left MV for Honda he gave me the hardest rides I'd ever experienced.'

Film star

There is no doubt that Giacomo Agostini could have been a successful film star, had it not been for his love for and commitment to racing. As an example, during the close season of 1968–9 he was offered a starring contract by a major Italian film company, but decided to turn it down unless the filming schedule could be altered so as not to interfere with his racing commitments for the start of the 1969 season. Giacomo underwent a series of screen tests in Rome during early December 1968. His performances were so impressive that he was offered a starring role in a film which was to be filmed, mainly on location, in Egypt. The problem, as Giacomo explained, was: 'that the film will take three months to make. We should be on location in Egypt for two months and then filming in the studios in Rome for another month – and this would interfere with the start of the racing season.'

Mike Hailwood had once said: 'I don't know why he doesn't take up acting with his looks. He'd make more money and I'd have nothing to worry about.' As it was Giacomo did go on to star in several films, in more minor roles, which did not clash with his racing programmes.

If it had not been for his motorcycle racing career Giacomo Agostini could have been a really big film star. As it was he still managed to appear in smaller parts in several movies, beginning in the late 1960s.

The new year began with headline stories of Bill Ivy signing to race the recently developed Jawa three-fifty V4 two-stroke (Yamaha having quit at the end of 1968) and Mike Hailwood going to cars full time.

Ago tries a six-cylinder MV

Just prior to the start of the 1969 Italian racing season, Giacomo Agostini tested a pair of new six-cylinder MVs at Modena. First rumours of six-cylinder machines had leaked from the factory when Giacomo said he 'hoped they would be ready for the TT'. The engines followed the Honda layout, with the cylinders set across the frame. These sported four valves per cylinder, while the three-fifty featured a 7-speed gearbox. The cylinders were inclined forward by 10 degrees, while the three-fifty version (348.8cc – 43.3 x 39.5mm) was reputed to put out 72bhp at 16,000rpm. Unfortunately no details of bore and stroke measurements of the five-hundred were ever revealed. Although more powerful than the existing three-cylinder, the six had two major problems. One concerned its race tuning. Originally, the design called for the use of electronic ignition. But this was at an early stage in its evolution and had to be abandoned in favour of points ignition with coils. This proved almost impossible to set up correctly. Then there was the introduction of new FIM rulings for 1970 which saw the limit of six-speeds only for the gearbox. So although it appeared during various test sessions, the 'new' six was destined never to be raced in a GP. Instead Giacomo Agostini continued with the existing, but improved triples, until new lightweight four-cylinder models were introduced during the early 1970s.

The season opener at Rimini on 16 March 1969 saw Renzo Pasolini achieve a big ambition when he beat Giacomo Agostini after a tremendous battle which had the partisan crowd (Pasolini's home town was Rimini) roaring. The duel raged for 18 of the 24 laps of the two-mile seaside circuit. Then, to the joy of the locals, 'Paso' began to draw away from the world champion, eventually winning by 3.6 seconds. In the 500cc event Ago won easily from the Paton of Angelo Bergamonti and the Linto of Alberto Pagani.

Next came Modena, where Pasolini again took the 350cc race after Giacomo had retired with a stuck throttle slide on one of his machine's three Dell'Orto carburettors. Then came Ago's customary victory in the 500cc race – this time from Giuseppe Mandolini on an ex-works 1957 Moto Guzzi dohc horizontal single. Renzo Pasolini made it three wins in a row when he once again got the better of Giacomo Agostini at Riccione, which although an international meeting was also the third round of the Italian Senior Championships.

In the 500cc race Agostini played cat and mouse with Mike Hailwood (who had been persuaded out of retirement together with his fellow former Honda teammate Ralph Bryans) for half the race, before clearing off to win by some distance. Angelo Bergamonti (Hannah-Paton) looked set for third place until clutch problems put him out. Teammate Bertarelli took over, beating off a challenge from Alberto Pagani (Linto), who eventually stopped with a broken rev counter.

500cc Riccione – 25 laps – 51.26 miles
1st	G. Agostini (MV 3)
2nd	M. Hailwood (Honda 500 4)
3rd	S. Bertarelli (Hannah-Paton)
5th	P. Campanelli (Seeley)
5th	L. Trabalzini (Norton)
6th	L. Tondo (Gilera)

With the arrival on the scene of a Benelli which seemed to have the legs of the three-cylinder MV, and the brand new production TR2 three-fifty Yamaha twin, for the first time since Honda had officially quit it appeared that Giacomo Agostini would have problems retaining his 350cc world title in 1969.

Shattering race and lap records, Renzo Pasolini and his Benelli four scored a fourth victory – and his most unexpected one – in the 350cc race at Imola during early April. The 3.1-mile circuit was a true road course, unlike the stop-go Adriatic street circuits on which Paso excelled. Out for the first time on a brand-new TR2 Yamaha, Silvio Grassetti was third. Giacomo won the 500cc race, breaking his own lap record with a new speed of 100.85mph.

Hitting back after suffering four defeats in a row, Ago finally beat arch rival Pasolini in the 350cc race at Cesenatico in mid-April. The Italian double World Champion rounded off his day

Pasolini in winning form on the Benelli 350 four at Imola.

by winning the 500cc race on his larger-engined three-cylinder MV. The meeting had got off to an excellent start, with not only Renzo Pasolini and Giacomo Agostini in the entry, but Bill Ivy making his debut on the works V4 Jawa. Unfortunately Ivy was plagued by misfiring problems, leaving the field open for the two Italians. In the 500cc race Ago was unchallenged.

The Grand Prix season begins

The Grand Prix season began with a war of words between MV and Benelli, with Benelli team manager, Innocenzo Nardi-Dei, accusing MV of alleged 'bad sportsmanship' at the Jarama circuit, near Madrid, before official practicing was due to begin. Anxious to learn the circuit, being used for the first time, Pasolini asked track officials if he could practice (MV and Ossa were already using the circuit), but was told that MV and Ossa had 'exclusive' rights and he must ask them. They both refused (having paid a considerable sum for the privilege). So Nardi-Dei said: 'If Agostini wants to practice alone he can race alone' and withdrew the Benelli from the 350cc class (Pasolini still riding the two-fifty four in the 250cc event).

The 2.12-mile circuit was a difficult one, especially in the wet – and, yes, it did rain in Spain – most of the races being staged in either wet or damp conditions (but not the blue riband 500cc event). The *Motor Cycle* dated 7 May 1969 had the following headline: 'Two falls, two wins for wet Ago'.

The first accident occurred when the double World Champion dropped his three-fifty and, as *Motor Cycle* said, 'went bowling end over end down the track'. But within five minutes he was out on his reserve machine. Crash number two occurred in the 500cc race, although this time it was not Ago's fault. Last but one away, Giacomo was pressing early leaders Angelo Bergamonti (Hannah-Paton) and Kel Carruthers (382cc Aermacchi) hard when Kel slid off right under the MV's front wheel. Down went Ago. 'I helped him pick the MV up, and gave him a hand starting it. That was the least I could do', said the Australian (whose own machine was jammed under a wire fence). Although Bergamonti was in fine form, Giacomo still caught and passed him to win the race.

In the 350cc race the MV star led all the way, although challenged in the early laps by Carruthers (Aermacchi) and Rod Gould (Yamaha). In driving rain Ago pulled away, with Gould losing ground when water got into the drum of his twistgrip and caused the throttle cables to stick, eventually bringing about the Englishman's retirement.

Renzo Pasolini was in more trouble when, at the next round of the world championships at Hockenheim in West Germany, he crashed in practice, breaking his collarbone.

Monza

During 1986, when Giacomo Agostini was interviewed about his favourite circuits by racing journalist Alan Cathcart, he came up with two names – the Isle of Man and Monza. Giacomo said:

I am Italian, so I very much like Monza – but Monza as it was, not like today, which is a bit sad. I loved the Monza of my youth, when I lived close to the circuit. When I hear the name 'Monza', something makes my blood start to run faster: just driving slowly in a car round Lesmo or Curvone or Parabolica fills me with special fascination, a sense of tradition mixed with deep nostalgia. If I just stand beside the track I can hear the echo of the machines we raced there nearly 20 years ago: the deep roar of my MVs, the shriek of the Hondas. It all comes back to me each time I hear the simple name 'Monza'.

The story of how Monza (to the north-east of Milan) came about is enthralling in itself. The autodrome, set in the spacious confines of the Monza royal palace – its official title then being the *Regio Parco di Monza* (Royal Park of Monza) – was the venue of the assassination of King Umberto I in 1900.

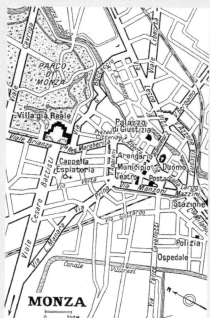

It seems strange that in Italy, which for most of the 20th century was so passionate about motor sport, there was no permanent racing circuit before the construction of Monza's autodrome began during the early 1920s. Great Britain had Brooklands (built in 1907) and the United States of America had Indianapolis (opened in 1909), while Italy only had long-distance road events such as the *Milani–Napoli* and the *Circuito del Lario* (the Italian TT), which took place in the hills above Lake Como. The *Autodrome di Monza* was constructed from scratch in an amazingly short time – just 110 days – by around 3,500 workers.

Vincenzo Lancia (the founder of the famous car company which carries his name) and Felice Nazzaro laid the first stone in February 1922, but a couple of days later protesters interrupted the project. Work was finally started on 3 May, finishing on 15 August, with the circuit being opened on 28 August 1922. There were 6.25 miles of tarmac with two vast banked curves, interlinked with the road course. Monza has changed several times since then but somehow the spirit (albeit severely restricted in recent years) has survived everything.

Though a 'run-out' with cars was staged in August 1922, the first major event was the inaugural Italian motorcycle Grand Prix, then, as for many years, dubbed the *Gran Premio delle Nazione* (Grand Prix of Nations) which took place on Friday 8 September 1922. The winner was Amedeo Ruggieri on an

American Harley-Davidson. The legendary Tazio Nuvolari was one of the early stars of Monza on both two and four wheels; he won the 350cc motorcycle Grand Prix four years in a row (twice also beating all the 500s!).

A series of fatal accidents on four wheels meant that the 4.5km banked oval circuit was not used for car events after 1933, although it continued to comprise part of the 10km motorcycle course until it was demolished prior to the outbreak of World War Two.

Like its British counterpart, Brooklands, Monza suffered at the hands of the military authorities during the war, but at least the Italian course survived. Its badly damaged track surface was not repaired until the end of the 1940s. When it reopened in 1949, there was a 6.3km circuit which followed much of the pre-war road section. This was shortened in 1955 to 5.75km by the construction of a fearsome banked oval, which was to prove over-bumpy (a 1957 speed record attempt by Bob McIntyre on a four-cylinder Gilera had to be restricted to a 350cc model and not the full 500cc version).

Nonetheless, the new road course was very fast, with wide, open sweeping curves that ensured it was one of the very quickest circuits in the Grand Prix calendar. The first 100mph lap was achieved by Englishman Geoff Duke on a works Norton in 1950. In 1967 Giacomo Agostini had the distinction of becoming the first and only man to average more than 200kph (125mph), when winning the 500cc Italian GP on his 3-cylinder MV Agusta. Then in 1971 he set an all-time lap record (again riding an MV triple) at 127.13mph. The following year, 1972, a series of chicanes was introduced, mainly because of fears expressed by the car racing fraternity. This also saw a series of Armco steel barriers erected. These were largely responsible for the terrible two-wheel fatalities which were to occur at Monza in 1973. First, in May that year, both Renzo Pasolini and Jarno Saarinen were killed in a 15-bike pile up on the first corner of the 250cc Italian GP. Hardly had this tragedy occurred than three more riders lost their lives on the same corner in a terribly familiar rerun of the crash some seven weeks later at an Italian Championship meeting. This caused Monza to receive, rightly, a fierce barrage of criticism from around the world.

Extensive alterations were carried out, providing adequate run-off and a host of other safety measures, partly funded by the car Grand Prix, which had continued at Monza. These meant that the circuit was declared safe for motor-cycles during the safety conscious era of the late 1970s and early 1980s. In 1983 the famous circuit once again hosted the Grand Prix of Nations. Tighter chicanes severely restricted lap times. Those riders, including the likes of Giacomo Agostini, who had raced in the old days before the chicanes were introduced, found much to dislike about the so-called improvements.

There is no doubt that Ago dislikes Monza as it is today:

With all the chicanes, it's not any more the real Monza. They made a big mistake putting so many artificial corners in which are so tight. It would have been better to spend a little more time and money to make a big, sweeping second-gear S-bend instead of a narrow chicane which makes everybody slow down too much and use bottom gear. A chicane is nothing: everybody takes it at more or less the same speed, and a good rider can't get any advantage because there's only one way to do it. On a fast corner at a circuit like Monza, if you are good and another rider is not so good, you can take half a second from him, but in a chicane you never gain any time.

In the old days at Monza, you see groups of riders with ten, maybe 12 machines slipstreaming each other all the way around the

> *track. It was very exciting for spectators, and for us too, because we know that all would be decided on the last lap. But now the chicanes break the groups up too much, and many of the races get strung out into a procession.*

Monza was also special to Agostini because it was his 'home' circuit in the GP year and of his 13 Italian Grand Prix victories, no less than nine were achieved there. He said:

> *In my day, the atmosphere there was incredible. For the Gran Premio [Grand Prix] there were always 80 to 100,000 spectators, and for three days it seemed to be the centre of the world. The proudest moment of my life was when I won my first world title at Monza in 1966. Afterwards, it seemed every single fan came to the MV truck to celebrate my title. All of Italy was with me in those days, because I was the first Italian for many years to win the blue riband of motorcycle racing, the 500cc world title.*

The second round in the title stakes had everything that the previous Sunday's Spanish GP had lacked – hot sunshine, 100,000 spectators and, above all, close racing in all six classes. The 350cc race was a good example, with Rod Gould (Yamaha) giving Giacomo an early scare by leading the race on the opening lap with Bill Ivy (Jawa) within striking distance. But Gould's bid was short-lived, for the left-hand cylinder of his TR2 Yamaha seized on the second lap. Even so, Ivy remained a serious threat, hounding Giacomo Agostini for several laps before the Italian slowly edged away. Not only that, but Ivy's teammate, the veteran Franta Stastny, carved his way through the field after an awful start to annexe the last rostrum position – giving Jawa fours what *Motor Cycle* said was: 'a very well deserved success'. On the final lap Ivy's machine faltered, but it was lack of fuel rather than a seizure.

In the 500cc race, again there was considerable pressure, with several of the new Linto twins and a four-cylinder entry in the shape of the Helmut Fath URS Metisse ridden by the German Karl Hoppe. But again Giacomo came out on top, setting the fastest lap in the 500cc race at 116.58mph.

350cc West German GP – 23 laps – 96.72 miles

1st	G. Agostini (MV 3)
2nd	B. Ivy (Jawa 4)
3rd	F. Stastny (Jawa 4)
4th	J. Findlay (Yamaha)
5th	G. Visenzi (Yamaha)
6th	K. Carruthers (Aermacchi)

500cc West German GP – 30 laps – 126.16 miles

1st	G. Agostini (MV 3)
2nd	K. Hoppe (URS-Metisse)
3rd	J. Findlay (Linto)
4th	J. Dodds (Linto)
5th	R. Fitton (Norton)
6th	G. Marsovszky (Linto)

Le Mans

Round three of the championships was staged at the 2.74-mile Le Mans circuit. And with no 350cc class, Giacomo Agostini had only the 500cc race to look forward to in the French GP. A heavy rain-shower completely spoilt the race for riders and race-goers alike. As the field got away, with Kel Carruthers (382cc Aermacchi) in the lead, the sun was shining, but on lap three of the 35-lap, 96.14-mile race the heavens opened. By this time Giacomo was in the lead with Carruthers second and Angelo Bergamonti (Paton) third. Several riders were then to suffer retirement, either through crashes or mechanical failure. Towards the end of the race, Billie Nelson sped through the field to come home runner-up behind winner Giacomo Agostini.

Back in Italy, Giacomo was a spectator at the big San Remo meeting – he had already sewn up the 500cc class of the domestic championship and had been beaten by Pasolini in the 350cc category of the 1969 Italian Senior Championships – so Count Agusta had ordered him not to ride, because the Isle of Man TT practice was only days away.

Early in TT practice, MV tested new front forks and brakes on two of its 350 triples. The 4LS front stoppers were manufactured especially for MV by the Ceriani concern. One of the forks, a lightweight version, was also from Ceriani, whereas the other was produced by MV itself.

'Untouchable Ago' was the *Motor Cycle's* headline for the Junior TT. In fact his only real problems were molten tar and dead flies on his goggles! Of the eight TR2 Yamahas, only two survived. There were 53 finishers from over 100 starters, the hot weather being responsible for many retirements. On post-race inspection a matt-black coating on the piston crowns of the three-cylinder MV showed carburation to have been a trifle rich, probably as a result of the weather getting considerably hotter during the afternoon.

Two days later and Ago added the Senior TT his haul of successes. After his winning ride on the larger MV, Giacomo said conditions had been much better than during the Junior race, apart from 'disconcerting heat mirages on the road over the Mountain'. He had had time to enjoy the ride – as he'd shown by waving to the crowds on many of the corners on his last lap.

Following the TT came the annual Post TT meeting at Mallory Park. And here, for the first time, Rod Gould showed what the following year would be World Championship form (by becoming the 1970 250cc champ), beating Giacomo Agostini and his three-cylinder MV 500 on a TR2 Yamaha three-fifty twin in the 20-lap 1000cc final.

Dutch TT

A fantastic battle took place at the 1969 Dutch TT at the end of June. Riding the V4 Jawa two-stroke was ex-Yamaha 125cc World Champion Bill Ivy. At this, the fifth round of the title series, urged on by a record-breaking crowd of over 150,000 spectators, 'Little Bill' hurled the Czech machine around the superb 4.8-mile Van Drethe circuit to challenge Giacomo Agostini to such good effect that he passed the Italian before the end of the first lap. Ivy then clung on to the lead for two laps, but just as the crowd sensed that an upset was on the cards the Jawa started to misfire slightly on one cylinder. Ago then regained the lead and began to pull away. However, the Jawa came back on to all four cylinders and the race was on again – and by lap 12 Ivy was leading once more. Then, as *Motor Cycle* said: 'The Jawa ignition system played tricks again and back on three cylinders, it had no answer to the MV,' and, with a new lap record, Giacomo Agostini regained the lead and went on to victory.

The World Champion's task in the 500cc class was a whole lot easier – in fact the fastest lap of the day was Ago's 350cc record breaker, when chasing Ivy and the Jawa. And things were not going well for the new Linto machines, with numerous breakdowns being notched up – and lots of unsatisfied customers who had paid a lot of money. Because of this, support had been withdrawn from Jack Findlay (2nd in the 1968 500cc championships on the McIntyre Matchless) who had been signed up to race the Linto in all the 1969 rounds. But he was now having to borrow single cylinder bikes for the 500cc races.

350cc Dutch TT – 20 laps – 95.75 miles

1st	G. Agostini (MV 3)
2nd	B. Ivy (Jawa 4)
3rd	S. Grassetti (Yamaha)
4th	K. Hoppe (Yamaha)
5th	J. Findlay (Yamaha)
6th	G. Visenzi (Yamaha)

During 1969 the new 350 six-cylinder MV was extensively tested. However, it was not proceeded with for a number of reasons, which are explained in the main text.

500cc Dutch TT – 20 laps – 95.75 miles

1st	G. Agostini (MV 3)
2nd	P. Williams (Arter Matchless)
3rd	A. Barnett (Kirby Matchless)
4th	G. Milani (382cc Aermacchi)
5th	J. Findlay (382cc Aermacchi)
6th	G. Marsovszky (Linto)

Ago beats the 130mph barrier in Belgium

Setting yet another milestone in his career, Giacomo Agostini became the first man ever to lap a Grand Prix circuit at over 130mph in the Belgian GP on 5 July 1969 – his exact speed being 130.66mph. And Giacomo's performance went a long way towards silencing critics who accused him of 'having an easy time.'

As riders formed up on the line for the start of the 500cc race a swarm of insects descended on the starting area. There were no less than six different types of machinery on the front row of the grid – MV Agusta, Aermacchi, Arter Matchless, Linto, Paton and Triumph. The crowd roared their approval as Ago obligingly provided Percy Tait (works Triumph) and Alan Barnett (Kirby Metisse) a tow clear of the pack on the first lap. Then he pulled away and, thereafter, went on to annihilate the lap and race records. The surprise performance of the race was undoubtedly Percy Tait's ride on a works-prepared production-based pushrod Triumph unit twin: he finished runner-up and was the only rider to remain unlapped by the end of the 13-lap, 113.89-mile race, averaging 116.58mph compared to Giacomo Agostini's 125.83mph figure.

A week after the Belgian round came the East German Grand Prix at the Sachsenring. But even though Giacomo clinched his fourth successive 500cc world title, equalling the record set up by Mike Hailwood on the four-cylinder MV in the early 1960s, it was Bill Ivy's fatal accident when the lower left-hand crankshaft of his Jawa V4 seized during practice that was, sadly, the big talking point of the meeting.

A sombre affair

The following is an extract from *Motor Cycle's* race report of 16 July 1969:

On Sunday morning the drizzle returned, dark grey clouds hanging just over the pine woods that cloak the hills within the circuit. It was a sombre setting for a last farewell to Bill Ivy. For as the 350cc starters filed out to the start, a wreath was placed on the place Bill had earned on the grid as second-fastest in practice. A few words were spoken; the crowd in the vast wooden grandstand stood in silence; and the Sachsenring seemed a very grim place indeed.

However, the show had to go on and Giacomo Agostini took the lead almost as soon as the starter's flag fell, with only Rod Gould (Yamaha) keeping him in sight, both men pulling away from local star Heinz Rosner (MZ). By the end of the race the roads were beginning to dry, with Giacomo winning from Gould and Rosner. The rain returned for the 500cc race, sweeping across the circuit as competitors wheeled their bikes to the grid behind a row of schoolboys carrying the flags of the competing nations. Adding a touch of variety was a pair of Russian Vostock fours, ridden by Ehdel Kiska and Juri Randla, but they were well off the pace. Again Giacomo led all the way; while private battles were waged all the way down the field. At the end – as in several other GPs that year – the MV World Champion had lapped the entire field at least once.

350cc East German GP – 18 laps – 96.31 miles

1st	G. Agostini (MV 3)
2nd	R. Gould (Yamaha)
3rd	H. Rosner (MZ)
4th	G. Visenzi (Yamaha)
5th	B. Stasa (CZ)
6th	M. Lunde (Yamaha)

500cc East German GP – 20 laps – 107.06 miles

1st	G. Agostini (MV 3)
2nd	B. Nelson (Hannah-Paton)
3rd	S. Ellis (Linto)
4th	W. Begold (McIntyre-Matchless)
5th	T. Dennehy (Drixton-Honda)
6th	P. O'Brien (Matchless)

Czech sunshine

After the wet weather of the Sachsenring, the conditions a week later at Brno, Czechoslovakia, were in complete contrast, with hot, sunny races.

Alberto Pagani

Alberto Pagani, born in Milan on 29 August 1938, the son of a famous father, was, as one journalist described him: 'A first class stylist and a man who kept his emotions very much under control.'

Pagani's father, Nello, had become the first 125cc World Champion on an FB Mondial in 1949; the same year he had also finished runner-up in the 500cc championship on a four-cylinder Gilera. During much of the 1950s he held the official title of team manager for the MV Agusta marque. Nello was very much a gentleman of the old school and could have easily been mistaken for a career diplomat. Alberto followed very much in his father's shoes, at least in temperament, being one of the 'most gentlemanly and well-educated men in the world of Italian motorcycling', as he was described in the book *MV Agusta* (Mario Columbo and Roberto Patrignani).

Alberto's racing career began in 1956, when, thanks to his father, (who was then MV team manager) he was able to borrow a 125 MV Agusta. By 1960 he was a works development rider for Aermacchi – in fact it was Alberto Pagani who debuted the brand-new Ala d'Oro (Gold Wing) ohv horizontal single during the 1960 Dutch TT. He was to remain associated with the Varese factory throughout much of the 1960s. Another highlight came in 1963, when he finished third in the Lightweight (250cc) Isle of Man TT on a twin-cylinder dohc Paton (behind the Honda four of Jim Redman and the MZ twin of Alan Shepherd).

Alberto was also closely linked with the development of the ultimately unsuccessful Linto five-hundred twin (essentially a pair of Aermacchi cylinders in a common crankcase) – the Linto's only real success was victory in the 1969 Italian 500cc GP at Monza with Pagani aboard.

Alberto had to wait patiently for his chance to join MV, which came in 1971, following Angelo Bergamonti's tragic death at Riccione in April that year. Alberto Pagani was certainly a more stable and reliable rider than his predecessor – and ultimately more suited for a role as second-string rider behind Giacomo Agostini. This he played with dignity and courage. In the course of 1971 and 1972 his best results came with wins at Monza (1971, 500cc) and Opatija, Yugoslavia (1972, 500cc). He also finished runner-up at Assen, Spa Francorchamps, the Isle of Man TT, Imatra, Imola and the Nürburgring (all in the 500cc class).

After ending the 1972 season as runner-up in both the Italian and World Championships behind team leader Agostini, Alberto Pagani decided to retire from competitive riding. His decision was probably provoked by the events surrounding Gilberto Parlotti's fatal accident on a 125cc Morbidelli at the 1972 Isle of Man TT, which are described in detail elsewhere.

However, Pagani Junior was not lost to motorcycling entirely, as for a further two years he followed in his father's footsteps by becoming MV's team manager. It could not have been an easy role, given the open warfare between Agostini and Phil Read, which began from the moment the Englishman joined the Italian team for the 1973 season. Once he left MV, Alberto Pagani concentrated his energies into expanding his various business interests and his family.

Ago leads Linto-mounted Alberto Pagani (24) during the 1969 Czech 500cc Grand Prix. Later Pagani was to join MV and partnered Giacomo during 1971 and 1972.

Although he was ultimately to win, and thus become 350cc World Champion for the second year running, Yamaha-mounted Rod Gould gave Giacomo one of his hardest races for some time over the 8.7-mile Brno road course. For almost half the 11-lap, 95.32-mile race distance, Gould duelled with the Italian ace. Time and time again he nosed his twin-cylinder air-cooled TR2 Yamaha ahead of the three-cylinder MV. And, although Gould had to eventually settle for runner-up position, he notched up the fastest lap of the race at 98.5mph. Third was Silvio Grassetti, racing the Jawa V4 for the first time.

In the 500cc event Ago was some 3½ minutes ahead of the second place man Gyula Marsovszky (Linto) at the completion of the 13-lap, 112.59-mile race.

Giacomo on the 500cc MV in winning form during the 1969 Czech Grand Prix at Brno.

GP riders threaten strike

The Finnish Grand Prix, staged on Sunday 2 August 1969, came very near to being called off, when most of the top stars, including Giacomo Agostini, threatened to strike because of the perceived dangers. It was saved only when, a few hours before the first race, the FIM jury reversed a decision they had made the previous evening and ordered the organisers to run the sidecar race at the end of the meeting.

On the day before the racing, Giacomo Agostini had joined the growing band of riders who were asking for a change, pointing out that rubber and oil shed by sidecars would present a 'formidable hazard on the tricky, bumpy, tree-lined Imatra circuit'. Offering no reason, the organisers refused to budge, and the flash-point came on the Saturday evening when riders learned that the FIM jury had rejected Giacomo's pleas. Then came a mass petition to have the right to pull out. But after a last-ditch stand by the organisers, the jury finally caved in to the riders' arguments.

After all the brinkmanship Giacomo still managed to score his by now customary double victory – and as a bonus broke the race and lap records in both classes. Once again, his biggest challenge came in the 350cc race, from Rod Gould, who Giacomo was 'content to sit behind', as *Motor Cycle* described it, for several laps before 'Agostini did his disappearing act and Rod settled for second spot.'

Riot-torn Ulster

After the problems in Finland, another 1969 GP was nearly cancelled at the last minute, but for very different reasons. With smoke still billowing from the fires of riot-torn Belfast barely five miles away, the 41st Ulster Grand Prix got under way amid what *Motor Cycle* called 'a tense, uneasy atmosphere'. Many feared that just one incident among the crowds thronging the 7.4-mile Dundrod circuit might turn the meeting into a shambles at the very least. However, the Irish love their racing, and these fears proved to be unfounded.

As for the racing itself, Giacomo Agostini gave the spectators more than their money's worth with a series of lap records in the 500cc race. These culminated in a searing 107.66mph and a 15-lap race average of 103.74mph – respectively 0.95mph and 0.86mph faster than Mike Hailwood's Honda figures set in 1967. The only rider to remain unlapped at the end of the full 15-lap race distance was Belfast's rising star Brian Steenson, riding a G50 Seeley. Steenson could well have repeated this performance in the 350cc race, had the engine of his Aermacchi not seized.

After the Ulster GP was over, Giacomo announced that he would not take part in the two remaining rounds of the championship (in Italy and Yugoslavia). Instead, he would ride in four major British internationals – Oulton Park on Bank Holiday Monday 1 September; Cadwell Park on Sunday 14 September; Mallory Park 'Race of the Year' a week later; and finally at Brands Hatch on Sunday 5 October. This programme had been chosen with Count Agusta's 'approval'. Asked why he had decided to miss the remaining GPs, Giacomo replied: 'I prefer to race in England'. Observers in Italy thought that Ago's decision to not race in his home GP was because the venue had been switched from Monza to Imola – the Count having a luxuriously appointed suite in the pits area of the former circuit.

The British visit

During his stay in Britain, Giacomo took delivery of a brand new Triumph 750 Trident street bike; finished in dark metallic green it was the early model with 2LS drum front brake and 'raygun' silencers. Four friends near his home already owned similar models.

Hopes of a great battle between Giacomo and Rod Gould during the 350cc race at Oulton Park were dashed on the first lap when Gould crashed his Yamaha. This left Giacomo to win comfortably from Phil Read on another TR2 twin. Then, in the 500cc race, his victory was even more clear cut after John Cooper, riding Mike Hailwood's Reynolds-framed 500 Honda four, was put out with a broken engine shock absorber while holding second place on the last lap.

Phil Read became only the third man to beat Giacomo in 1969, when the Englishman raced his Yamaha TR2 to victory over the works MV star in the 350cc final at Cadwell Park's international races during mid-September.

But the day was Giacomo's. Despite being able to use only five of his 500 MV3's six speeds, he thrilled the crowd with some fabulous Mountain wheelies, including one that I shall never forget, which ran half the length of the paddock straight, before he finally brought the front wheel of his MV down to earth again!

175-1000 Wills Trophy Cadwell Park – 10 laps – 22.5 miles

1st	G. Agostini (MV 3)
2nd	K. Redfern (750 Norton)
3rd	D. Croxford (500 Seeley)
4th	A. Jefferies (750 Norton-Metisse)
5th	J. Hedger (650 Triumph)
6th	P. Smart (500 Seeley)

Technique

To win the number of world championships and Grand Prix which Giacomo Agostini did takes not only dedication, skill and professionalism, but also consistent performance, coolness under pressure and reliability of machinery. Actually, on this latter point Ago could easily have won at least two more titles if his bike had not given trouble at just the wrong moment.

But how did Giacomo see things himself? There is no doubt that he had a great ability to learn quickly. He once said:

During the practicing I study the circuit and make sure my machine is right – carburation, suspension and so on. It's not necessary to try to go really fast in training and, because of my temperament, I find that I cannot make good times in practice. But, as the nervous tension builds up, I go faster and faster.

Of course, during the final stages of his career, he had to cope with the new qualifying lap system (for example at Daytona in 1974), but even then he was a master at hiding exactly what he was likely to do in the race, both from other riders and their teams.

Did he have any favourite circuits – ones where he had a definite advantage? 'Not really. There are so many circuits. In racing you have to make the best advantage at each track to do well in a season-long championship.'

What did he think of the wet?

I certainly didn't like racing in the wet, it is far too easy to fall off when it is dry let alone when the circuit is wet. However, it's the same for everyone so I did my best and went as fast as I could – safely. Rain also spoils the racing for everyone: the riders, spectators and organisers.

Like John Surtees, Giacomo Agostini once commented: 'I like racing. I can't think of any other way in which I would rather earn my living.'

Fitness was always important to Giacomo Agostini, and his personal fitness was one reason why he remained at the top for so long. To achieve peak fitness, and thus maximum track performance, he even had a fully equipped gymnasium installed in his home. 'This was good for mind and body', he said in 1976.

There is also no doubt that the younger Giacomo Agostini did not see the potential dangers of racing, although as he grew older and more experienced he became more acutely aware of them The deaths of close friends in racing definitely altered his view; none more so than Gilberto Parlotti's fatal accident in 1972 in the Isle of Man TT. Agostini had always been a thinking man's rider, but from then on until he finally quit at the end of 1977 he became even more concerned about circuit safety.

His great experience of racing – and his professionalism – were also to play a key role in his ultimate reappearance at the highest level as a team manager; the riders who rode for him also respected what he had achieved.

Lapping Mike Hailwood

Giacomo not only won his second 'Race of the Year' at Mallory Park seven days after his Cadwell Park success, but also lapped five-times winner Mike Hailwood (riding a Seeley) in the process! Rod Gould, his Yamaha TR2 outpaced by the five-hundred MV in the 'Race of the Year', threw away an almost certain second place in a spectacular crash at the Esses section. All this was watched by a record crowd of almost 60,000 spectators.

Race of the Year Mallory Park – 30 laps – 40.5 miles

1st	G. Agostini (MV 3)
2nd	K. Redfern (750 Norton)
3rd	D. Croxford (750 Kuhn Norton)
4th	M. Uphill (700 Rickman-Metisse)
5th	M. Hailwood (500 Seeley)
6th	P. Smart (750 Francis Norton)

Although Phil Read repeated his Cadwell Park 350cc success at Brands Hatch in early October, the MV star hit back with an impressive double as the Kent circuit basked in brilliant sunshine for the season's last big British meeting of 1969.

Race of the South Brands Hatch – 20 laps – 53 miles

1st	G. Agostini (MV 3)
2nd	M. Andrew (750 Kuhn Norton)
3rd	P. Read (350 Yamaha)
4th	J. Hedger (650 Triumph)
5th	C. Mortimer (650 Curtis Norton)
6th	R. Heath (650 BSA)

Although Giacomo Agostini's contract with MV was due to expire at the end of 1969, it seemed certain to be renewed, as he now had six world titles under his belt. During the close season Giacomo spent time racing in South Africa, making his racing debut in that country during January 1970, at Pietermaritzburg. But it was not to be a victorious debut, as he was outpaced by Phil Read (350 Yamaha). Ago suffered engine trouble, which prevented him turning out at the Kyalami circuit, near Johannesburg, a week later.

The problem stemmed from a leaking head gasket. The engine was then rebuilt and taken to Kyalami. There the gasket went for the second time, and the cylinder was too badly distorted to be repaired, so Ago was reduced to the role of spectator for the remainder of his South African tour. He was in good company: Mike Hailwood, Jim Redman and former Suzuki star Frank Perris were also watching the action, rather than taking part.

As in 1969, the 1970 early season Italian meetings did not give much indication of form for the forthcoming World Series. In truth, Giacomo was saving his energies for the big action, whereas rival Renzo Pasolini, while matching Ago at the domestic short circuits, wilted when faced with the longer Grand Prix type events.

An endurance test

Near-zero temperatures, drifting fog and almost continuous drizzle turned the qualifying and races of the first round of the 1970 World Championship – the West German GP – into grim tests of endurance. To complicate matters further, this was the first German Grand Prix to be staged over the long, ultra-demanding 14.2-mile Nürburgring lap since 1958. Many riders, including Giacomo Agostini, had to learn one of the world's most difficult circuits in truly appalling conditions. But, enhancing his reputation, Giacomo scored two clear-cut victories with a display of superb, professional riding. Compare this with what happened to one of his main challengers, fellow Italian Renzo Pasolini. Even before official practice had begun, the Benelli teamster had come off one of the factory's 650cc Tornado road bikes while he was 'learning' the Nürburgring, resulting in a badly swollen ankle which put him out of the meeting! It was almost a case of history repeating itself, for Pasolini had crashed in practice for the previous year's West German GP (at Hockenheim) and broken a collarbone, an injury which put him out of action until the Dutch TT and robbed Paso of his chance of winning the 250cc world title.

350cc West German GP – 6 laps – 85.13 miles

1st	G. Agostini (MV 3)
2nd	K. Carruthers (Benelli)
3rd	C. Mortimer (Yamaha)
4th	K. Hoppe (Yamaha)
5th	H.D. Gorgen (Yamaha)
6th	J. Curry (Aermacchi-Metisse)

500cc West German GP – 6 laps – 85.13 miles

1st	G. Agostini (MV 3)
2nd	A. Barnett (Seeley)
3rd	T. Robb (Seeley)
4th	K. Hoppe (Münch-URS)

| 5th | G. Molloy (360cc Bultaco) |
| 6th | W. Rungg (382cc Aermacchi) |

At the next round, which featured classes for 350 and 500cc machines, at Opatija in Yugoslavia, Giacomo again completed the double. Once more the nearest challenge came in the 350cc race – in the form of the 1969 250cc World Champion, Benelli-mounted Kel Carruthers. Giacomo also broke the lap record in both capacity classes with speeds of 94.32mph and 95.44mph respectively. With the 350cc speed nearly as quick as the 500cc, it was evident in which race he had to ride the hardest. Even so, in the 30-lap, 111.82-mile 500cc event he still lapped the entire field.

When Mick Woollett asked 'Who will win?' in his column in the 10 June 1970 issue of *Motor Cycle* he answered his own question:

> *To ask who will win the Junior and Senior TT is pointless. We all know that, barring some sort of disaster, Giacomo Agostini will score his third successive double on the magnificent MV racers, the Italian bikes that not even the mighty Japanese factories could subdue.*

If the Italian did succeed he would set a new record, for no man in the 63-year history of the Isle of Man races had ever scored the coveted Junior-Senior double three times in a row. John Surtees had come close, but failed when his 350cc MV let him down in 1960, gearbox trouble dropping him

Giacomo Agostini with his larger MV at the foot of Bray Hill during the 1970 Isle of Man Senior TT.

Ago during his winning ride in the 1970 Junior TT on his three-cylinder MV. Alan Barnett (Aermacchi) and Paul Smart (Yamaha) finished 2nd and 3rd respectively.

to runner-up.

Giacomo became the first man to equal Jim Redman's 1963–5 Honda-mounted Junior TT hat-trick when he scored his third successive victory in the 350cc class on his MV Agusta triple. Troubled by molten tar, he had stopped to examine his bike on the second lap – exactly as he had done the previous year. But the road, not the machine, was at fault, and the extremely hot conditions accounted for 58 retirements out of 99 starters; including both works Benellis.

As the 17 June 1970 issue of *Motor Cycle* said:

> *First continental rider to win a Junior TT; then, two years later, in 1968, to score the coveted Junior-Senior double. Giacomo Agostini, so frequently the maker of motorcycle history, became the first rider in the 63-year story of the famous races to win both the Junior and Senior TTs three years in succession.*
>
> *... the handsome 28-year-old Italian, dashing darling of racing fans throughout Europe, averaged 101.52mph on his three cylinder MV Agusta. It carried his personal total of TT victories to seven and that of MV Agusta to 30. Now the factory are within striking distance of the all-time record of 34 held by Norton.*

Several times during the race it had seemed that the jinx that prevented

John Surtees from notching up the triple-double on the four-cylinder MVs in 1960 would strike again. As Giacomo revealed:

After two laps the engine started misfiring. Sometimes it ran on two cylinders. Sometimes three. The fifth and final laps were the worst. I did half a lap on only two cylinders. I thought to myself that I should stop but then decided it was better to go on.

It proved a wise decision. The MV kept going – and after the race the misfire was traced to a faulty electrical component.

Race and lap records were broken by Ago at the Post TT Mallory Park meeting, the result of the main race being:

1000cc Mallory Park – 20 laps – 27 miles

1st	G. Agostini (MV 500 3)
2nd	J. Cooper (Yamsel 350)
3rd	R. Gould (Yamaha 350)
4th	K. Redfern (Dunstall 750)
5th	P. Read (Yamaha 350)
6th	P. Mahoney (Kuhn Seeley 750)

Double Dutch

It was a double again at the Dutch TT, but the 350cc race was an exciting affair, with a close race between Giacomo, Renzo Pasolini (Benelli) and Phil Read (Yamaha) – others such as Kel Carruthers, Rod Gould and Kent Andersson (all on Yamahas) providing close racing not too far behind. The MV rider set a new class lap record of 91.47mph.

Giacomo dominated the 500cc event from start to finish. For three laps, veteran German rider Karl Hoppe (Münch URS) kept the MV in sight until a piston packed in, then it was all over, with the remainder of the field well behind at the finish of the 20-lap race.

At the Belgian GP a week later, Giacomo Agostini broke yet another record by clinching his fifth successive 500cc title – and in doing so became the first rider in any class to have won five world titles in a row! His win also meant that the famous Italian marque had taken the manufacturers' world championship for the 13th time. A dismally wet morning did not prevent a crowd of 80,000 from lining the spectacular 8.8-mile course – the fastest of all bike circuits – to watch the afternoon's races.

With such poor weather conditions (it remained wet all day) no speed records were broken, but even so in winning the 13-lap, 113.9-mile race, at

Instead of contesting the final round of the 1970 World Championships in Spain, Giacomo Agostini came to England. One of the meetings he took part in was at Cadwell Park in the Lincolnshire Wolds. He not only dominated the event but gave racegoers all round the circuit a display that they would remember for a long while. And when cresting Cadwell's famous 'Mountain' section he usually got the wheel of his MV triple high in the air!

111.04mph, Giacomo was certainly not hanging about. By way of comparison, runner-up Frenchman Christian Ravel (Kawasaki) averaged 'only' 105.76mph, with Tommy Robb (Seeley) third with a speed of 104.70mph.

A massive crowd of some 250,000 spectators attended a sun-drenched Sachsenring circuit for the East German GP at the beginning of July. The 350cc race proved to be a cracker, with a determined challenge to the MV's dominance from both Benelli and Yamaha. But still Agostini emerged victorious. There seemed little that men such as Pasolini, Carruthers, Gould, Andersson and Findlay could do. Pasolini got the nearest but still finished over 20 seconds behind. As usual the 500cc race victory was far more decisive, runner-up Johnny Dodds being a massive 3 minutes and 10 seconds astern at the end of the 21-lap, 112.34-mile race.

The 1970 Czech GP had all sorts of problems – first a near strike over low start money – then just before the 350cc race got under way Silvio Grassetti dumped his V4 Jawa on the tarmac, putting a hole in the tank and depositing seven gallons of fuel on the start-line. The race was then delayed for over half-an-hour while officials attempted to clean up the mess! When the riders eventually got under way, Giacomo tore ahead on his MV to win, clinching the 350cc world title for the third year running, his eighth world crown and only one short of the record held jointly by Carlo Ubbiali and Mike Hailwood. There was no 500cc race in Czechoslovakia.

And so Giacomo Agostini's complete dominance of the 350 and 500cc classes of the 1970 Grand Prix season continued, with more double victories coming in Finland, Ulster and Italy.

Bergamonti joins MV

At Monza Agostini had been joined by a teammate, Angelo Bergamonti, who, like Ago, had served his racing apprenticeship aboard the ohv Settebello and Gran Premio dohc Moto Morini singles, before going on to

Rod Gould (2) and Kent Andersson (3) both riding Yamaha's, lead Giacomo Agostini (1) with his MV during the 350cc Ulster GP on 15 August 1970. Ago won, as he did in all but one round that year – and this was because he didn't take part, having already retained his title.

ride the Paton dohc twins, notably in the 500cc class, plus Aermacchi and Benelli machines.

After finishing runner-up to Ago in both the 350 and 500cc races at Monza, Bergamonti was dispatched to contest, by himself, the final round of the world championship series. Held over the twists and turns of Montjuich Park, Barcelona, he scored an impressive double; beating Rod Gould and Kent Andersson (Yamahas) in the 350cc race and Ginger Molloy and a 3-cylinder HIR Kawasaki two-stroke in the 500cc class.

Meanwhile, Giacomo Agostini had visited England to race once again. When he turned out at Cadwell Park, he, together with Phil Read, got top billing. However, Phil had a very public row with circuit owner Chas Wilkinson (regarding wanting to ride a 250 instead of his 350 Yamaha) and when Wilkinson refused to allow the change, he promptly left Cadwell and went home!

Next Giacomo Agostini's MV broke down on the first lap of the 350cc race, while John Cooper's Yamsel expired in the main race of the day. So the 30,000-strong crowd who had packed the Lincolnshire circuit never did see the three superstars battling it out together. Still, Ago did win the 1000cc race, from local hero Derek Chatterton (Yamaha 350).

But a week later at Brands Hatch the three riders did finally meet. The results in the 12-lap, 31.8-mile 'Race

Introduced for the 1969 season, the Yamaha TR2 350 twin-cylinder two-stroke provided top privateers (and factory backed riders) with a viable machine, which could put up a competitive performance against the Agostini/MV threat.

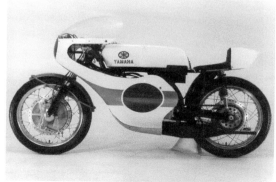

In the 500cc class Read also rode the new Ducati V-twin which debuted in 1971.

of the South' were: 1st Agostini; 2nd Cooper; 3rd Read. But John Cooper had the satisfaction of setting the first ever over 90mph lap on a three-fifty at the Kent circuit.

Giacomo's final race meeting of the 1970 season came at San Remo, a week after Brands Hatch. Needled by Italian press reports hailing Angelo Bergamonti as his latest rival, Ago scored conclusive victories over his new MV teammate. He gave Bergamonti no chance to recover from a slow start and led him over the line by 9 seconds in the 350cc race; third man Kel Carruthers (Yamaha) was lapped by both MVs.

The mayor of San Remo dropped the flag for the 500cc race while Giacomo was still pulling on his gloves. But this only acted as a spur and Ago piled on the pressure to finish the race more than 40 seconds ahead of his teammate Bergamonti, lapping everyone else in the process.

Ago signs for 1971

At the beginning of December 1970, and after the rumour machine had produced many column inches of largely unfounded information, Giacomo Agostini signed a new contract to race MV Agustas in 1971. Although the

Phil Read won the 1971 250cc world title on a Helmut Fath-tuned TD2 Yamaha - and on occasion also rode a 350 version.

rumours said he had been offered a big money deal by Benelli, Ago sensibly chose to stay where he was – enabling him to realistically plan adding two more world titles to his existing tally of eight. He had already said that one of his ambitions was to break the present record of nine, held jointly by Mike Hailwood and Carlo Ubbiali.

Then, as reported elsewhere, Count Domenico Agusta died of a heart attack in February 1971, while visiting Milan on business. Nevertheless, during the 1971 Grand Prix season everything continued much as before – with Giacomo dominating the scene. As one journalist of the period put it: 'His indomitable superiority, combined with his powerful MV machines, meant that the outcome of the race was known as soon as it was started.'

In the first eight 500cc races counting towards the World Championship, Ago won all eight and thus scored his ninth title – drawing level with Hailwood and Ubbiali. The victories were at:

Salzburg (Austria)
Hockenheim (West Germany)
Isle of Man TT
Assen (Holland)
Spa Francorchamps (Belgium)
Sachsenring (East Germany)
Anderstorp (Sweden)
Imatra (Finland)

During the 500cc Belgian GP Giacomo used a full-face helmet (a Bell) for the first time, replacing the old 'pudding basin' type he had used since he began racing in 1961.

Meanwhile, in the 1971 350cc championship, Giacomo Agostini also contested the first eight rounds of the series, with Brno in Czechoslovakia replacing Spa Francorchamps in Belgium; otherwise the venues remained the same. However, in two of these races he struck mechanical problems – engine failure in the Junior TT and gearbox gremlins in the Czech GP – forcing his retirement in both. Even so, having won six of the possible eleven rounds Giacomo Agostini became, as *Motor Cycle* said in their 4 August 1971 issue, 'champion of champions', with one more title to his name than either Mike Hailwood or Carlo Ubbiali.

Ago then decided to miss the Ulster Grand Prix – even though bikes had already been sent! With Count Domenico Agusta dead, the control of the MV racing team was not as it had been before. Nominally, Domenico's youngest brother Corrado was now the head man of the Agusta Group. But in truth his control was never tight – and in fact over the coming years it

---

MV Agusta Riders 1949–76

G. Agostini	F. Gastaldi	N. Pagani
R. Amm	M. Giani	C. Poggi
R. Armstrong	L. Graham	T. Provini
A. Artesiani	S. Grassetti	P. Read
A. Attolini	F. Gugielminetti	G. Ronchei
C. Bandirola	M. Hailwood	G. Sala
F. Benasedo	J. Hartle	C. Salt
A. Bergamonti	G. Hocking	C. Stanford
B. Bertacchini	J. Keller	T. Shepherd
F. Bertoni	G. Leoni	B. Spaggiari
G. Bonera	F. Libanori	J. Surtees
E. Brambilla	W. Lomas	L. Taveri
G. Cantoni	V. Lucchi	A. Toracca
C. Cavaccuiti	R. Magi	C. Ubbiali
D. Chadwick	U. Masetti	R. Venturi
R. Columbo	G. Matucci	E. Vezzalini
A. Copeta	E. Mendogni	H. Williams
R. Dale	G. Milani	G. Zillard
T. Forconi	H. Müller	L. Zizani
B. Francisci	A. Pagani	A. Zyland

All the above are riders who officially represented MV Agusta.

would be government appointed officials, rather than the Agusta family, that would make the really important decisions. But back in 1971, in the months following Domenico Agusta's death, Giacomo Agostini had far more say in what would happen at the team than he ever had before Domenico's passing.

More competition

Giacomo had decided he would rather race at a big forthcoming non-championship British meeting, than the Ulster Grand Prix where he had nothing to gain, having already sewn both titles up. His chosen venue was Silverstone. And as *Motor Cycle* said in their 25 August 1971 issue:

> *Silverstone had seen nothing like it since the great days of the early 1950s when Geoff Duke reigned supreme on works Nortons. Every road to the 2.9-mile Northampton circuit was jammed two hours before the meeting was due to start and programmes were sold out before racing got under way.*

Why? Well it was quite simple, everyone was there – Phil Read, John Cooper, Jarno Saarinen (who was just coming to the fore and had won the 350cc Czech GP when Ago's gearbox had gone on the blink), Paul Smart, Barry Sheene, Bruno Spaggiari, Dave Simmonds, Rod Gould, Mick Grant, Chas Mortimer – the list was endless – plus Giacomo Agostini and Mike Hailwood!

I was there that day and it was a fantastic experience. In the 350cc race Hailwood (riding a TR2 Yamaha) was left struggling in the pack after a poor start, the front runners being Cooper, Saarinen and Agostini. But Hailwood didn't give up and was soon passing riders of the calibre of Phil Read and Tony Rutter until he was fourth. But there was no catching the three leaders, who had opened up a big gap. And Giacomo went on to win from Saarinen and Cooper.

In the 500cc race Barry Sheene (Suzuki) shot to the front at the start and stayed there for five laps. Then Giacomo seized the lead, although he seemed content to play with Sheene for a few laps,

Another Yamaha rider who achieved considerable success was the Swede Kent Andersson. he finished 4th in the 1970 350cc championship; 3rd in the 250cc the same year and was also 125cc champion in 1973 and 1974.

'Mooneyes' John Cooper

Nicknamed 'Mooneyes' because of the famous 'eye' motifs on his 'pudding basin' red-painted crash helmet when earning his living on the British short circuits with a pair of Manx Norton singles during the mid-1960s, John Cooper was born in Derby during 1938, just prior to the outbreak of World War Two a few months later.

His first racing motorcycle was a 197cc Villiers-engined James two-stroke, which he rode in the mid-1950s at local circuits. Progressing from club level, to national and then international, his first victory at the latter level came in Scarborough during 1961.

At this time, at least in the 350 and 500cc classes, British short-circuit racing meant big four-stroke singles such as the Manx Norton, AJS 7R and Matchless G50. Cooper's choice was for many years a pair of Nortons tuned by Ray Petty.

In 1966 he became double (350 and 500cc) British Champion – the last honours the Derby man would win with the Petty Nortons. Although he rode Seeleys for a while in the 350 and 500cc classes, Cooper also began to take part in the smaller categories and in 1968 became the 250cc British Champion (on a Yamaha two-stroke). This led John and Colin Seeley to develop the Yamsel machine. This was essentially a TR2 Yamaha engine in one of Seeley's excellent chassis. This combination proved an instant success. He won countless races on this bike, including the big money Race of the Year at Mallory Park in 1970.

Then, after being loaned a factory BSA Rocket 3 for the 1971 Easter Match Race series (held annually over the Easter weekend at venues such as Brands

Hatch, Mallory Park, Oulton Park and Snetterton between teams from Great Britain and the US), Cooper managed to secure full works backing from BSA. At last John Cooper had machinery to realise his true potential – and with it was to come the most successful period in his racing career.

As described elsewhere he beat Giacomo Agostini on the three-cylinder five-hundred MV in one of the greatest races of all time at Mallory Park's Race of the Year in September 1971. He also beat Ago at Brands Hatch later that year. Then he travelled to the US for the first time where he won the 250-mile Ontario Classic in California, with its massive payout. Then back home the readers of *Motor Cycle News* voted their hero 'Man of the Year' by a clear margin.

Sticking with BSA in 1972, Cooper won the *Motor Cycle News* superbike championship title, but at the end of that

John Cooper, the co-star together with Giacomo Agostini of what many still consider to be one of the greatest races of all time – the Mallory Park Race of the Year 1971 – when John and Giacomo duelled on a 750 BSA Rocket 3 and an 500 MV 3.

season, and with the entire BSA Group on the verge of financial collapse, he signed for Norton. But after crashing at Brands Hatch at the beginning of the 1973 season and breaking a leg, John Cooper quickly decided it was time to hang up his leathers after almost 20 years in the sport.

Although he was tempted to consider a comeback he never did. However, he retained an interest in bikes and helped several riders, including Heron Suzuki teamster John Newbold, while building up a garage business in his native town of Derby.

Later still, with the advent of the classic scene, John Cooper was to be seen parading, but not racing his Seeley G50, at events such as the Post TT at Mallory Park.

before pulling away to win easily. Read and Spaggiari both made poor starts on the new works v-twin Ducati machines, then came tearing through the field. Read had just snatched third place when big-end failure put him out. Spaggiari took over, then joined Read in the pits after his machine went on to one cylinder. Dave Simmonds held second place after passing Sheene until his Kawasaki triple seized. Then Barry went on to finish runner-up behind a victorious Giacomo, who once again had proved he was the master.

350cc Silverstone – 20 laps – 58.54 miles

1st	G. Agostini (MV 3)
2nd	J. Saarinen (Yamaha)
3rd	J. Cooper (Yamsel)
4th	M. Hailwood (Yamaha)
5th	A. Rutter (Yamaha)
6th	B. Ditchburn (Yamaha)

500cc Silverstone – 20 laps – 58.54 miles

1st	G. Agostini (MV 3)
2nd	B. Sheene (Suzuki)
3rd	J. Cooper (Seeley)
4th	J. Harvey (Kirby-Metisse)
5th	G. Marsovszky (Linto)
6th	T. Robb (Seeley)

An interesting aside to the Silverstone meeting was a 'Parade of Champions' in which 10 world champions took part in a parade. These were Geoff Duke, Eric Oliver, John Surtees, Jim Redman, Mike Hailwood, Phil Read, Dave Simmonds, Rod Gould, Horst Owesle and Giacomo Agostini. Jim Redman rode an MV loaned to him by the Italian company, as did John Surtees, the latter only managing a single lap, having been delayed in traffic jams around the circuit.

Sunday 12 September 1971 was a black day for MV. Not only did its new, long-awaited four-cylinder three-fifty (349.8cc – 53 x 38.2mm) behave badly (misfiring before eventually retiring with a broken bearing) when ridden for the first time by MV new boy Alberto Pagani (as a replacement for Angelo Bergamonti, the latter having been killed at a non-championship Riccione meeting before the GP season got under way), both the MV 3s ridden by Giacomo Agostini in the 350 and 500cc races also expired. The only bright spot was Pagani's victory in the 500cc race on another three.

Race of a lifetime

Billed as the 'Race of the Year', Mallory Park's big meeting of the year on 19 September 1971 became, for many British fans at least, the 'race of a lifetime'. As *Motor Cycle* reported:

> *British dreams came true at Mallory Park on Sunday when John Cooper on the latest 750cc three-cylinder BSA beat Italian world champion Giacomo Agostini fair and square to win the 'Race of the Year'. This was without doubt both Cooper's and BSA's most famous race victory ever.*

Giacomo Agostini was at the very peak of his career – and he was riding his 500 MV 3 Grand Prix machine, which had not been beaten in a straight fight (apart from the rare mechanical breakdown) since Mike Hailwood and Honda faded from GP racing after 1967. The 30-lap Mallory Park race was one of the most exciting ever witnessed at a British circuit – and I know just how exciting as I was there. Cooper and Ago were never more than a few yards apart and were absolutely on the limit all the way, with both bikes and riders in 100 percent condition from start to finish.

From the moment the flag dropped, Cooper shot ahead with the MV star in hot pursuit. Then Ago outbraked the British pairing to take the lead at the hairpin. But Cooper responded by riding the wheels off his bike. By lap four he was right in the MV's slipstream. And Barry Sheene was in third on a 500cc Suzuki twin. But then Sheene slid off in spectacular style at Gerards.

This left Giacomo and Cooper way ahead of Ray Pickrell, Percy Tait, Paul Smart and Jarno Saarinen. Mike Hailwood's works Yamaha 350 was down on power and, after holding 10th, he eventually retired with broken piston rings. Cooper got back ahead after 10 laps, but although he could out power

Agostini round the tricky Gerards sweep and the following Steibe Straight, the Italian regained the lost ground at the hairpin section. And so it went on, lap after fabulous lap. Then, on lap 26, Cooper got his nose into the lead as they came out of Devil's Elbow for the last time to win an incredible race.

Earlier, Giacomo had won the 350cc class with surprising ease, none of the Yamaha stars getting to grips with the MV. And he also took the 500cc class, pursued by Sheene, Charlie Sanby and Dave Croxford.

Mallory Park Race of the Year – 30 laps – 40.5 miles

1st	J. Cooper (750 BSA)
2nd	G. Agostini (500 MV 3)
3rd	R. Pickrell (750 Triumph)
4th	P. Smart (750 Triumph)
5th	P. Tait (750 Triumph)
6th	J. Saarinen (350 Yamaha)

A week later, local circuit specialist Derek Chatterton won the main race at Cadwell Park before a massive crowd, with Giacomo Agostini chasing hard on a badly misfiring MV 3. These two were a long way ahead of John Cooper, the latter being unable to repeat his Mallory performance.

Finally came another defeat (again by Cooper) in the prestigious 'Race of the South' at Brands Hatch on Sunday 3 October 1971. Ago's only consolation was a fine victory in the 350cc race when, as *Motor Cycle* described, he shattered the Yamaha-mounted opposition. First Cooper (Yamsel) held second place, until he was slowed by gear selector problems. Then Derek Chatterton, who had vanquished Ago at Cadwell a week before, moved into second place, pursued by Alan Barnett and Phil Read. But all three retired, Chatterton following a crash, Barnett with broken piston rings and Read on the last lap with a seized engine. All this let Paul Smart into second, ahead of Barry Sheene.

Beaten three times on British circuits over three weeks, Giacomo Agostini returned to his invincible ways on his homeland course at San Remo on Sunday 10 September 1971. Riding his factory three-cylinder MVs, he won the 350cc and 500cc races over the picturesque 2.1-mile seaside course. Finland's Jarno Saarinen provided him with an early scrap, but then Ago gunned the MV away to establish a comfortable lead. Saarinen was later to retire with suspected big-end failure on his TR2B Yamaha, leaving Ago's old Benelli rival Renzo Pasolini (now riding an Aermacchi two-stroke) to finish runner-up. In the 500cc event Giacomo came home ahead of Phil Read on the works Ducati V-twin, with Gilberto Parlotti, on another of the Ducatis, third.

By early November it was known that a larger four-cylinder model would be raced by MV in 1972, with a 498.6cc (58 x 47.2mm) engine and six-speed gearbox. At the same time MV Agusta announced that both Giacomo and Alberto Pagani had been re-signed to ride in 1972. The latter would also act as a test rider, especially of the new 750cc four-cylinder model, being developed to take part in Formula 750 racing. A prototype of the 750 Super Sport was displayed at the international Milan Show held at the end of November. As soon as this was over Giacomo Agostini flew to Australia to compete in two meetings – the first at Calder Raceway, Victoria, on 10 December, the second at Oran Park, New South Wales, a week later. This was the Italian World Champion's first visit 'Down Under'; the man behind the visit being Melbourne millionaire Bob Jane.

But Giacomo was delayed because his flight had to make a detour to miss India and Pakistan (who were at war). Despite his later arrival he was greeted at Melbourne Airport by an enthusiastic crowd – including several banner-waving Italians. This was not only Giacomo Agostini's first-ever visit to Australia, but also the first time that an Italian works machine had competed there since Geoff Duke raced a factory 500 Gilera four back in 1955. He celebrated by winning his three races at Calder. Then it was on to Sydney, where he was due to practice on the difficult Oran Park circuit. But a shock was in store at Oran, when in the 350cc event Giacomo was beaten by the Australian Brian Hindle (Yamaha). During practice Ago had complained to officials about concrete walls on the outside of two bends of the 1.3-mile course. After being forced to pull out of the 12-lap unlimited race with rear wheel trouble, he then won his final two races, featuring 16 and 20 laps on his 500 three cylinder MV. The visit generated considerable press and television coverage throughout the Australian continent – and brought Giacomo Agostini's 1971 season to a close.

Although no one knew it then, the following year, 1972, was to be one of major changes, including the emergence of Formula 750 style racing (the forerunner of today's Super Bike class), the arrival of a controversial new teammate, and a new World Class star.

Chapter 6

Ago v Phil

AS GIACOMO AGOSTINI approached the 1972 season he could not have realised just how difficult it would prove to be. His years of dominating the sport with little or no opposition were about to come abruptly to an end.

A defeat at Imola

A sensational upset for both Giacomo and MV Agusta came at Imola on 23 April 1972, the pairing tasting defeat in the inaugural 200-mile race. The race for Formula 750 machines is remembered now as being a legendary 1-2 victory for the then new Ducati V-twin design, ridden by Paul Smart and Bruno Spaggiari. But it had been Giacomo Agostini and his racing version of MVs 750 S sportster that had started the day as favourites. The MV name had been responsible for much of the pre-race hype, with a vast crowd of spectators – and much of the world's press – expecting the World Champion to come out on top.

Formula 750 had largely come about since the FIM and the American AMA governing bodies had buried their 50-year feud and decided to co-operate a few months earlier. And it was this new racing formula that had given racing such a boost in 1971 – and made possible a truly star-studded entry from both sides of the Atlantic. The result was probably the widest ever range of motorcycle marques and engine types ever seen for a single race. In 1972 – before the class was effectively taken over by the Yamaha TZ 700/750, Kawasaki KR 750 and Suzuki TR 750 two-strokes – the Imola event attracted not only MV and Ducati, but also BSA and Triumph triples; Moto Guzzi V-twins; Norton and Laverda parallel twins; BMW flat-twins; and Honda fours, as well as two-strokes from Suzuki, Kawasaki and

The 1972 season didn't begin well for Giacomo Agostini, with a defeat at Imola in the inaugural 200-mile F750 event; by the Ducati V-twins of Paul Smart(16) and Bruno Spaggiari (9).

Pilot's eye view of the MV 500 four-cylinder model which Giacomo Agostini rode from 1972 onwards.

Yamaha. All these were factory or works-supported entries.

Formula 750 regulations stated that a motorcycle had to be production based, so MV were immediately hampered by having to use shaft instead of chain final drive. The engine tuning allowed was more a case of special attention (blueprinting in other words), than a radical redesign. So again MV had to use the major components from their 750 S roadster. All in all, even though it sported a few special bits (such as a pukka racing Fontana front brake) the MV Giacomo was to ride suffered against more suitable machinery from rival manufacturers.

The crescendo of noise and colour at the course as the race got under way (for the full 200 miles, rather than split 100-mile sections like the following year) was a sight anyone who was there will never forget – and has been unmatched up to the present time. Ranged against Agostini, Smart and Spaggiari were riders of the calibre of Phil Read, Walter Villa, John Cooper, Peter Williams, Ray Pickrell and Jack Findlay. As if to prove the pundits correct, Ago and the 750 MV streaked away from the drop of the starter's flag, retaining the position for four laps, before having to submit to the flying Ducati V-twins. But Giacomo refused to throw in the towel and clung on to third position, within striking distance of the two leaders, until lap 42, when the 750 MV retired at the Acque Minerali section of the circuit. This retirement was due to a fault which has always plagued the production MV fours – the set of bevel gears located within the gearbox cover behind fifth gear, which turns the drive through 90 degrees to mate with the final drive shaft.

As if this was not bad enough, then came the start of the World Championships. And although Giacomo (and Alberto Pagani) dominated the 500cc series, the picture in the 350cc class was totally different. At the first two rounds (Nürburgring and Clermont-Ferrand), MV were totally outsped by works Yamaha-mounted Jarno Saarinen. The 'Flying Finn' simply pole-axed the MV at the Nürburgring. Although Ago finished runner-up, his teammate Pagani could only come home a lowly eighth. Besides the Yamaha challenge (the second works Yamaha ridden by Hideo Kanaya finished third), there were the new Aermacchi twin-cylinder two-strokes of Renzo Pasolini (fifth) and Frenchman Michel Rougerie. Saarinen took the lead on the second lap, shattering the German circuit's lap record three times before setting a new outright lap record at 90.85mph.

Even worse was to come in France, when Giacomo was relegated to fourth, with Pagani not even turning out!

350cc French GP – Clermont-Ferrand

1st	J. Saarinen (Yamaha)
2nd	T. Länsivuori (Yamaha)
3rd	R. Pasolini (Aermacchi)
4th	G. Agostini (MV 3)
5th	J. Drapel (Yamaha)
6th	D. Braun (Yamaha)

Stung by these emphatic beatings, MV responded by bringing out their new four-cylinder model, further developed since its debut at Monza the previous year. The arrival of the four signalled a reversal of fortunes, with Giacomo winning at the next round – at the Salzburgring in Austria – with Kanaya second, Pasolini third and Saarinen fourth. This form was continued at Imola, the scene for the Italian GP that year, where Giacomo scored victory number two in the 1972 350cc title race. The top six positions were:

350cc Italian GP – Imola

1st	G. Agostini (MV 4)
2nd	H. Kanaya (Yamaha)
3rd	R. Pasolini (Aermacchi)
4th	J. Saarinen (Yamaha)
5th	J. Drapel (Yamaha)
6th	T. Länsivuori (Yamaha)

Parlotti's accident

Then came the Isle of Man TT, and an event which would change the course of racing history. This was the fatal accident suffered by fellow Italian, and Giacomo Agostini's friend, Gilberto Parlotti. Parlotti was then leading the 125cc World Championship, but was being closely challenged by the likes of Angel Nieto (Derbi), Borje Jansson (Maico), and Kent Andersson and Chas Mortimer (Yamahas). Gilberto Parlotti was a newcomer to the ultra-demanding 37.73-mile Mountain circuit, and to help the learning process he had brought with him a Ducati 750 street bike. In addition, when time allowed, Giacomo had helped show his friend round; including a session the night before Parlotti's race.

Many argue that the 125cc race should never have been allowed to start – there was heavy rain and thick mist up on the Mountain – and Parlotti died when his Morbidelli twin left the road and ploughed into a series of concrete pillars that lined a section of the circuit called the Verandah. Travelling at around 100mph, the Italian suffered serious injuries midway through the second lap. The rescue helicopter arrived at the scene, but Gilberto Parlotti was dead before he arrived at hospital.

Two days after the joy of winning the Junior TT in June 1972 came the death of close friend Gilberto Parlotti riding a works 125cc Morbidelli twin in the Ultra Lightweight TT.

Giacomo, teammate Alberto Pagani and MV Agusta team manager Arturo Magni were all deeply shocked by this terrible incident. In addition their own 500cc race the same day was delayed by 2½ hours because of the weather conditions. In the interim Magni tried to contact the MV factory in Italy, but without success. So it was down to Magni and his riders to make a decision. After much heart-searching it was finally decided that as professional riders they had to race in that afternoon's Senior TT. As Ted Macauley said in his 1973 *International Motor Cycle Racing Book*:

> *It was left to Agostini, the star performer, the man who had to put his fears and apprehensions behind him and not even think about coming second. He had to win. His reputation demanded that and his own bravery would support it. I do not suppose he has ever faced such a difficult problem – but he opted to race in what was most certainly his last TT appearance.*

And even though Giacomo went on to win the 1972 Senior TT (to add to the Junior race he had won a couple of days earlier) it was to be his last Isle of Man race. It was also his fifth consecutive Senior victory. As for Alberto Pagani, he too raced in the Senior TT. But in many ways Parlotti's crash affected him even more than his teammate. And at the end of that season – as runner-up in both the 500cc World and Italian championships – he hung up his leathers.

While the 500cc championship presented little problem for the MV men – of the 13 rounds Ago won 11, Pagani one (Yugoslavia) and with no MV opposition Chas Mortimer (Yamaha) won the final round in Spain – the 350cc contest was completely different. Quite simply Pagani was not able to help Agostini in the smaller class, so MV recruited a new teamster, Phil Read. Yes, Phil had the ability to mix it with the best, but he was not an ideal team member, being someone who was only interested in winning. A collision course had been set.

Read's debut

A despondent-looking Giacomo Agostini awaiting the start of the 1972 Senior TT - a few hours after Parlotti's fatal accdent. it was a mark of the man that Ago was able to put aside his grief and do the job of winning the race for MV. But he was never to race in the Isle of Man TT again.

The 1972 Junior TT; 1st Giacomo Agostini MV (3); 2nd Tony Rutter Yamaha (16); 3rd Mick Grant Yamaha (27).

This signing came as a real shock, at least for Giacomo Agostini and race fans – if not MV Agusta themselves. Initially Phil rode only in the 350cc class. His first MV success came at the East German GP – and it was also his first-ever race on the Gallarate factory's four-cylinder 350. He finished 19 seconds ahead of Renzo Pasolini (Aermacchi), Dieter Braun (Yamaha) and Silvio Grassetti (MZ). Jarno Saarinen and Giacomo Agostini both retired. The Finn went out when the nut holding his Yamaha's engine sprocket came off, while Giacomo's machine stopped with what were officially described as 'ignition troubles'.

But why had Phil Read been recruited? In *MV Agusta*, Mario Columbo and Roberto Patrignani put forward the following case:

> *What MV saw in Phil Read was more than just a matter of class. They were looking for an aggressive rider who was not prepared to play second fiddle to anyone. Although this latter quality can be a headache for team managers, because it can easily spill into disobedience (something Read himself had already proved when he flouted Yamaha team orders to 'steal' the world 250 title from Bill Ivy in 1968), it is possible that MV signed Read precisely because Agostini needed shaking out of his unwanted timorousness in face of the Japanese challenge.*

My own view is that for the first time in years MV had serious competition. And in addition it had just lost its central figure, the man who had been the driving force, Count Domenico Agusta. So not only had the company been slow to act, it did not always respond in a rational manner. For example, Corrado Agusta had ordered that Giacomo: 'was no longer to race 750cc class machines on his 500cc MV at British meetings'. But he had sanctioned entering the Imola 200 with a machine which was clearly not good enough (even though Giacomo rode superbly). The company had also been caught out by the arrival of the new breed of high performance two-strokes from the likes of Yamaha and Aermacchi. And, finally, there had been the arrival of a man who, potentially, was the greatest prospect since Giacomo himself, Jarno Saarinen.

Previously all this would have been overseen by Count Domenico Agusta; but in 1972 things were vastly different. Another factor was that Alberto Pagani, although an excellent support rider when the competition was sparse, was not a competitor of the first ranking – and thus not able to provide true back-up in the hotly contested 350cc class. Read certainly was – but at what cost? The team now had two world champions of near equal

Phil Read

Phil Read, born in Luton, Bedfordshire on 1 January 1939, has always courted controversy, yet there is no question of his right to be regarded as one of the truly great riders of all time. In fact, had it not been for a certain Mike Hailwood, Phil would now be even more highly regarded. However, his private life, both relationships and business interests, has proved difficult. Then there have been the comments, fuelled by a press ever-hungry for a story regarding other competitors and events (such as the Isle of Man TT), which have polarised public opinion. The author has known Phil on a personal level for a long time; we have always got on well. And there is no disputing his track record of seven world titles – equal to no lesser man than John Surtees – with only Mike Hailwood, Carlo Ubbiali, Angel Nieto and Giacomo Agostini holding more.

Phil began racing on a BSA Gold Star (encouraged by his mother) in 1957, but his big break really came when he won the Senior Manx Grand Prix on a Norton in September 1960. Then, again on a Norton, he won the Junior (350cc) TT the following June. Other excellent places during the remainder of the year marked him out for future stardom.

During 1962 he mainly confined his activities to the British short circuits, winning many races. His results that year probably prompted Geoff Duke to sign him up to support John Hartle in the Scuderia Gilera team, after Derek Minter was injured on his own Norton early in 1963. Although the Gileras (which had been mothballed since 1957) proved no match for Mike Hailwood and his MVs, Read still did enough to provoke an offer from Yamaha to race their RD56 two-fifty twin, his first outing for his new employers coming at the Japanese GP in October 1963. In 1964 Read was top man in the 250cc World Championships, giving Yamaha their first title. It was also the first time a two-stroke had won the class. His win broke a three-year run of success by the Honda factory. Phil kept his grip on the title the next year – then Honda signed Mike Hailwood and 'Mike the Bike' snatched the championship from Phil in 1966, after a season-long attempt by Phil to sort out teething problems with the new four-cylinder 250 Yamaha. These glitches had been resolved in time for the 1967 season and that year Read and Hailwood fought out one of the closest championships in the history of the sport. Read actually had a higher total of basic points, and was runner-up, whereas Hailwood, with one victory more, was crowned champion. He also finished runner-up to teammate Bill Ivy in the 125cc title chase.

The following year, 1968, Phil won back both the 125 and 250cc titles. But even though both Honda and Suzuki had pulled out, this was no easy season, as a bitter rivalry erupted between Read and Ivy. In an effort to make peace Yamaha ruled that Phil could win the 125cc, with Bill being lined up for the 250cc crown. However, the two men had other plans, resulting in a season-long battle between the two. At its end Read had won both titles but in the process not only upset Ivy and Yamaha but also many race fans. For many years thereafter Yamaha were none too happy with the man who had given them their early successes, although all this now seems to be in the past. Meanwhile, on a private TD2B, Read won the 250cc title again in 1971, on a machine tuned by the German Helmut Fath.

In 1972 came news that Read would be joining MV Agusta. At first this was to ride in the 350cc class, but for 1973 this was broadened to include the 500cc too. The reasons why and the consequences of Phil joining the Italian team are

Eight times world champion Phil Read was a past master at needling other competitors.

Phil Read, pictured here astride a Honda CB1100R at Brands Hatch in 1981, had a racing career which began in the mid-1950s and ended three decades later. During this time he rode BSA, Norton, Gilera, Yamaha, Benelli, Ducati, MV Agusta and Honda machinery and won eight World Championship titles. He was also a controversial character.

fully discussed in the main text, but the move was like putting a fox into a hen house. Read and Ago simply didn't hit it off, almost from day one. This resulted in Giacomo joining rivals Yamaha for 1974, after Phil won the 500cc title in 1973. With Ago's departure Phil went on to retain the 500cc crown in 1974, but he was not to be found in the 350cc results that year, for the simple reason that MV withdrew from the class. Giacomo Agostini took the title for his new team.

In 1975 a fierce battle developed between Read and Agostini for the 500cc championship. Giacomo came out on top, even though he had to wait until the last round to know the outcome of the titanic struggle. There is absolutely no doubt that both men wanted to win. It was to be Ago's final championship, and MV Agusta and Phil Read were never again to win a world crown in the Grand

Prix series. Phil continued to race after Ago retired at the end of 1977, but he never reclaimed the form of earlier years.

Today, both riders are often to be seen riding at historic race events throughout the world – quite often on MV Agustas!

ability. Giacomo felt that his position as MV's number one was under threat, while Read was a past master at needling opponents, including other team members.

More problems

By the end of the 10th round of the 13-strong world championship season at Brno, the scene of the Czech Grand Prix, Jarno Saarinen's challenge had become a reality. The Finnish Yamaha star had closed to within five points of Giacomo Agostini in the 350cc championship table. In attempting to keep the Yamaha at bay, Giacomo had blown up his MV four – the final ignominy being a crash caused when his rear tyre became drenched in oil from a hole punched in the MV's crankcase by a broken connecting rod.

The race had begun when Read, on the other MV, led off the grid, with Renzo Pasolini (Aermacchi), Giacomo and Saarinen in pursuit. By the end of the lap, Giacomo was ahead of Read and Pasolini, while Saarinen still lay fourth. Then Saarinen caught and passed Pasolini, and when Giacomo came off on his own oil on lap four the Finn was catching Read. There was nothing that Read could do about it. Completing the eighth lap, Saarinen was right in the MV's slipstream. And, as they passed the pits, he signalled that the race was in the bag. And he was dead right. Two laps later he sped through alone to start the lap. Read limped in, his engine running on three cylinders; an inlet valve having broken.

MV then slapped in a protest alleging that the Yamaha's engine was oversize. It was measured and found to be 349cc. So Saarinen was confirmed as the winner, with Pasolini second – and the MV team went away to lick its wounds.

MV Agusta had been so busy working on the new four-cylinder 350cc racers that they had not had sufficient mechanics to spare to prepare a machine for Alberto Pagani to race in the 500cc class, so he was a non-starter in Czechoslovakia. After Brno the position was even worse, as the blown-up 350cc engine had to be rushed back to the factory, rebuilt and tested before they could leave for Sweden. As it was impossible to get the bikes transported to Anderstorp by road in time for practising, MV were forced to charter a plane and fly the bikes direct from the airfield next to

The new four-cylinder 500 MV Agusta as raced by Giacomo Agostini and his new teammate from the end of 1972. The engine produced 70bhp at 14,800rpm, giving the bike a top speed of over 165mph.

their factory to the landing strip at the Swedish circuit.

Success in Sweden

After his success in Czechoslovakia, it was Saarinen's turn to strike problems in Sweden, when the Yamaha rider's gearbox started sticking. And after several times having to wrench the pedal with his hand to make a change he lost ground to Giacomo Agostini who had led from the start. Jarno soon dropped back into the clutches of Phil Read on the other MV. At one time the trouble cleared and he regained second place, but eventually dropped back to finish third. This victory now put Giacomo back in the driving seat to retain his 350cc title.

350cc Swedish GP – 34 laps – 84.32 miles

1st	G. Agostini (MV 4)
2nd	P. Read (MV 4)
3rd	J. Saarinen (Yamaha)
4th	R. Pasolini (Aermacchi)
5th	D. Braun (Yamaha)
6th	J. Findlay (Yamaha)

As he had already clinched his 11th World Championship by winning the

1972 500cc title, Giacomo Agostini was a relieved and excited man when he finally secured the 350cc crown – thus bringing his championship haul to 12 – with victory at Imatra, Finland, at the end of July.

In finishing runner-up, Saarinen finally had to accept defeat, saying: 'Ago was trying very hard, and my best chance of a title was in the 250cc race, so it was better to finish second than to take a risk'. Later during the same meeting Saarinen headed his rivals over the line to take victory in the 250cc event, thus becoming the new World Champion for the quarter-litre class.

1972 500cc World Championship

If the 1972 350cc championship had been difficult (Giacomo Agostini eventually winning it by 102 points to Jarno Saarinen's 89), the 500cc title race was much easier, with the final points tally as follows:

1st	G. Agostini (MV)	105 points
2nd	A. Pagani (MV)	87 points
3rd	B. Kneubuhler (Yamaha)	54 points
4th	R. Gould (Yamaha)	52 points
5th	B. Granath (Husqvarna)	47 points
=6th	C. Mortimer (Yamaha)	42 points
=6th	D. Simmonds (Kawasaki)	42 points

Giacomo Agostini won 11 of the 13 rounds, with victories at the Nürburgring (West Germany); Clermont-Ferrand (France); the Salzburgring (Austria); Imola (Italy); TT (Isle of Man); Assen (Holland); Spa Francorchamps (Belgium); the Sachsenring (East Germany); Brno (Czechoslovakia); Anderstorp (Sweden) and Imatra (Finland).

Then came the start of appearances at non-championship meetings, both at home in Italy and in Great Britain. The biggest news was a double victory at Pesaro by Jarno Saarinen on Benellis in the 350 and 500cc races, over Agostini. In both races the tussles between Ago and Jarno were intensely close. And ultimately mechanical trouble played its part in the Italian's defeat on both occasions.

Snetterton debut

After a crash at Brands Hatch earlier in the month and then the double defeat at Pesaro the previous weekend, Giacomo returned to Britain needing a confidence-boosting victory. He actually scored two – although as *Motor Cycle* said: 'The dice were loaded against him.' These successes came at Snetterton, Norfolk – Ago's first visit to the East Anglian circuit.

The first victory came in the 500cc race. The 2.9-mile circuit was greasy after a light drizzle; Barry Sheene, who had just won both the 250 and 350cc

Giacomo leading the field at Brands Hatch, October 1972.

races, was on the line with a 354cc TR2B Yamaha. Ago did not really know the circuit, and to add to his problems, the big MV refused to fire first bump.

As Sheene shot ahead, Giacomo was left pushing and was last away. By mid-race he was only fifth, but lapping faster and faster Giacomo 'sliced hunks' (*Motor Cycle* 30 August 1972) off Mike Hailwood's lap record (set on the works 500 Honda four). But still the Italian lay only third as Sheene and local hero Paul Cott started the last lap. Then, with a supreme effort – and a new 500cc lap record of 96.02mph – Ago caught and passed his Yamaha-mounted rivals to win the race. Minutes later the Italian MV star was out on the same 500cc MV to do battle with the factory 750cc machines (conveniently forgetting the Count's previous orders!). This was an even more incredible performance, as not only did Giacomo's race average of 96.29mph beat his recently set 500cc-lap record, but he also succeeded in beating the best 750cc riders around, in the 'Race of the Aces' event.

Snetterton Race of the Aces – 10 laps – 27 miles

1st	G. Agostini (MV 4)
2nd	J. Cooper (750 Triumph)
3rd	P. Williams (750 Norton)
4th	R. Pickrell (750 Triumph)
5th	P. Tait (750 Triumph)
6th	M. Grant (750 Norton)

When interviewed at Snetterton, Giacomo confirmed that he 'had no

Another Ago shot from Brands Hatch, circa 1972.

intention of retiring, even though his world title score was now up to 12 championships' and that he 'would again race MV Agustas in 1973'. He went on to say: 'we are like a family now – MV Agusta, Agostini'. And there was certainly no hint of the problems between Phil Read and himself which were to come to a head in such a dramatic fashion the following year, 1973. Giacomo also said he would be 'returning to England for the big Scarborough meeting on 9-10 September, but I am doubtful for the Mallory Park Race of the Year'. He continued: 'Count Agusta is against my racing the 500cc MV Agusta in big bike events' but he was 'very much hoping to persuade the Count to change his mind.'

Scarborough debut

Another debut ride came at Oliver's Mount, Scarborough, where on 12 September 1972 Giacomo and Jarno Saarinen both made their debuts at the North Yorkshire seaside venue. This was one of the most star-studded Scarborough International Gold Cup meetings ever, with not only Saarinen and Ago, but also the likes of Barry Sheene, Phil Read, Chas Mortimer, Mick Grant, Derek Chatterton, Tuevo Länsivuori, Ray Pickrell, Dave Croxford and Peter Williams.

Giacomo gave an impressive performance on one of the three-cylinder MVs, scoring a convincing victory in the 500cc race, finishing 21 seconds ahead of Barry Sheene (Yamaha). In the process he not only collected the impressive Gold Cup trophy, but also smashed John Cooper's existing lap record by a staggering 2.6 seconds, with an average speed of 70.68mph.

Barry Sheene

Barry Sheene will forever be remembered as having done more to raise the profile of the rider – and to give the sport a wider audience – than any other previous rider. It was Sheene who, together with Americans such as Kenny Roberts, Eddie Lawson and Freddie Spencer, ensured that racing was financially more rewarding for the competitor than the organisers.

Born in London on 11 September 1950, Barry was encouraged by his ex-racer father, Frank, who also ran a successful engine-tuning business. Barry Sheene's race debut came on a Bultaco TSS 125 at Brands Hatch during 1968, but he crashed after the engine seized. His father had close ties with the Spanish Bultaco factory and this resulted in works bikes for the following year. Then came the purchase of Stuart Graham's ex-works Suzuki 125cc twin. With the little Suzuki the youthful Sheene almost snatched the 1971 125cc World Championship title, only failing at the final hurdle in Spain when he was beaten by factory Derbi rider Angel Nieto.

In 1972 Barry switched to Yamaha machinery, without any real success, but on his return to the Suzuki fold, via its British importers Heron – and its team manager Rex White – his luck changed. At first he rode the air-cooled TR500 twin and later the 180mph (290kph) TR750 triple, and it was on one of the latter that Barry suffered a horrific accident at Daytona in March 1975. He made an amazing recovery, and was back racing, and competing against Agostini, a mere five weeks after the crash.

As recounted elsewhere, Sheene's first victory over Agostini came at Assen during the 1975 Dutch TT. He also won at Anderstorp, home of the Swedish GP, later that year.

However, it wasn't until 1976 that Sheene really found his form in the blue riband category of GP racing. Armed with one of Suzuki's latest XR14 (RG500) liquid-cooled disc valve square fours, he won five of the 10 rounds of the 500cc championship (France, Austria, Italy, Holland and Sweden). Actually, this was even more convincing than it would appear, as he didn't ride or finish in four

Barry with a group of *Motor Cycle News* girls – including his sister Maggie (far right of picture), – circa 1972.

Barry Sheene pictured in 1974 with his Suzuki TR750 leading Norton mounted Dave Croxford at Brands Hatch.

rounds (which included the Isle of Man TT) and finished runner-up in the remaining round. In retaining his crown the following year Barry recorded six victories (Venezuela, West Germany, Italy, France, Belgium and Sweden).

During 1978 (runner-up) and 1979 (third) Barry fought out some truly memorable duels with the American Kenny Roberts. Ultimately Roberts won both contests, and Sheene began to consider a switch to four wheels, although after testing a Surtees F1 and a BMW saloon he decided to stick with bikes. This time he used production Yamaha machinery (a four-cylinder five-hundred), backed by the Akai electrical concern.

Barry soon discovered that his privateer effort was no match for the works-supported teams and he struggled; but eventually, at the end of 1981, Yamaha relented and handed Sheene a works ride. He responded by winning the final round in Sweden to finish the season fourth in the 500cc World Championship table.

In 1982 he had another serious accident while practising for the British Grand Prix at Silverstone, and although he recovered this really was the end of the big time. He then switched back to a private RG500 Suzuki before retiring in 1984, going to live with his parents in Australia where he became a television presenter.

As the 21st century dawned he began a new career as an historic racer, aboard a 500cc Manx Norton. In fact it was following a victory in a support race at the British Grand Prix in the summer of 2002 that he was diagnosed as having cancer. Sadly this proved terminal and he passed away in March 2003, aged 52.

Saarinen and Ago's only clash came in the 350cc race, but after a poor start Giacomo eventually retired, although before this Jarno had built up a commanding lead.

Scarborough Gold Cup – 10 laps – 24.1 miles
1st   G. Agostini (MV 3)
2nd   B. Sheene (Yamaha)
3rd   P. Cott (Yamaha)
4th   M. Grant (Yamaha)
5th   D. Chatterton (Yamaha)
6th   B. Adams (Cowles Seeley)

After Scarborough came the annual 'Race of the Year' at Mallory Park, but Giacomo Agostini was not there, having been effectively prevented from attending by Count Corrado Agusta's orders. Besides Ago, John Cooper was not able to ride at Mallory, due to a practice injury sustained at Scarborough the previous weekend. But it would have been tough for either man, as the big Mallory race was won by Jarno Saarinen, who, on his latest water-cooled 350 Yamaha, also set a new outright lap record for the Leicestershire circuit. Instead of turning out at Mallory, Giacomo was sent to the Spanish Jarama circuit near Madrid, where he spent three days instructing local riders in the art of racing big capacity bikes, with a special emphasis on 750cc models.

At Cadwell Park on 24 September 1972, Giacomo Agostini became the first man to lap the demanding Lincolnshire circuit at over 80mph and thus collected a special silver tray which had been waiting for this event on circuit owner Chas Wilkinson's office desk. But it was Mick Grant on a 350 Yamaha who pushed Ago the hardest in both the heat and the final of the 10-lap, 22.5-mile race. The precise record lap speed was 80.84mph.

Back in Italy, at San Remo, Giacomo chalked up double 350/500cc victories, his main opposition coming from Aermacchi-mounted Renzo Pasolini. In the 500cc race Paso, riding a 380cc (an overbored 350 two-stroke twin) Aermacchi, was forced out after his engine seized. After his victories at San Remo, Giacomo became Italian Senior Champion for the 13th time. The previous top scorer had been Tarquinio Provini with 12.

Grand Prix of Paris
Billed as the Grand Prix of Paris, the meeting held on Sunday 22 October 1972 at Rungis in the French capital's suburbs (near Orly airport) was not one Giacomo Agostini will want to remember – for two totally different

reasons. Firstly there was his own failure to complete a single racing lap after being torpedoed by Englishman Mick Grant, and secondly there was the sad death of former 125cc World Champion Dave Simmonds in a caravan fire at the circuit.

When Phil Read flew out to Italy in November 1972 to discuss the renewal of his MV contract, Count Corrado Agusta confirmed that it would 'suit the factory perfectly if the team did not contest the Isle of Man TT in 1973'. This came after Phil had said that he did not wish to take part in the event. It was also revealed that Giacomo Agostini had the same feelings on the subject. Like Ago, Read's new contract meant only riding MVs – no more Yamaha or Norton machinery in 1973.

In early December one of MV's main racing challengers, Aermacchi, became Harley-Davidson, after the American company who had a 50 percent holding in the Varese marque purchased the remaining shares. Harley-Davidson at that time was owned by AMF (American Machine & Foundry).

After a proposed three-meeting trip to Australia in late 1972 had fallen through, many wondered if Giacomo Agostini would actually make a planned journey to South Africa to race in January 1973. But he did, though he arrived in the country just two days before the South African TT race at Pietermaritzburg. This first appearance ended in failure – his MV three misfiring from the start – and he was forced into an early retirement.

The latest development of the 500 four-cylinder MV was finished the day Ago left to race in South Africa. Plans were afoot for him to test it upon his return. He said: 'We are developing this machine just in case Yamaha decide to use their four-cylinder racer in the 500cc class.' This was in reference to rumours from Japan that Yamaha were experimenting with a four-cylinder two-stroke GP machine.

Giacomo Agostini's second race meeting of his South African tour was celebrated with a morale-boosting victory at the Kyalami circuit. Mechanics had traced his misfiring faults to an ignition wire which had broken inside the insulating casing. But he had to work hard for his win. Mick Grant (350 Yamaha), winner of the South African TT the previous weekend, made a superb start and clung on to the lead for two laps. Then Ago screamed ahead, but Grant, Les van Breda (500 Suzuki) and Errol James (750 Ducati) kept the Italian champion in sight.

By early February 1973 the Yamaha challenge to MV's five-hundred had been confirmed. *Motor Cycle,* in their 10 February 1973 issue, asked: 'Who will win?' going on to say:

It will certainly be a clash of the Titans, with all the ingredients of a feature film. On one side, Giacomo Agostini, established and handsome idol of the grand prix crowds, his mount built by MV Agusta, who have dominated the 500cc class for 15 years. On the other, Jarno Saarinen, the dashing young Finn with the baby face, who, last year, established himself as the world's most promising rider by winning the 250cc championship, his challenge backed by Yamaha, one of the world's biggest motorcycle names.

When interviewed in Japan, Yamaha works rider Hideo Kanaya told the reporter: 'Agostini is my target this year – I am happy to have a chance to challenge the greatest rider the world has ever known.' 28-year-old Kanaya, who worked as a development rider for Yamaha, had started racing 10 years earlier and from 1965 until 1970 raced for Kawasaki. Switching to Yamaha in 1972 he proved that he had world-class potential by winning the 250cc

Nuovo MV Agusta 500 Four

The *nuovo* MV five-hundred four arrived at the beginning of 1973 as a replacement for the long-running 3-cylinder (itself a development of the three-fifty triple which Giacomo had debuted at the Nürburgring in the spring of 1965). The new four was in many ways an excellent machine, but as John Surtees says, it 'was a motorcycle which I had long campaigned for during my time at MV, but with no success'. So by the time it finally arrived it was hardly cutting edge technology.

The 'old' four, as ridden down the years by the likes of Surtees, Hocking, Hailwood and finally Agostini himself, was a large, heavy and unwieldy piece of metal – even though it won many Grand Prix and a host of world titles. Then of course came the much more compact and lighter three-cylinder, before finally, what MV should have built all along for the blue riband 500cc GP category, a lightweight four.

At first it was not a full size five-hundred. Instead it displaced 433cc (56 x 44mm). Early examples also came equipped with wire wheels. But very quickly the capacity of the air-cooled across-the-frame power unit was upped to 498.6cc (58 x 47.2mm).

The *nuovo* 500 four was, without doubt, subjected to a more intense – and quicker – development programme than any previous MV Grand Prix design. This was necessary because of the ever-growing threat from the new wave of two-stroke machines which were by then arriving from the likes of Kawasaki, Suzuki, König and Yamaha.

For example, in 1974 a new frame was adopted with tubes running from the cylinder head to the swinging arm pivot point, in a fashion pioneered by racer/constructor Colin Seeley. In addition cast alloy wheels were now standardised, and there was a disc rear brake, rather than the old drum. This latter modification now meant that the racing MV relied exclusively upon hydraulically operated discs – two at the front, making three in all. The rear swinging arm fork was also modified in an attempt to improve handling.

In 1975 experiments were carried out with a frame featuring multi-adjustable angle for the twin rear shocks. In addition, a Yamaha-type horizontal monoshock frame was used; an interesting feature of this latter type was that small hydraulic dampers were also employed at each side of the rear wheel.

For 1976, with sponsorship from Marlboro, the frame was changed once again, reverting to a traditional duplex cradle affair, with detachable bottom rails for easy engine removal. Twin rear shock absorbers were also specified. Besides its new Team Marlboro graphics, other changes included the fuel tank design and the exhaust system, with the megaphones of the latter being not only upswept but kinked towards the end furthest away from the exhaust pipes. The tyre combination that year was usually a slick at the rear, with a treaded component at the front. And it was with one of these machines that Giacomo Agostini scored MVs last ever Grand Prix victory in the 500cc class, at the Nürburgring in August 1976.

In its final guise the engine put out 98bhp at 14,000rpm and could reach 177mph (285kph). Other details of the 1976 machine's specification included:

11.2: Compression ratio
Four Dell'Orto 32mm E154 carburettors with integral float chambers
Magneto ignition
Dry multi-plate clutch
Twin front 250mm discs, with a single 230mm at the rear
18-inch tyres
An 18 litre (3.96 imp gal) fuel tank
Dry weight of 120kg (264.5lb)

West German GP at the Nürburgring.

Saarinen wins Daytona and Imola

The 'Flying Finn' Jarno Saarinen shocked the racing world by winning both the Daytona and Imola 200-mile races on his works water-cooled 350 Yamaha twin, in March and April 1973 respectively. So with Saarinen and their 250, 350 and 500cc machines, Yamaha reasoned that they could win all three world titles.

As the opening rounds of the Grand Prix season got under way this looked ever more likely. In the 250cc class, which of course held no interest for MV Agusta, Saarinen won the first three rounds – West Germany, France and Austria. This was good enough to place him well in the lead. But it was in the 500cc where the Finn and Yamaha were really grabbing the headlines, after victories in France and Austria with the brand new four-cylinder machine, which had proved a reality.

Things didn't seem to be going MV's way when, after taking a 1-2 victory (Agostini and Read respectively) in the opening round of the 350cc championship at Le Castellet, France, Giacomo was forced to retire when leading

Jarno Saarinen with Rod Gould (centre) and Yamaha mechanics as they prepare one of the new four-cylinder Japanese bikes; spring 1973.

in Austria with a drowned ignition distributor.

Finally, at the third round of the 500cc championship at the Nürburgring, Phil Read gave the Italian factory their first win over the seemingly unbeatable four-cylinder 500cc Yamahas. MV had built a special bike for Giacomo Agostini consisting of a 430cc four-cylinder engine (based on the latest 350cc unit) in a 350cc frame, Giacomo 'not liking the 500 four-cylinder model's handling'. However, this debut ended when a valve broke; in the 350cc race both MVs retired with blown up engines.

Things did not look good for the Italian team. Then came the Monza tragedy when a horrific first-lap crash saw both Renzo Pasolini and Jarno Saarinen killed. This came after a 350cc race which had seen Giacomo Agostini score a popular victory on his four-cylinder MV over the Yamaha, Aermacchi and Benelli opposition. As the *Motor Cycle* race report of 26 May 1973 said:

> It was one of the worst tragedies in the history of grand prix racing. And the 150,000 crowd, overjoyed half an hour earlier after a

thrilling, dramatic, 350cc battle which at times involved four riders, streamed home silently from the Monza autodrome circuit near Milan, many in tears.

The meeting was subsequently abandoned, with no 500cc race being held.

The next round on the championship trail was the Isle of Man TT, which as we know MV had already decided not to contest. Nor did they go to Opatija for the Yugoslav GP – again on safety grounds. So it was not until Assen and the Dutch TT that MV returned to the GP scene. Before this the question was already being asked: 'Will Read give Ago the treatment?' This was because with six of the 12 rounds run, Read had 27 points, Agostini none in the 500cc title race. Everyone remembered that Read did not take much notice of team orders... Mick Woollett commented:

Of course, MV may step in to stop their teamsters fighting it out, but Agostini's position with the team is not as strong as it was. For a start, Read is on very good terms with young Rokki Agusta, team manager and son of factory boss Count Corrado Agusta. Secondly, Agostini is rumoured to have annoyed Count Agusta by talking to Honda about riding for them if they decide to make a comeback to racing next year. All in all, it adds up to a very interesting situation in the 500cc class – despite the absence of the Yamaha team.

It should be pointed out that Yamaha had officially withdrawn following Saarinen's untimely death, at least in the 500cc class.

Without the Yamaha challenge, MV elected not to race their troublesome 500cc fours at the Dutch round. Instead, both Read and Agostini were mounted on near identical three-cylinder models. Besides the already reported valve problems, Giacomo Agostini had been thrown off when an engine locked up while testing at Misano. The failure was found to be in the train of gears which drove the double overhead camshafts. One gear broke, locking the engine. Subsequently the engine which

Renzo Pasolini, who by early 1973 was riding for the Aermacchi Harley-Davidson team, had together with Jarno Saarinen become a serious challenger to the might of Agostini and MV Agusta. Tragically, both Renzo and Jarno were to die in a horrific crash at Monza in May 1973.

Read had used to win at the Nürburgring was stripped and examined to see if this too had any problem, or if it was an isolated fault. In addition, as Giacomo had always maintained, he: 'preferred the three to the four'. Finally MV, knowing that there was no real opposition in the 500cc class, put their riders out on the three-cylinder models at Assen.

Before the race Rokki Agusta confirmed that there were no team orders: 'Agostini and Read are both top-class professionals. It's not sport to give orders – they will ride their own race.' The *Motor Cycle* dated 30 June 1973 carried the following headline: 'Lucky Read takes the points.' Earlier in the 350cc race a great duel had taken place between the two MV stars and Tuevo Länsivuori on a works Yamaha, with victory finally going to Giacomo.

When Read and Ago lined up for the 500cc race, Giacomo had obviously decided he must win at all costs. From the start he shot into the lead. And, setting a new absolute lap record for the 4.8-mile van Drenthe circuit of 96.97mph, Giacomo pulled relentlessly away from Read who, as *Motor Cycle* said: 'was absolutely on the limit'. Then luck played into Read's hands. Agostini's gearbox began to give trouble, and, after one slow lap with the MV jumping out of gear, the reigning champion pulled in to retire.

At this stage of the season neither Read or Giacomo led in the championships – these honours went to the New Zealander Kim Newcombe (König) in the 500cc and Länsivuori in the 350cc classes.

Then came the final rounds of the series. Giacomo won in Finland and finished runner-up in Czechoslovakia and Sweden, thus taking the 350cc title. Phil Read took the 500cc championship with victories in Sweden and Spain. But Agostini won three of the remaining five rounds that he contested (Belgium, Czechoslovakia and Finland). And in fact, although MV gained both the 500cc and 350cc World Championships, the remainder of the season was spent with a war of words between the two so-called 'team members'.

Hideo Kanaya, the Japanese Yamaha rider who was later to become a teammate of Agostini's at Yamaha, pictured in summer 1973 with one of the new TZ 350 twins.

Giacomo felt that he was not being given equal treatment as the season progressed. He also complained about Phil Read's 'boastful attitude.' But a lot of that really stemmed from Read's ability to 'wind up' the opposition – including Ago!

Although the big international meeting at Silverstone in August 1973 was not part of the official World Championships, Giacomo suffered a psychological defeat when he was convincingly beaten not only by Read but also by the up-and-coming youngster, Barry

Sheene. This meeting also saw Kim Newcombe suffer a fatal crash, although he had still amassed enough points to finish runner-up in the 500cc championship.

After the GP season was over, in September 1973 Giacomo himself suffered a particularly heavy crash at Misano while testing the new lightweight four-cylinder MV. In this accident he badly injured his left leg and did not make any more appearances on MVs that year. Then came the real battle for hearts and minds at MV. As Giacomo put it:

> My contract with MV ends in October. Before I sign one I intend to speak to Count Corrado Agusta and to clear some matters with Read, to whom I have given so much this year – even to the point of leaving myself with just one bike to defend the 500cc title. Instead of being grateful, he has stolen some important victories from me.

Jarno Saarinen

As *Motor Cycle News* said in its 23 May 1973 issue: 'History will not do Jarno Saarinen justice.' The record books show that the 'Flying Finn' was the 250cc World Champion in 1972 and that in 1973 he won the world's two major races at Daytona and Imola. On Sunday 20 May 1973, while leading both the 250 and 500cc World Championships, he was killed together with Renzo Pasolini during the 250cc Italian Grand Prix at Monza, because of unattended oil left from the previous race.

Many believed that Jarno would have become one of the world's greatest-ever riders, and as *MCN* said: 'His exciting brilliance helped lift European racing out of the doldrums!'. He was also one of the most intelligent and approachable of riders. For example, despite the fact that he had already earned thousands of pounds that year, he and his wife, Soili, continued to drive their faithful old Volkswagen camper van around the circuits. Saarinen revealed his 'thinking man's character' by commenting: 'why should I change my car just because I am a World Champion? In any case, if we bought a fast sports car we would have to live out of suitcases. We can carry more of our possessions in the VW.'

Jarno Saarinen was born on 11 December 1945 in the Finnish port of Turku. Right from his formative years his great passion was racing. The late Lewis Young (a former GP rider) once recalled:

> I remember him when he was a boy. He used to come round the paddock and make a nuisance of himself. He had handlebars on his push-bike sloped down in just that peculiar way he has on his racing bikes. Naturally, as soon as he got a motorbike he wanted to race. He raced on the dirt and ice and in 1965 he became Finnish ice racing champion.

This experience gave Jarno an incredible sense of balance and enormous

Jarno Saarinen was killed in a fatal crash at Monza shortly after the start of the 1973 250cc Italian GP, robbing racing of a potentially great star.

self confidence. So fellow competitors, rather too hastily, dismissed him as trying too hard.

During 1967 he raced a Puch 125 for the Finnish importers, but the following year he purchased his own Yamaha. A year later came his GP debut, but on more than one occasion he almost quit because of lack of money. Then, in 1970, the Helsinki-based Yamaha importers, Arwidson & Co., came to the rescue with a pair of new bikes. But still Saarinen thought he might have to quit even after winning the 350cc Czech GP at Brno in 1971.

He was offered works bikes by the Yamaha factory for the 1972 season and at last his dream of becoming a champion was coming true – his perseverance and hard work had paid off, and they brought him that year's 250cc championship title.

An engineering student, he maintained his own bikes. And even when in 1973 he had his own factory mechanics, he always made the final check himself. So it was all the more tragic that a man who set so much store by safety was to be killed by the slackness of race officials. The crash caused Monza to lose its World Championship status as home of the Italian GP for many years thereafter.

The crash – which in total involved some 15 riders – was not in a class contested by Giacomo Agostini at the time, but there is no doubt that had Saarinen lived he would have proved the biggest threat to Ago since the days of the Hailwood-Agostini duels of the late 1960s. In 1973 he had already shown world-beating form in the 500cc World Championships on the new four-cylinder Yamaha. Finally, one has to ask, would Giacomo Agostini have joined Yamaha some 18 months later if Saarinen had been there?

In reply Read said: 'He's an absolute superstar. Nobody can really work with him. Being Italian he is flamboyant and he likes to be number one.' Actually, the real problem was that both men had a burning desire to win. Certainly, in my opinion – and that of many others close to him – Giacomo Agostini was very non-Italian in his temperament, and could never be accused of being hot-headed.

Finally, in December 1973, Phil Read had gone to Italy and signed a contract to ride for MV in 1974. Giacomo, meanwhile, not receiving any assurances that he would be number one, did not resign. Instead, as related in the following chapter, he was courted by both Honda and Yamaha before ultimately signing for the latter. So, after nine highly successful years the Agostini-MV partnership was over. But the battle between himself and Phil Read was set to continue, but on rival makes of machinery, rather than as teammates.

Another Yamaha contender at the top level in 1973 was Englishman Mick Grant.

FOLLOWING Jarno Saarinen's tragic and untimely death at Monza during the first lap of the 250cc Italian Grand Prix in May 1973, Yamaha were effectively out of the running in the 500cc World Championship. They had a new bike, which in Saarinen's hands had shown it was capable of mixing it with the best, but they didn't have a star rider, unlike their big rival MV Agusta which had

Giacomo Agostini at Silverstone in August 1973 with his 500 MV Agusta.

Phil Read, pictured here with his late wife Madeline in 1973, was a man who wanted to win. This was to cause the two teammates at MV to enter a bitter, often verbal rivalry that year.

two, Phil Read and Giacomo Agostini. However, as recorded in the previous chapter, these two men were very much rivals rather than team-mates. And Agostini felt his position as the long-running number one of the Italian company was threatened.

Meanwhile the 1970 250cc World Champion Rod Gould had been installed at Yamaha's European Headquarters in Amsterdam as team manager for the Japanese company with which he had gained the majority of his racing successes.

A chance meeting

Obviously Gould and Agostini had known each other for some time, as not only had the former also raced with considerable success in both the 350 and 500cc classes, but as the two men were both title holders they also had a degree of mutual respect for each other – friendship even – on a rider-to-rider basis. This then was the setting when Gould visited the MV team truck at Assen towards the end of June 1973, while Giacomo

Read's 350 MV Agusta at Brands Hatch in late 1973. By this time matters had developed to the point where Giacomo Agostini was on the verge of quitting the factory he had been with for the last nine years and with which he had won a record-breaking 13 World Championship titles.

Giacomo on the latest four-cylinder MV on his way to victory over Phil Read at the Czech GP at Brno, July 1973.

Ago winning on the 500cc four-cylinder MV, Finnish Grand Prix, 29 July 1973.

was there to take part in the Dutch TT, Gould himself having retired from riding at the end of 1972.

This 'visit' came only a few weeks after Saarinen's fatal crash, but Gould says he: 'had no ulterior motive in mind, just the need for old friends to enjoy a chat in a calm oasis, amidst the hustle and bustle preceding the following day's racing.' Rod Gould remembers that after the half-hour chat – mainly just general 'chit chat' – Giacomo finished off by remarking, half-jokingly, 'Don't forget Rodney, my contract with MV expires at the end of this year.' And that really was it, no other mention having been made about the possibility of joining Yamaha or anything else of any real significance.

The seeds are sown

However, even if the two men didn't realise it, this off-chance meeting was to kick-start one of the greatest coups in racing history. With Phil Read winning the 500cc race the next day in Holland, Ago was well on the way to losing the 500cc title he had held every year since he had first won it back in 1967. As Ted Macauley commented in his book *Yamaha*, published in 1979:

Chapter 7

Yamaha

Giacomo Agostini stunned the racing world when he signed for Yamaha at the beginning of 1974. Here he poses with of one the Japanese marque's four-cylinder models.

... his [Agostini's] always tense relationship with Read was deterio-rating rapidly. The bitter differences between the two men were now being aired both publicly and privately, and the atmosphere in the MV camp was becoming intolerable. Agostini, for so long the hero and idol of all Italy, felt he was being squeezed out and that Read, the rider brought in to support him, was being given the best machines. He was conscious of internal pressures building up around him, and his mood sank lower as each Grand Prix came and went.

Even though Gould says he didn't visit Ago for anything other than a social call, it would still make sense to say that during the half-hour he spent with the Italian he must have noticed that things were not as happy as they should have been in the MV camp. The full story of the Read v Agostini controversy is laid out in the previous chapter, so suffice it to say here that as the 1973 season ebbed away Giacomo Agostini became ever less settled at MV, although there was no more contact between Rod Gould and Giacomo before the Grand Prix season came to an end.

Gould goes to Japan

Meanwhile, on 14 August 1973, Rod Gould jetted to Japan, this visit including a meeting with factory officials concerning the following year's race programme. It wasn't until this meeting that Gould says he: 'realised that the factory would be returning for a full crack at winning the 500cc championship title.' Prior to that Rod could only hazard a guess at what the future held. All Yamaha's top brass attended this meeting – which in itself was proof that important events were planned. And as Gould says: 'At the top of their agenda was the need for a rider – a world class one – and someone capable of beating Agostini.' The Japanese officials still saw Ago as the biggest name in the sport.

Several names were mentioned, including Barry Sheene, Dieter Braun and Johnny Dodds. But none, not even Sheene, was an automatic choice for the job of wrestling the crown from MV Agusta's grasp. Then, as Macauley says: 'Gould suggested: Why not Agostini?' None of the Japanese officials had realised that Agostini was not happy where he was. But of course Gould knew and he filled them in with the details. Although everyone could see why Agostini should be their top choice, this did not sit well alongside their principle of not wishing to be seen to 'buy' success. Yamaha, and the Japanese in general, do not conduct business in this way. So they reasoned that as Agostini was the current 500cc world champion, he was the one man they could not attempt to lure away from his existing employer. And that was that, the meeting ended with no firm decision about who to sign for 1974, but Agostini had been ruled out.

There was another name on the table– Mike Hailwood. Back in Holland at Yamaha NV, Amsterdam, the company's European base, workshop manager Gerry Wood, a close friend of Hailwood, said he felt it might be a good time to put out feelers. Wood had been staying at the Hailwood home in England and he discovered that Mike was still interested in two wheels. When news got back to Gould he made contact directly, inviting Mike to a top-secret test session at the French Paul Ricard circuit. But after organising everything Mike decided to continue his four-wheel activities.

Back to square one

So where did all this leave Yamaha? The answer was: back to square one! They all agreed that Agostini was their top choice, but for reasons already

The Finn Teuvo (Tepi) Länsivuori was Giacomo's teammate at Yamaha in 1974.

given he could not be approached while he remained champion. This led Yamaha to sign Tepi Länsivuori, a close friend of the late Saarinen, and he was signed to ride both 350 and 500cc factory Yamahas for 1974. So what about former Yamaha World Champion Phil Read? Well, he was not even considered an option, because of his highly publicised rows with teammate Bill Ivy during the 1968 season.

Back at his Amsterdam office Gould received a telephone call from Volker Rauch – a German journalist and photographer who was also a close friend of Giacomo. Rauch told Gould that Honda were now on the scene, considering a full comeback, with Agostini as their number one target! This put Gould in a difficult position, and as he says: 'we certainly could not afford to allow Honda to get his services and I was determined not to be beaten.' Gould also thought that, because he and Agostini had been both close rivals and friends on the circuit, he could 'swing a deal'. But he still needed authority from head office.

With authority gained – around six people within the Yamaha organisation knew – Gould, after getting Giacomo's ex-directory home telephone number from Rauch, arranged a meeting at the Agostini home in Italy. This lasted most of the night and was very comprehensive. As Gould was to reveal later:

> He was interested, okay; but he wasn't sure. Remember he'd been most of his racing life with an Italian factory, MV, and he understood everything about their ways. Now a Japanese company was after him, and he, naturally, was curious about the way they worked. He had what seemed a million questions to ask. How they treated riders, how they looked after their mechanics, the bikes, the problems with getting parts, would they do exactly as he wanted; just about everything you could think of, he asked.

As the meeting went on it became clear just how much the partnership between Agostini and MV had eroded. Gould learned that apparent preferential treatment of Read by Rokki Agusta (Corrado Agusta's son) had alienated Giacomo to a point where divorce from MV seemed the only option. Actually the real reason why Rokki Agusta treated the long-time loyal MV man in this way had nothing to do with the actual racing and riding, but stemmed from the fact that the young Agusta resented the way that Giacomo Agostini stole all the limelight. Strange, but entirely true!

Commuting between Amsterdam and Milan

Rod Gould

Rod Gould was born in Banbury, Oxfordshire, on 10 March 1943 and made his racing debut on a BSA DB32 Gold Star three-fifty in 1961, in club races. By 1964 he had acquired his first Manx Norton (a 350), which was followed by a 500 version the following season. On these machines he was to establish himself as someone who was going places.

During this early stage of his career he concentrated on the British short circuits, places like Mallory Park (where he won the title Master of Mallory in 1966), Castle Combe, Snetterton and Cadwell Park.

Local star Dan Shorey also lived in Banbury (and raced Nortons) at that time and it was Dan who advised Rod to go professional in 1967. And with his Nortons and a very fast Yamaha TDIC-engined Bultaco special, the name of Rod Gould began to make its mark; not just in Britain, but as a member of the Continental Circus in Europe. His first Grand Prix success came aboard his five-hundred Norton, during the 1967 East German GP at the Sachsenring, where Rod finished fifth – the race being won by Giacomo Agostini on a 3-cylinder MV.

In 1968 Gould got the GP season off to a good start with a fourth in the 250cc class at the Nürburgring. With a succession of top six finishes (his best being third places in Belgium, Finland and Ulster) Rod finished the season fourth in the World Championship ratings. By now he was concentrating on both the 250cc and 350cc classes, exclusively riding factory-supported Yamahas; but although he finished runner-up no less than half a dozen times in the GPs, these results were split evenly in the two classes.

In 1970 Gould dominated the 250cc class, winning six of the 12 rounds and beating the 1969 class champion Kel Carruthers. In 1971 Phil Read became the new 250cc World Champion, with Gould as runner-up; Rod winning in Sweden and Finland. His final riding season was 1972 when he finished third in the points rating behind Jarno Saarinen (Yamaha) and Renzo Pasolini (Aermacchi-Harley Davidson). He then retired and was appointed racing manager for Yamaha, based in Amsterdam. Rod directed the Japanese firm's fortunes in all four classes (125, 250, 350 and the new 500cc four-cylinder model Yamaha introduced at the beginning of the 1973 season).

As described elsewhere, it was the signing of Giacomo Agostini that was by far Rod Gould's biggest coup as Yamaha manager. Ago was unsettled at MV Agusta after Phil Read had joined the Italian team, and Gould stole Agostini's services right under the noses not just of MV Agusta, but also of Honda – who were seriously considering a comeback if they could get the Italian star to join them.

The Agostini-Yamaha partnership was a success right from the start, with their debut victory together at Daytona in early spring 1974. After eventually quitting Yamaha, Rod Gould opened a motorcycle business in Birmingham, together with Mike Hailwood, during the late 1970s. However, the deep recession in motorcycle sales and the death of Mike in a road accident in March 1982 signalled the end of the Hailwood & Gould dealership. Rod Gould subsequently faded from the two-wheel scene.

Following this meeting Rod Gould became a frequent commuter between Amsterdam and Milan. With the Japanese officials at head office back in Hamamatsu on his back, serious contract negotiations began. And Gould had been correct in thinking that he had an advantage in the negotiations

Länsivuori seen here
testing one of the four-
cylinder Yamaha's, spring
1974.

due to his personal relationship as a former rider – whereas Honda were
using a third party (the McCormack Sports Promotion Company). After
weeks of trying, Rod Gould was finally to capture the big prize – Giacomo
Agostini's signature. The entire wheeling and dealing exercise had lasted
some six weeks and was conducted in the greatest secrecy. As Ted Macauley
says: 'After exactly six weeks of dealing and persuading, of secrecy and
worry, Gould watched triumphantly as Agostini added his name to the
contract and gave the world of motorcycle racing its biggest story in years.'

Relaxed at last

For Giacomo, his nightmare was over and for the first time in many a day
he felt, as he was later to describe: 'happy and relaxed'. The move really had
been because of just that, he wanted to move and join forces with Yamaha,
MVs main rivals in the battle for the ultimate prize in Grand Prix racing, the
500cc title. He also took great pains to explain that Yamaha were not
paying him more than he would have received at MV. Giacomo provided a
personal insight as to why he had quit his old team by saying: 'Read won
once or twice and suddenly I am a nobody in their eyes. I don't have any
trust in MV any more. All I want to do is win races. I want to show them
that I can win on anything – not only an MV.' And of course this latter
reason was, as Giacomo saw it, another reason for joining Yamaha, a
chance, at last, to silence his critics, who had long promoted the idea that it
had been the bikes, rather than his skill, that had given him his record

Daytona, February 1974 and Giacomo (far left) gets ready to take his factory TZ750 Yamaha out on the Florida circuit for the first time.

number of world titles.

Read's view

What did Ago's former teammate, Phil Read, make of this? When interviewed in January 1974 by my friend and fellow author Mick Woollett, Read had this to say in answer to Woollett's question of how Phil rated Agostini's chances on the works Yamahas:

> *If we've got to be rivals, I'd rather he was riding Yamahas than MVs. Agostini has been racing MVs for nine years – riding them is second nature to him. He can do unbelievable things on them. I think it will take him a season to get the best out of the Yamahas. Remember that, in addition to switching from a four-stroke to a two-stroke, he's also changing from a four cylinder to a twin for the 350cc class.*

Phil went on to comment:

Yamaha – the company

If precision engineering can be judged by the art of the clockmaker, Torakusu Yamaha could fully claim this distinction. Born in Nagasaki in 1851, the young Torakusu, at the age of 20, took a 10-year apprenticeship under the guidance of a British clock manufacturer. This was to provide an excellent basis for a working life in the field of engineering. Not content with his decade of learning, Yamaha then took up another apprenticeship, this time in the field of medical equipment at Osaka, and it was during this period that he decided to move to the Hamamatsu area. This was 1883 and four years later, in 1887 – now self employed as a general engineer – Torakusu Yamaha was asked to repair an organ at the Hamamatsu Primary School.

It was this task which set Yamaha on a course that would eventually lead his company, Nippon Gakki, to become one of the world's foremost manufacturers of musical instruments. Before the turn of the century, the company was not only a major supplier on the home market, but had already begun an export drive, which involved shipping instruments to Europe.

Expansion continued unabated, but in 1916, Torakusu Yamaha died at the age of 64. By then Nippon Gakki was firmly established. After Yamaha's death the company went through some industrial unrest, but in 1926 a new president, Kaichi Kawakami, was appointed. And it was this man who guided the firm through the Great Depression of the early 1930s and the subsequent years when Japan was virtually under military rule.

During early 1945 many of Nippon Gakki's production facilities were badly damaged by Allied bombing, and the road back to peacetime production was a hard one.

During 1951, Kawakami, who had suffered from ill-health for some time, passed the presidency to his 38-year-old son, Gen-ichi Kawakami. And this was to prove the stepping stone to Yamaha's emergence as a motorcycle marque. Like fellow industrialists in Germany and Italy, Kawakami saw the potential of providing affordable transport for a population hungry for personal independence.

The biggest problem was deciding on the type of machine. It was finally decided to concentrate on a motorcycle based around the highly successful German DKW RT125 design. This had first appeared in 1935, and in the post-war era was destined to be copied not only by the Japanese company, but also by BSA, Harley-Davidson and the Russian Voskhod factory, among others.

The success of this first bike, coded the YA1, was helped considerably by its domination of the Mount Fuji and Asama races in 1955. By the end of that year, work had already begun on a larger-engined model. This was a 175cc single. But the really big development was the two-fifty twin-cylinder (coded YD1). Although a German Adler had been imported for evaluation, this new bike was largely the work of the Yamaha development team headed by Zenzaburo Watase. Adler influence could be seen through the 54x54mm bore and stroke dimensions, the crankcase layout and the crankshaft mounted clutch, but otherwise most was new.

In November 1957, Yamaha entered racing versions of its twin in the Asama races. And these specially constructed machines took the top three places in the 250cc class, defeating rivals Honda, much to the latter's chagrin!

After sending works rider Fumio Ito to the US in 1958 (making Yamaha the first of the Japanese firms to venture to the States), Yamaha tended to take a back seat, compared to Suzuki and Honda, in international racing. They were subsequently the last of the 'big three' to come to Europe (briefly in 1961).

After Honda, Yamaha was the number-two motorcycle marque in the world during the mid-1970s. The operation was vast, as this photograph of the company's drawing office shows.

So it wasn't until 1963 that the company was really ready to make a serious challenge for honours with their new 249.7cc (56 x 50.7mm) disc valve RD56 twin. But even then they only contested the Isle of Man TT, the Dutch TT and the Belgian GP. In Holland, Ito gained runner-up spot, going one better a few days later at Spa Francorchamps – soundly beating the mighty Honda team in the process.

The final round in the 1963 championship was at Suzuka, Japan – the first time the country had been granted GP status. Yamaha also had their new signing, Phil Read, riding for the first time. The Englishman led for most of the race, before finally having to settle for third after experiencing plug trouble.

It was Phil Read who gave Yamaha their first world title, the 250cc, in 1964; a feat the same rider repeated in 1965. In 1967 Bill Ivy gave Yamaha its first 125cc world crown. Phil Read was double 125 and 250cc champion in 1968.

Then Yamaha retired. However, the excellent TD2 (250) and TR2 (350) air-cooled piston-port twins ensured that Yamaha had the top privateer bikes in 1969. On developments of these machines, Rod Gould became 250cc champ in 1970, followed by Read in 1971, the Finn Jarno Saarinen in 1972 and German Dieter Braun in 1973. But Giacomo Agostini and MV dominated the 350cc class during those same years. Then in 1974 Ago switched from MV to Yamaha. As covered elsewhere he went on to win the 350cc title in 1974 and the 500cc (Yamaha's first) in 1975.

Since that era Yamaha has won many other championships at all levels of competition – from club to Grand Prix. More recently the marque has been closely associated with both World Super Bike and the new Moto GP series, the latter being introduced in 2002.

As for Giacomo Agostini, after his days of riding were over, he later rejoined Yamaha as team manager of the Marlboro GP squad, gaining much new success for the Japanese company throughout the 1980s, in both the 500 and 250cc classes, with a number of riders including Eddie Lawson and Luca Cadalora.

Frankly, I'm sorry Ago has left MV. At one time I thought that we had achieved a good relationship. We were both getting well paid and, although he went through a bad patch, he still ended the year with the 350cc title.

However, Read's next statement revealed something of the feud which had gone on between the two superstars:

The trouble with him [Agostini] is that he must be in the limelight. He must be the star. After so many years at the top, he just couldn't take a few defeats. I think I'm a good loser. I expect to be beaten a few times in a season. But Ago got used to winning all the time and couldn't accept the fact that we can all be beaten. It's made him a bad loser.

But if one comment above all in the January 1974 interview was off the mark, it was how Phil Read viewed Agostini's chances Stateside at Daytona, which was only a few short weeks away:

One thing's for sure, he's in for a shock when he makes his debut on the TZ 750 Yamaha at Daytona in March. I'm sure he expects to go out and clean up – but they have more fine big bike riders in the States than we have in Europe. He'll have a fight on his hands.

As a parting shot, Phil promoted his then 'friend' Barry Sheene (things were not always so rosy in later years!) by saying:

He's the man Yamaha should have signed. He's young and has already proved that he can handle 170mph two-strokes. To my mind he's a better bet than Agostini. I only wish we'd known Agostini was going before Suzuki signed Barry for 1974. I'd have picked Barry for my teammate without hesitation ... then again, I'd have thought that Yamaha would have signed him to support Ago. I'm really surprised they are sticking with Länsivuori. But Ago will be pleased. It makes him the number one, with Länsivuori unlikely to steal any of his thunder.

Agostini in Amsterdam

The headline read: 'Agostini and his Yamaha in Amsterdam.' This was in response to questions posed by Dutch journalist Erich Winter when Ago was in Amsterdam towards the end of January 1974 discussing plans with Yamaha's European publicity manager and race chief Rod Gould. Ago was able to confirm 'that my number one target is to regain the world 500cc championship title I held from 1966 until Phil Read took it from me last year.' Then the 13-times world champion told Winter:

> Some people have suggested that I only signed for the cash and that I will soon retire. That's not true. I did not switch to Yamaha for money. I switched because I did not like the atmosphere in the MV Agusta team and because I want to win my title back.

He also went on to reveal that he would 'only give up racing when I find that I cannot win anymore.' It was also clear that he was still bugged by his former teammate, saying: 'I quite easily beat Read in the Belgian Grand Prix and the Czech Grand Prix and in Finland. So I'm not finished yet – in any case I'm two years younger than Read.'

Agostini also went on to say that he was very pleased to be with Yamaha and be able to compete in the American races, something he was not able to do when with MV because: 'they do not have a machine eligible for Formula 750 racing.' By then he had already ridden the four-cylinder TZ 750 in a test session in Japan – and from Amsterdam he was flying out to Japan again for 'an extended test session'. During this session he intended 'trying all the racing Yamahas; the twin-cylinder 125, 250 and 350cc models as well as the four-cylinder 500 and 750cc bikes.'

Preparing for Daytona

After that Giacomo Agostini would be flying to America for his debut on a works Yamaha – at the Daytona 200 in Florida on 10 March. He was scheduled to arrive in the States two weeks prior to the race so that he and the rest of the seven-strong Yamaha team could 'carry out further testing at Daytona before official practicing begins on Monday 4 March.'

Actually, as my friend Nobby Clark (Ago's race mechanic) reveals:

> His [Agostini's] first race for us was to be Daytona and we went out there a month before the event so that he could get the feel of racing a two-stroke, something he had never done before, and the circuit which was part flat infield but mainly high speed banking.

This was also where Giacomo first met Kenny Roberts, the number one rider in the United States. They both received a Corvette car with their name written on the doors; beside the name of Giacomo Agostini were the words

'Thirteen Times World Champion'. Kenny was not at all pleased and made a big fuss, saying that the 'world' was the United States of America, that he was No.1 and so was world champion. Giacomo calmly looked him in the face and said: 'We'll see tomorrow'.

Ago does it

'Ago does it!' shouted the *Motor Cycle* front page headline in the 16 March 1974 issue. The magazine went on to report: 'In a sweltering 90 degrees which left him completely exhausted, Italy's 350cc World Champion Giacomo Agostini silenced his critics on Sunday with a record-breaking win in America's fabulous Daytona 200 race.' And this was certainly no easy victory, as ranged against him was the elite of the big-bore racing world: men such as Kenny Roberts, Barry Sheene, Paul Smart, Yvon du Hamel, Gary Nixon, Gene Romero, Dick Mann, Mick Grant, Peter Williams and a host of other stars.

After qualifying, the front row comprised Smart (who had been quickest), Japanese works Yamaha rider Hideo Kanaya, Roberts, Sheene and Agostini. After an action-packed race in which Agostini's winning average speed of 105.01mph took 1 hour and 43 minutes, 30.39 seconds, the top six places were:

Daytona 200 Miler – 47 laps – 180 miles

A young Kenny Roberts after winning at Ontario in 1974. Earlier that year at Daytona he had been forced to accept runner-up spot following a brilliant Yamaha debut ride by Giacomo Agostini in the famous 200 miler.

Giacomo Agostini's works YZR500 Yamaha Grand Prix machine, 80bhp at 10,000rpm; 6 speeds; dry clutch; cantilever (monoshock) frame.

1st	G. Agostini (Yamaha)
2nd	K. Roberts (Yamaha)
3rd	H. Wilvert (Kawasaki)
4th	D. Castro (Yamaha)
5th	T. Länsivuori (Yamaha)
6th	G. Romero (Yamaha)

Giacomo's mechanic Nobby Clark says:

So it was a triple first. Our first event together and his first on a Yamaha, his first on a two-stroke and his first at Daytona. He was very clever and professional about it. He went out every day and learned the circuit section by section. He never showed anyone just how quickly he could lap either during our private sessions or during the race qualifying. He would ride every lap in sections – flat out and really trying for half a lap – then slow down fractionally – then off again. Everyone had a false idea but come race day he put it all together and won the race. People said he was lucky but the truth was it all worked out just as he planned it.

Mick Woollett, writing in *Motor Cycle* on 23 March 1974, said:

That win at Daytona proves it. Giacomo Agostini is a great cham-

pion, one of the finest in the history of motorcycle racing. For him it was the most important event of his life. At 31 he was switching from the four-stroke MV Agusta he had raced for nine years to two-stroke Yamahas. He was also changing from an Italian to a Japanese team and, just to make things even more difficult, the switch had come at a time of personal crisis – he had lost his 500cc world title and then suffered a heavy and painful crash while testing an MV in Italy in September. Heaping problem upon problem, this was Agostini's first appearance at Daytona, and he faced what was probably the strongest entry ever assembled for a single race. In practice he was outpaced by four of his rivals. With nerves which must have been close to breaking point he faced the starter, his whole future hanging on the next hour and a half. That he triumphed brilliantly, overcoming heat and track problems that eliminated ace after ace, is now history.

So how did Giacomo himself view the 1974 Daytona race?

It was so hot and the race so long. About halfway I started to dream – like a man in the desert. I imagined I was diving into the swimming pool at my motel, sinking deep into the cool, clear water. My concentration had gone completely. I had to slow down and get such thoughts out of my head – then I got my, what do you call it... second wind. Then I was okay.

After the race Ago had been so completely exhausted that even after lying on the floor of the Yamaha workshop for a quarter of an hour and then being driven to the garlanding ceremony in Daytona's 'Victory Lane' he had been unable to string more than a sentence or two together. Even at the prize giving on the Sunday evening he seemed bemused and exhausted by the noisy crowd of well-wishers.

Clutch rather than bump start

Even though this had been his first race with a clutch start, rather than the then traditional bump-and-run start used by European organisers, Giacomo was still second into the first corner on race day and took the lead soon after. How had he achieved this?

To make a good clutch start you need a little luck. You cannot keep your engine at the same revs all the time – you have to open and close the throttle so that the revs are between [on the TZ 750

Yamaha] 7,000 and 9,000. If the flag goes down when you have only 7,000 it's not so good.

I watched the starter carefully. When I saw the muscles of his

Daytona Speedway

William (Bill) Henry Getty France was, like the track he created, larger than life. France moved to the north-eastern coast of Florida in 1934, near to Daytona Beach. The following year he witnessed that ultimate speedman, Sir Malcolm Campbell, make his land speed record run, the last man to gain the 'world's fastest' crown on the golden beach at Daytona.

France first became a motorsport promoter in 1938, running both motorcycle and stock car races at Daytona Beach, but these early events were not without their problems. Noise, population growth, crowd control, accidents – all were headaches for France and his team. And although his events on both two and four wheels gained in stature Bill France could visualise the day when racing on the beach would be unacceptable. So, in 1953, he began planning the ultimate solution: a purpose-built circuit complex in the Daytona area. But this was no easy task and the transition from dream to reality took six long years. But there was to be a happy ending: the creation and subsequent opening of the new Daytona International Speedway complex.

The new venue's first event was not concerned with bikes, being the Daytona 500 stock car race. The year was 1959. With its successful adoption by the four-wheel brigade it may seem strange that the first motorcycle meeting was not staged until February 1961. However, even then this was not held under AMA (American Motorcycle Association) rules, but instead was the first FIM sanctioned road race ever held in the US.

The first AMA event at the new Daytona track was the famous 200-mile Experts race, run for many years previously on an oval comprising a 2-mile stretch of beach linked by two sweeping turns. This first event on the purpose-built circuit was won by Harley-Davidson works rider Roger Reiman, riding one of the Milwaukee factory's side-valve 750cc V-twins.

The new Daytona Speedway complex was built for use by almost any branch of motorised events, from motorcycles to sports cars, Formula Junior, stock cars and even drag racing. The facilities available were second to none at the time. There was covered pit accommodation and ample workshop space. All the leading trade support companies were looked after – spark plug, fuel, tyre and other specialists having permanent sites and equipment installations.

There were five basic circuits. The outer banked course was 2.5 miles in length; others that took in artificial bends and straights across the infield varied from 1.63 to 1.66, 3.1 and 3.81 miles, and there were a number of variations, one of which was used by the AMA for the 1961 200-miler.

The infield, which included a 45-acre lake suitable for speed-boat racing, could accommodate more than 65,000 spectators and their vehicles. The six grandstands, one of which was covered and held 6,500, catered for some 35,000 people. The press facilities were truly first class and the public address system ensured that everyone could hear the announcements at all times. There was also a hospital which could cope with virtually every emergency.

On the infield too was the box-tower scoreboard called 'Times Square', which could be seen from all areas of the complex. Illuminated 'telesigns' spelt out confirmed positions and times. The lap scoring and time keeping box had a photo-finish camera. A cafeteria for the competitors ensured that the 'inner man' was taken care of from dawn to dusk. Access to the infield areas was by tunnel underneath the speed bowl circuit.

The whole complex covered 446 acres next to Highway 92, the main carriageway between Daytona Beach and all points west and north. The imposing entrance even had its own main office block, press reception and fuelling station. All were in constant, instant contact with any part of the track and all the control points by telephone.

One of the reasons why it took almost two years from the first stock car meeting in 1959 until motorcycle racing began in 1961 was that the AMA Competition Committee initially had reservations about the safety of racing bikes on the 33 degree steeply banked turns on some sections of the circuit. Finally a compromise was reached between the AMA officials and the pairing of Bill France and the amenable mayor of Daytona Beach, whereby motorcycles would be restricted to a 2-mile road course in the infield portion of the track.

In 1963 motorcycles were allowed streamlining for the first time at Daytona. This rule not only increased maximum speeds, but also forced riders to adopt a European riding style. Also in 1963 the track length was increased to 3.81 miles. By the late 1960s the famous races were beginning to align themselves to the European-type racing scene. Then in 1970 the AMA officially decided to scrap the rules limiting four-stroke engines (except side-valve 750s) to 500cc. Instead, all manufacturers were allowed to race 750cc bikes regardless of valve type. There is no doubt in my mind that this rule change was responsible more than any other event for road racing becoming popular throughout the States. It also ended the 50-year split between the AMA and the FIM. This led to a vast international entry for the 1970 200-miler, with an armada of foreign bikes and riders. With factory machinery from Harley-Davidson, BSA, Triumph, Suzuki, Kawasaki, Honda and Yamaha, it looked like being a great race. Although the BSA and Triumph triples had dominated the qualifying sessions, the one remaining Honda 750 four (of a quartet entered) lasted the distance to give rider Dick Mann a famous victory, after the majority of the works entries had expired, so fierce was the competition.

Mann won again in 1971, but this time on a BSA Rocket Three. Then in 1972 Don Emde gave Yamaha their first victory aboard a production TR2B Yamaha three-fifty twin. Next, in 1973, Jarno Saarinen scored a much publicised victory, again aboard a three-fifty Yamaha twin; the lap distance having now increased to 3.84 miles.

Then came 1974 and Giacomo Agostini's fabulous victory, at record speed riding a seven-fifty four-cylinder Yamaha two-stroke, his average speed being over 105mph. The race was shortened to 180 miles, due to fuel rationing. It was also Ago's first ever race for Yamaha – what a debut! And although he returned the following year (to finish fourth), that 1974 result remains one of the truly great Daytona performances of all time. But this was not to be the end of Giacomo Agostini's involvement with the Daytona 200, because in 1982 he was the man behind New Zealander Graeme Crosby's victory (again on a Yamaha 750).

So the American venue has played a special role in the Agostini story – from both riding and team manager standpoints. Because Crosby's success came right at the beginning of our hero's management career, it was also an important step in a new career for the 15-times world champion, which he was to pursue over the next decade with first Yamaha and later Cagiva.

arm start to flex, I go. Don Castro beat me into the first corner but I soon passed him. My idea was to ride hard for five laps. I wanted to get away from the pack because the first few laps are dangerous – a crashing rider can put you out.

How did it feel to win at Daytona?
When asked how he felt about his win, Ago replied:

It was the best way to reply to my critics. Now I have won on a bike that was no faster than 20 other bikes in the race. But I don't expect to win every race. There are many good riders and to win you have to have the best combination of rider, machine and mechanics – it's a team.

But while the American stars could relax and soak up a few more days' sunshine in Florida before travelling home, Giacomo Agostini was jetting back to Italy to make his European debut aboard the YZR 500 four-cylinder model at Modena in Italy the next week. The bike he used to win the debut appearance was a version of the works five-hundred with cantilever monoshock rear suspension, developed from Yamaha's motocross bikes. This featured a single suspension unit concealed under the fuel tank. But the first clash between Phil Read (MV) and Giacomo fizzled out when the Italian superstar retired from both the 350 and 500cc races at Misano a week later.

The winning formula returns at Imola
Just five weeks after his Daytona triumph, Giacomo Agostini rode the same Yamaha TZ 750 to victory in the Imola 200 – the race styled by the organising *Moto Club Santerno* as the 'Daytona of Europe' – on Sunday 7 April 1974. After being presented with the winner's laurels by Soili Saarinen, widow of former Yamaha star Jarno Saarinen (who had won at Imola a year earlier), near hysterical fans mobbed Ago, as the *Motor Cycle* reported: 'crushing in on the Yamaha van and actually climbing on top of it just to be near their idol'. As for Agostini himself, he said: 'Daytona was very important to me – and so is Imola. Now I've also shown the Italian fans that I can win on a Yamaha in a hard race – I'm very happy.'

But Giacomo had to fight to hold off the challenge of America's Kenny Roberts, who was riding in his first race in Europe. In the first 98.24-mile leg the 22-year-old Californian shocked the Agostini fans as he opened up a 12-second advantage over the Italian. However, a slowish refuelling stop, a misunderstanding about his race position, and a frightening 150mph slide let the cool and calculating Giacomo Agostini build up a sufficient lead so that he was able to refuel and roar back into the race still at the front of the field. Then, making a storming comeback, Roberts set a record lap at 95.07mph, closing to within 4 seconds of Giacomo at the finish.

In the second leg the two men from opposite sides of the Atlantic fought for the lead – first Ago ahead, then Roberts. At one time the American seemed to be getting away just as he had in the first leg, but Giacomo pegged him back, regained the lead and pulled away to save European honour by scoring a decisive and important victory. Over the two legs, the first six finishers of the 1974 Imola 200 were:

1st	G. Agostini (Yamaha)
2nd	K. Roberts (Yamaha)
3rd	T. Länsivuori (Yamaha)
4th	G. Romero (Yamaha)
5th	B. Sheene (Suzuki)
6th	R. Guili (Yamaha)

The GP season begins

Next, at the end of April, came the first round in the 1974 Grand Prix season. Although the reigning 500cc champion Phil Read won on his MV Agusta in the French round held over the near five-mile twisting, mountainous circuit at Clermont-Ferrand in the centre of the country, it was not the clear-cut success that many had predicted for the Englishman.

In fact, arch rival Giacomo Agostini set the pace on his four-cylinder two-stroke Yamaha, shattered the lap record with a lap of 84.78mph and was pulling away from Read until his bike faltered and stopped with bearing failure. The 350cc race saw Read exit to an early retirement after being outpaced by the leading Yamahas. Agostini came through from a slow start to win from teammate Tuevo Länsivuori.

A week later a riders' strike crippled the West German round at the Nürburgring, which was reduced to virtually a sidecars-only meeting when the majority of solo riders – Agostini included – walked out in protest after a long wrangle with the organisers concerning the amount of unprotected Armco barrier. In a remarkable display of solidarity, riders from all countries refused to ride. This was the first real strike in the history of road racing – the only other collective action prior to this had been at the Dutch TT in 1955 when half the field pulled in after one lap of the 350cc race. Then the problem was poor starting money. In Germany the problem was a lack of

Tuevo Länsivuori in vivid action at Mallory Park, summer 1974.

straw bales in front of the steel barriers. As this was in clear breach of FIM regulations, no action was forthcoming against the riders concerned – unlike in Holland a decade earlier, where several riders including reigning 500cc world champion Geoff Duke were banned for several months.

Ago scores a double

Giacomo Agostini scored his first Yamaha double victory in early May at the Salzburgring, the home of the Austrian GP. This put him well ahead in the 350cc title chase and in a challenging position in the 500cc class. And what a brilliant double it was too, fought out in bitterly cold and wet conditions. He outsped and outlasted his rivals to score two impressive victories. It proved a disastrous weekend for Phil Read and his MVs. First he was outpaced during 500cc qualifying by new teammate Gianfranco Bonera; then on race day he twice suffered machine troubles.

Only a few hours before the start of an international meeting at Misano a week after the Austrian GP, Read received a phone call from Count Corrado Agusta saying that the team would no longer race the 350cc model. This in effect meant that the MV challenge had ended in this class, almost handing the championship to Yamaha – if not to Giacomo himself!

Imola shocks

The next round in the 1974 World Championships came at Imola, Italy, in late May. The move to this circuit followed the tragedy at Monza a year earlier, which had seen both Saarinen and Pasolini killed. MV's new star Gianfranco Bonera won the 500cc race, but only after Barry Sheene and Giacomo had broken the lap record, together with Bonera, a dozen times or more in a hotly contested race. Then Sheene crashed and Ago ran out of fuel while leading with one lap to go. But most amazing of all was the sight of Phil Read, MV's number one, being almost lapped by the end of the 36-lap, 114.08-mile race! But Read still managed to come home third – behind Bonera and Länsivuori (Yamaha).

Imola was not all bad news; Giacomo not only won the 350cc race to strengthen his grip on the championship, but also had the satisfaction of setting the fastest lap in the 500cc race – a new course lap record at 96.38mph.

Off to Japan

Although Agostini didn't take part in the Isle of Man TT (then still a round of the World Championship series), he did race at the big Post TT meeting at Mallory Park, together with a host of GP names including Read, Bonera, Länsivuori and Sheene. However, it was a day he wanted to forget – his best place by far being in the 500cc race where he came home third. Then it was off to Japan to test new Yamahas – for the 500cc class. Although the 750 and 350cc model had been going great guns, the class he most wanted to succeed in that year, the 500cc, had so far proved a dismal failure, with too many retirements.

With a couple of record-breaking rides in the Dutch TT at Assen, Giacomo Agostini stamped his authority on the Grand Prix scene in the sixth round of the 12-event World Championship series. After winning the 500cc he was really beaming, and during the race he had been the first man to break the three-minute barrier for the demanding 4.8-mile van Denthe circuit.

At the midway stage Giacomo's victory in the bigger class was crucial, having retired in the French and Italian rounds while leading, and having missed the strike-bound West German GP and boycotted the TT he almost had to win to keep his championship hopes alive. Things were much easier in the 350cc class, as he already had a comfortable lead. As one journal of the period reported:

The atmosphere at the Dutch is always terrific and Saturday (race day) was no exception. All night long the roads to the normally sleepy little country town of Assen in Holland's north-east corner had been thronged with cars and motorcycles making their way to the circuit.

Read's revenge

A mere eight days later in early July, reigning 500cc champion Phil Read took his revenge on his arch-rival at the Belgian GP at Spa Francorchamps, set among the forests of the Ardennes region of eastern Belgium. Smarting from his defeat at the Dutch TT, Read blasted back into the headlines when he scorched around the 8.7-mile circuit on his MV four at an incredible 133.42mph – the fastest lap in the history of Grand Prix racing at that time. And he left Giacomo, having his first outing on a new, lightweight four-cylinder Yamaha, so far behind it was embarrassing. This victory lifted Read above his teammate Gianfranco Bonera to lead the championship with 50 points, four ahead of Bonera and eight in front of Agostini. There was no 350cc race in Belgium.

The 'new' 500 Yamaha was in fact a 'cleaned up' version of the existing bike. Yamaha's Rod Gould said:

> It's a completely new engine – an inch narrower and just over an inch shorter than the old one. Horsepower at 90bhp, revs at 10,500, and bore and stroke dimensions are all the same. But the machine is very much lighter, it weighs only 132.5kg (292lb) compared to 154kg (340lb) of the old one.

To achieve this significant weight saving, a lot had been pared off all round, but the frame retained the basic layout and geometry of the old, with wheels and tyre sizes remaining the same. Giacomo had previously tested the newcomer at the Nivelles circuit, near Brussels, before going to Spa Francorchamps, but on race day the newcomer simply wasn't competitive.

Another defeat

For the second Sunday in succession Giacomo's new super lightweight works Yamaha 500 four let him down. This time he was beaten by teammate Tuevo Länsivuori, riding one of the older, much heavier works machines, at a non-championship meeting at Zandvoort in Holland. Setting a new motorcycle record for the Dutch circuit at 92.92mph, the little Finn pulled away to beat his teammate by nearly half a minute.

After this shock, and wasting no time, the Yamaha mechanics immediately stripped Ago's motorcycle the same evening and the telephone wires to Japan nearly melted as the European-based racing team conferred with the design and development engineers in Hamamatsu. Agostini had a dilemma. Should he race the new, so far unsuccessful machine when he was due to meet Phil Read for their vital clash the following weekend in the Swedish Grand Prix, or should he revert to the older, heavier machine? Giacomo could not afford to make the wrong decision – as up to that time he had

A youthful Barry Sheene, with Heron Suzuki team manager Rex White.

finished in only three rounds out of seven; with only three to go he simply couldn't afford another DNF.

Crashing out

In the end Ago decided to ride the older Yamaha four and after setting the third fastest qualifying time in practice, with MV riders Read and Bonera plagued by suspension and tyre problems, languishing in seventh and eighth places, the Italian star must have fancied his chances of making inroads into Read's lead in the championship at Anderstorp in Sweden. But it was not to be, with Ago suffering a disastrous crash – an accident which virtually eliminated all hopes of regaining the 500cc championship title in 1974.

The crash occurred in the early stages of the race, as the pack swept off the main straight (the runway of the local airfield). At 130mph Barry Sheene's Suzuki went into a slide (caused by an engine seizure), then flipped over. Read, in Barry's slipstream, avoided the mêlée of bike and rider. But Giacomo, dicing with Jack Findlay on the second works Suzuki, had already drifted wide, having dived under the Australian. As the *Motor Cycle* race report dated 27 July 1974 stated: 'He went down in a cloud of sparks and dust and was picked up by an ambulance with a damaged right shoulder – and may miss next Sunday's Finnish Grand Prix.' Actually, Giacomo was flown home to Italy after the meeting for specialist medical attention at his local Bergamo Hospital. His injury turned out to be much more serious than at first thought, and it took some 1½ hours for his badly fractured right collarbone to be pinned. Doctors said it would be six weeks before the break was properly mended, but if progress was good he would be fit enough to ride in the Czech GP a month later, at the end of August.

With Giacomo Agostini out, Phil Read retained his 500cc World Championship title when he won the Finnish GP at Imatra a week after the Italian's accident. And although Giacomo did race at the Czech GP at Brno he was, as *Motor Cycle* reported: 'only a shadow of his usual self'; eventually coming home sixth.

Ago's 14th title

All the heartache of the previous six weeks was forgotten when, back in the groove and fully recovered from his Swedish collarbone injury, Giacomo shattered the absolute lap record for the testing 3.7-mile Opatija seaside circuit as he stormed to an impressive victory in the 350cc race at the Yugoslav Grand Prix in early September. This success clinched the 350cc World Championship for the Italian for the seventh year running – and lifted his record-breaking total of world crowns to an incredible 14, five more than Mike Hailwood.

Fastest in practice, Giacomo led the race all the way, upping the lap record of 96.66mph set by Dieter Braun on a Yamaha the previous year to an impressive 97.93mph. Easing up, he finished over 30 seconds ahead of Australian Johnny Dodds (Yamaha) with Braun snatching third place from Patrick Pons in the closing stages. Giacomo's teammate Tuevo Länsivuori was never in the hunt and retired with engine trouble.

Only the four smaller solo classes were run at the Yugoslav GP (the eleventh round of the 12-strong championship series), which was held in weather so hot that spectators were cooling off between races by swimming in the Adriatic only yards from the circuit. Ago didn't contest the final round in Spain, which in any case only featured a 350cc event.

Mallory Park

In mid-September came the annual 'Race of the Year' meeting over the 1.35-mile Mallory Park circuit in rural Leicestershire. The 1974 meeting really lived up to its name, as the most star-studded field ever to contest a race on a British mainland circuit set up to do battle over 40 gruelling laps in the main race. This had been hailed in previews as the 'Clash of the Giants'. The entry included Kenny Roberts, Phil Read, Barry Sheene, Paul Smart, Dieter Braun, Gianfranco Bonera, Dave Croxford, Yvon du Hamel, Patrick Pons, Oliver Chevallier, Eric Offenstadt, Stan Woods, John Newbold, Mick Grant, Roger Marshall, Barry Ditchburn – and Yamaha teamsters Tuevo Länsivuori and Giacomo Agostini. What a race in prospect!

1974 Mallory Park Race of the Year. Riders on the trailer include left to right: Percy Tait, Geoff Barry, John Newbold, Kenny Roberts, Paul Smart, Dave Croxford and Giacomo Agostini.

A scream of multi-cylinder engines heralded the start, as down went the starter's flag and away shot Giacomo on his Daytona-winning TZ 750 Yamaha. Swooping through the Esses, the Italian led from Read, Sheene and Roberts – the big four establishing their superiority right from the off.

Giacomo now takes up the story, in an extract from one of the post race reports:

I made a good start eh? And I tried hard for a few laps. But when the others started to pass me and I wanted to go faster the engine

Yamaha TZ 750

The TZ 750 was launched at the Tokyo Show in early 1973. Designated the TZ 750A, it was actually a '700' – 694cc to be precise – basically a pair of TZ 350 twins side-by-side. Its bore and stroke were also identical to the three-fifty at 64 x 54mm. But there were differences. For example, the squish band of the bigger bike was dropped 2mm on the TZ 350 to 1mm. In addition the exhaust port differed from the 350, sitting 1.5mm lower in the cylinder barrel. This provided more mid-range, at the expense of top end, making the TZ four-cylinder easier to ride.

Yamaha used 4-petal read valves (developed from their successful motocross engines) – and it should be remembered that at that time the production TZ 350 was only simple piston-port induction; and again was more aimed at broadening the power band. To accommodate the introduction of the read valve assembly the cylinder barrels were equipped with a fifth transfer port on the intake side – the pistons having cut-outs in their skirts. These modifications produced an extended inlet duration, which in turn allowed more complete filling of the crankcase. Because Yamaha engineers were worried that piston reliability would be compromised, a few of the early TZ 750s were supplied without the trimmed piston skirts.

A casual observer would have thought that the new Yamaha four, with its across-the-frame cylinder layout, would have featured a single crankshaft. But in fact there were two assemblies sitting side-by-side in the magnesium horizontally-split crankcases. On the inboard end of each crankshaft was a 10mm wide gear – this engaged a 20mm wide gear located at the rear of the cranks. The crankpins were set at 180 degrees apart which provided a firing order of 1, 4, 2 and 3.

The countershaft transferred drive from the crankshafts to a huge 7-plate dry clutch assembly. Power was also supplied via a primary gear to a magneto rotor, as well as to a transmission oil pump and a water pump. There was no two-stroke oil pump on the TZ four, lubrication being take care of by simple petroil mixture. A quartet of 34mm Mikuni carburettors were fitted. Yamaha's official figures gave the power output as 90bhp at 10,000rpm. This was combined with an all-up ready-to-race weight figure of 168kg (370lb). These figures were impressive for the time.

Chassis design comprised a tubular steel open-loop frame with box-section rear swinging arm and twin shocks – very similar to the original YZR500 four raced by Jarno Saarinen in early 1973. And although the engine sat fairly high in the frame, ground clearance was still something of a problem. This was not because of engine width, but was rather a case of the exhaust touching down. The four pipes were at first mounted beneath the engine, and to alleviate the grounding glitches, the two inside pipes were actually flattened in their mid-section – which from a performance point of view was a drawback. Another problem, as confirmed to the author by ace race mechanic Nobby Clark, was that these pipes were prone to fracture and had to be strengthened. Later models largely solved this problem by re-routing the left (near) side outer pipe up and around the carburettors. This allowed more room for all the pipes to be the desired shape, while at the same time curing the fracturing problem.

A pair of 298mm (11.73in) brake discs were specified for the front wheel, with an equally large single disc at the rear. A drum rear brake had originally been considered but this was axed after testing. Giacomo Agostini took the new machine to two brilliant victories – the Daytona 200 and a few weeks later the Imola 200 in spring 1974.

Towards the end of 1974 the TZ 750B, as it was known, was introduced, the cylinder bore having been increased to 66.4mm, giving a full 750cc. Along with the increase in engine displacement, specific components were upgraded – most notably the water pump and rear tensioner, both of which were considered not strong enough to cope with the additional 10bhp. Towards the end of 1975 the production TZ 750B became the TZ 750C, which was strange because the two bikes were virtually identical.

At Daytona in 1975, a trio of very special TZ 750s had been provided for Kenny Roberts, Steve Baker and Giacomo Agostini. These bikes were effectively 750 engines shoehorned into the 500GP monoshock chassis. Kenny Roberts openly admitted that: 'the new suspension cured the twin shock model's tendency for high speed weaving' and that the machine 'handled a lot better.' However, as it happened none of the special monoshock bikes won; instead this honour went to Gene Romero on a Kel Carruthers tuned production twin shock bike.

It wasn't until 1976 that Yamaha produced its ultimate F750 four-cylinder two-stroke, the much vaunted OW31. Lightened by some 18kg (40lb), it also gave more power. Yamaha had again looked at the 500GP chassis for inspiration. Factory sources alleged Roberts was clocked at 182mph during qualifying for Daytona that year.

For 1977 Yamaha produced a production version of the previous year's OW31 factory racer. But it wasn't really a proper replica, because the engine was virtually the previous year's production 'C' motor, while the chassis was made from heavier materials – so there was only a slight reduction in weight over the previous year's TZ. In search of rigidity, the frame gained an additional tube underneath the power unit at the front and between the loops of the cradle itself. In addition some changes were necessary to accommodate the new monoshock rear suspension, employed for the first time on a production TZ 750. Finally, new exhaust pipes complete with integral silencers were employed, needed to comply with the ever harsher FIM noise level regulations.

1977 marked Agostini's final season and besides finishing third on an OW31 in the 750cc World Championships, he posted his final victory in the last round of that year's championship with a magnificent victory at Hockenheim. Without doubt 1977 was also the high point of the TZ 750 series, and although the TZ 750E and F models were built between 1978 and 1983 the model would never quite dominate the circuits as it had done before.

In 1980 the FIM announced its decision to axe the F750 World Championship, a decision which ultimately meant the death of the TZ 750 itself. In January 1983 the final TZ 750F was sold, thus ending one of the most exciting chapters in modern motorcycle racing.

just would not rev, it should go to 10,700 but in practice it would only go to 10,500 – and in the race it just wouldn't go over 10,300. Then it started to overheat. So something must be wrong somewhere. Anyway I don't think that I could have gone flat-out for 40 laps round Mallory Park. My shoulder is not completely fit yet.

Mugello

The 1974 Italian road racing season came to a close at Mugello, a new circuit 20 miles north of Florence. The organisers had worked overtime removing tons of Armco barrier surrounding the many bends and clutch-slipping hairpins that were a feature of the 3.25-mile circuit.

The main race between the MV duo of Read and Bonera – and Giacomo's Yamaha – was a pulsating wheel-to-wheel affair which thrilled the 30,000 crowd, as the three men tried outbraking each other into every bend.

The 15-lap race ended when Ago overtook Bonera to gain second place behind Read and win his 13th Italian National Championship title. Giacomo also posted the fastest lap at 90.5mph, but he was clearly unhappy at finishing behind his former teammate, saying: 'I concentrated too hard in chasing Bonera. When I did attack the MV duo it was the final lap. I had left it too late.'

During a comprehensive Italian television interview in mid-November

Superb model of Giacomo
Agostini's 1974 Yamaha
YZR500 GP bike, built by
Ian Welsh of Edinburgh.

1974, Giacomo told viewers that he intended: 'quitting the 500cc class –
unless Yamaha build me a more competitive machine for 1975.' He told
millions of viewers that unless he had a machine he considered competitive
with the latest MV Agusta and Suzuki racers, then he would: 'prefer to
compete in the 250 and 350cc classes – and ride the TZ 750 Yamaha in
occasional big-bike events.'

There was absolutely no doubt that Giacomo had been bitterly disappointed with the five-hundred Yamaha. He had told close friends that what
he said was absolutely true. He also said that he did not expect Tuevo (Tepi)
Länsivuori, who had been openly critical of Yamaha in Finnish newspaper
interviews, to team up with him in 1975 – Giacomo expected Länsivuori to
race Yamahas for Finnish importer Arwidson.

1975 prospects

Not content with telling the Italian public that he didn't think much of the
500cc works Yamaha, Ago then repeated this at a reception in Modena at
the end of November 1974 hosted by Lux, a local tile-making company who
sponsored a number of riders, including himself. Speaking at the dinner,
Giacomo Agostini said exactly what he had said on TV. Although many
observers thought that this talk would upset Yamaha, it actually had the
effect of ensuring that they did produce an excellent bike for the 1975
season, as the results would ultimately show.

The prospects for 1975 did look good – for the race-going public – not
just with Yamaha, but also MV Agusta, Suzuki, Kawasaki and Harley-
Davidson (formerly Aermacchi) all taking a direct interest in the class, when

Phil Read, the 1973 and
1974 500cc World
Champion on his factory
MV four-cylinder.
However, in 1975 Giacomo
Agostini won the blue
riband title back, as a
follow-up to his 350cc title
on a Yamaha in 1974.

only MV had supported it three years before.

Giacomo spent most of the 1974/75 closed season back home in Italy with his long-time girlfriend Lucia Farrello. Yamaha got on with further development of their machinery – including the five-hundred GP four.

Meanwhile Phil Read had created problems for himself by going to Japan to test, among other bikes, the latest 500 GP Suzuki square-four. This was despite the fact that Barry Sheene, his declared 'friend', was hoping to be signed again as Suzuki's number one rider. Read created further publicity and controversy by organising a poll in a British specialist newspaper asking readers whether he should ride an MV or a Japanese bike. The result of the poll was an emphatic 'stay with MV'.

The pendulum swings

As 1974 became 1975 the fortunes of the two great rivals, Read and Agostini, began to change. As Ted Macauley said in his book *Yamaha*:

> *The Yamaha operation was smoothness itself. Agostini was now master of the two-stroke, the elementary errors of the previous year were behind him and his determination was in full flow. Read, on the other hand, was experiencing difficulties at MV, the machine did not seem to be running well and he wanted changes. Nor could he find satisfaction in his dealings with some of the personnel at the factory and in the team.*

Nobby at Daytona in 2002; he has worked for the MV Agusta, Honda, Yamaha and Cagiva Grand Prix teams throughout a career which has spanned over four decades.

Nobby Clark – Top Mechanic

As Mick Woollett said in the June/July 1996 issue of *Fast Classics* magazine, Rhodesian-born Nobby (real name Derek) Clark was the 'Mechanic of Champions'. Since first coming to Europe to help friend Gary Hocking at the start of the 1960 race season, Nobby has worked with virtually all the top riders and been a works mechanic for MV, Honda, Yamaha and Cagiva.

Nobby's first motorcycle had been a 146cc James two-stroke with 3-speed

hard-change gearbox. 'Little more than a moped really and certainly lacking any sort of glamour. I'd saved the money to buy the James from my meagre wages as an engineering apprentice with Rhodesian Railways' says Nobby. Old school friend Hocking was one of Nobby's fellow apprentices, before he set off to Europe in 1958, where he had immediate success riding Nortons lent to him by Reg Deardon. Hocking returned to Rhodesia towards the end of 1959 and, as Nobby says: 'looked me up and said "why don't you come to Europe?" I didn't need much persuading and I came over with Gary for the following season.'

Nobby then worked on Gary's MVs until the latter quit motorcycle racing after the Isle of Man TT in 1962. Next came an offer out of the blue from Jim Redman, asking if Nobby would like to work for him in 1963. Beginning as he says as a 'general gopher', Nobby gradually worked his way up until he was one of the official Honda team mechanics. He says: 'At first I just used to work on Jim's bikes, but gradually as I became accepted and as the workload increased so I began to work on all bikes as and when needed. Those were great days. We had twins, fours, fives and sixes – you never knew what would arrive from Japan next!'

Honda moved up to the 500cc class for 1966, and after Jim Redman retired following the crash in which he broke his arm during a very wet Belgian GP, Nobby transferred to Mike Hailwood – of whom Nobby says: 'He and I got along really well. He was very easy to work for.' But at the end of 1967 Honda pulled out of World Championship racing. The Japanese factory agreed to lend Hailwood bikes for non-championship events and they asked Nobby to carry on as mechanic. He says: 'I was happy to do so through the 1968 season, but it was a bit of an anti-climax after the hustle and bustle of the grand prix.'

Next he joined Bill Ivy for 1969 (maintaining his Formula 2 racing car – not the works V4 Jawa upon which Ivy was killed during practice for the East German GP that year). After Bill's death Nobby worked briefly in the car world until he switched back to two wheels to help the Australian Kel Carruthers in 1970 – Kel finished runner-up in both the 250cc and 350cc World Championships on Yamaha twins.

At the end of 1970 Yamaha were setting up a works team with headquarters in Amsterdam and invited Nobby to join them. In March 1971, as Nobby says: 'I set off with Rod Gould and Kent Andersson for the early Italian meetings. It was the start of a long association with Yamaha that lasted until the end of 1983 – first working for Yamaha Amsterdam, then Yamaha Japan and finally Yamaha

Nobby Clark (extreme right) with the Kenny Roberts Grand Prix team in 1980.

USA.'

Jarno Saarinen joined the team and won the 250cc title in 1972 and then in 1973 Yamaha moved into the 500cc class, to challenge the long-dominant MV Agusta (which meant Agostini!). After winning the first two races on the new bike, Jarno was killed on the 250 Yamaha at Monza.

That winter Rod Gould, who was by then managing the Yamaha team, 'pulled off an incredible coup by signing Agostini' as Nobby puts it. Nobby said of Giacomo: 'Agostini was, I found, very clever and professional in everything he did in racing.' Nobby was Ago's personal mechanic for both 1974 and 1975, during the Italian's time as Yamaha's number one rider.

When Nobby finally left the American Yamaha arm at the end of the 1983 season, Giacomo Agostini was running the works Grand Prix team in Europe, but with Marlboro money. Nobby reveals that: 'He [Agostini] rang me up early in 1984 and invited me back but when I arrived in Europe he said the budget was so small he couldn't afford to pay me.' Even though Ago offered to find Nobby a job elsewhere the latter declined. So for 1984 he joined the Italian Cagiva team, but says 'it was a complete disaster. The riders were former World Champion Marco Lucchinelli and Frenchman Herve Moineau. Between then they scored one single 500cc championship point all year.'

Nobby then joined American Randy Mamola, working on the latter's three-cylinder two-stroke Honda 500; 'A really good bike' says Nobby. Their best result that year was victory in the Dutch TT at Assen. Then came a series of problems trying to get travel visas. Nobby says: 'I went back to Bulawayo to try and get a Zimbabwean passport, but it was hopeless. The whole system seemed to have broken down. You couldn't even get a passport photo taken because there was no photographic paper available... it was a complete chaos. In the end I gave up trying and went to live in Durban (South Africa) for a

while.'
    Eventually, after working in Italy with a power-boat racing team, Nobby got a call from Rob Iannucci, boss of Team Obsolete. Among several ex-works bikes he had bought a Honda 250 six and wanted Nobby to rebuild it. This happened in the middle of 1993, and Nobby worked for Team Obsolete for several years, until a dispute caused him to leave the Iannucci team.
    By the time I spent five weeks travelling around the US with Nobby in spring 2002, he was working with my friend Stu Rogers on Bob MacKeever's Champagne Racing Team vintage Norton racers. I found Nobby a true motor-cycle enthusiast and now am proud to count him as a friend. His main occupation these days is with the Guggenheim Museum, maintaining their historic motorcycle collection. By a strange twist of fate, I myself had helped compile the Guggenheim book, published in 1998, entitled *Art of the Motorcycle*, which coincided with the successful launch of their exhibition of the same name in New York. The exhibition has now travelled to several other centres both in the United States and abroad.

Tepi Länsivuori switched to Suzuki for 1975; he finished 4th in the 500cc World Championship that year.

His closed season trip to Japan couldn't have helped his cause.

As revealed within the boxed section in this chapter outlining the development history of Yamaha's TZ 750, Giacomo rode one of the experimental models with a cantilever single shock frame in the 1975 Daytona 200 race. However, he was unable to repeat his success of a year before and had to be content with fourth place.

When the Grand Prix season got under way it was clear that not only had Giacomo become totally focussed on winning back the 500cc crown he had last held in 1972, but Yamaha had also succeeded in ironing out the glitches which had upset their title challenger the previous year.

The GP season begins

The 1975 GP season began with the French round at the Le Castellet circuit. After finishing runner-up to the Venezuelan youngster Johnny Cecotto in the 350cc race, Giacomo made no mistake by going one better in the 500cc race with a decisive victory. New teammate Hideo Kanaya (who had replaced Länsivuori) finished runner-up, with Read and his new teamster Armando Toracca (Bonera having suffered a pre-season crash at Modena) coming home third and fourth.

At the second round of the championships, in Jarama, Spain, there was no 500cc event. But here Giacomo beat Cecotto to victory in the 350cc event. Actually this was to be the Italian's only victory that year in the class; the title going somewhat easily to Cecotto, who was to score four victories (including the first round in France). Agostini was runner-up, with Korhonen, Braun and Pons taking the next three places on private Yamahas.

The next round of the 1975 500cc championship was staged at the Salzburgring in Austria. Agostini was a non-finisher with Kanaya taking victory from Länsivuori who was now a member of the Suzuki team; Read was again third and Toracca fourth.

High speed action at Hockenheim

The third 500cc clash of the season came at the ultra-fast Hockenheim circuit in Germany. Here Agostini showed that the combination of the revitalised Yamaha and his own trackcraft were going to be difficult to break down that year. The top six placings were as follows:

500cc German GP – Hockenheim

1st	G. Agostini (Yamaha)
2nd	P. Read (MV Agusta)
3rd	T. Länsivuori (Suzuki)
4th	H. Kanaya (Yamaha)
5th	S. Woods (Suzuki)
6th	D. Braun (Yamaha)

The next round came on home soil, at Imola, which again staged the Italian Grand Prix, with Giacomo winning and Read runner-up. The Isle of Man TT was missed, so the GP circus then went to Assen in Holland. Here Barry Sheene won his first 500cc GP race, with Ago second and Read third.

In 1975 Barry Sheene scored two wins in the 500cc World Championship series (in Holland and Sweden). Other winners that year were: Phil Read (2), Hideo Kanaya (1), Mick Grant (1) and the Championship winner Giacomo Agostini with four victories (France, Germany, Italy and Finland).

The complete top six listing was:

500cc Dutch TT – Assen

1st	B. Sheene (Suzuki)
2nd	G. Agostini (Yamaha)
3rd	P. Read (MV Agusta)
4th	J. Newbold (Suzuki)
5th	T. Länsivuori (Suzuki)
6th	G. Bonera (MV Agusta)

Read stages a comeback

With a win in Belgium and a second place in Sweden (when Giacomo was forced out with a puncture), Phil Read enjoyed a brief spell as leader in the championship. Then at Imatra, Finland, where Read had clinched the title the previous year (due to Ago's injury collected at the Swedish round), came a reversal of fortunes, with Giacomo Agostini getting firmly back in the driving seat; having already logged up three victories and a second, against Read's single win at Spa Francorchamps and a mixture of seconds and thirds. Quite simply Read knew he had to win the Finnish GP if the Englishman was to stand any hope of retaining his world crown. But halfway through the race, when leading, the MV's magneto failed. Then Bonera fell off the remaining Italian four and the title was Agostini's – provided only that he finished in the top seven at the final round in Czechoslovakia.

Ago takes the 500cc title

Giacomo didn't make any mistakes and at Brno he rode a superbly controlled race. Even though Read won, taking his tally of points to 96, Ago comfortably secured the greater prize, the 1975 500cc World Championship, by cruising home second. It was Yamaha's first 500cc title (in fact a first in this class by a Japanese marque), and the culmination of a vast amount of money, ambition, planning and sheer hard work. It was the ultimate accolade for Giacomo Agostini, who had given the entire Yamaha project a new life after it had faltered when Saarinen was so tragically killed. As Giacomo was to recall after winning what was to turn out to be his 15th and final world crown: 'It's been hard work, but I really wanted to win back my title. Yamaha gave me the best possible chance, and though it's been a tough two seasons I feel it has all been worthwhile.'

However, just as it appeared that Giacomo Agostini had reclaimed the very peak of his performance, the first seeds of decline had already been

Gianfranco Bonera, signed by MV to partner Phil Read after Ago's departure to Yamaha in 1974.

sown; perhaps more clearly to be seen in retrospect. This was highlighted by his relatively poor showing in the 350cc class, which he had totally dominated the previous year. Instead, on his twin-cylinder Yamaha, Ago just couldn't seem to match the youthful and largely inexperienced Cecotto in 1975. Amazingly, within two seasons of giving Yamaha the ultimate prize, Giacomo Agostini would announce his retirement, following what was to prove a surprisingly rapid decline.

Chapter 8

Swansong

AT THE end of the 1975 season Giacomo Agostini's contract with Yamaha was due to expire. And with new, younger stars now arriving on the scene our hero decided to form his own team. In fact, in many ways, this move was the forerunner of his later managerial roles, first with Yamaha and finally Cagiva during the 1980s and 1990s. Giacomo's main sponsor, both in his final years as a racer and later as a team manager, was the Swiss-based Philip Morris/Marlboro tobacco concern.

In the Italian superstar, Marlboro officials could clearly see a personality who was every publicity man's dream. With his record-breaking on-track successes, charm, film-star looks and clean-cut image, Ago inspired adula-

Backed by private sponsors, notably Marlboro, Giacomo Agostini returned to MV Agusta for the 1976 season. Here are the 350 (left) and 500cc four-cylinder machines as they were that year (without Marlboro livery).

tion from both sexes. One commentator once referred to him as 'an authentic idol of the crowds', which was absolutely true. Also his switch from MV Agusta to Yamaha at the end of 1973 had actually cemented his reputation; many so-called 'experts' had said he wouldn't be able to instantly make the transition from four-stroke to two-stroke (including his former teammate Phil Read). But Giacomo Agostini had proved these critics wrong, with not only two World Championships (one 350cc, one 500cc), but also by beating all-comers on the TZ 750 Yamaha at such prestigious events as the Daytona 200 and Imola 200. In achieving all this he had finally silenced those who claimed his previous successes at MV had been a case of simply having the right bikes at the right time.

Long before this, if anyone had asked his old teammate at MV, Mike Hailwood, they would have learned that Mike-the-Bike had a high regard for Giacomo Agostini – both on and off the circuit. Hailwood had spent three seasons in close company with the Italian, first while a fellow member of the MV team and then as bitter rivals while at Honda. Although their on-track rivalry produced the closest racing of either man's career, Mike and Giacomo were always good friends. In fact on many occasions Ago has named Mike as the man whom he most respected and admired. For example, when Alan Cathcart interviewed him for *Classic Racer* magazine in 1986, asking the question: 'Was Kenny Roberts your most respected rival over the years?' Giacomo replied:

Kenny is a friend now, and a great rider, but even he cannot compare to Mike Hailwood, who was a friend even when I raced against him. Mike was a real gentleman: he was very fast, but he respected other riders. He didn't try to win by putting out the other riders from his way, like some others do. He was very honest, but very fast – the best I ever raced against.

A return to MV

As Giacomo Agostini's decision to join Yamaha had created a sensation, so did his decision two years later to return to the MV fold. Apart from purely nostalgic considerations, the return of the prodigal son was important to the MV Agusta camp. First because its number one rider Phil Read had left following what had been a poor year in 1975, but second because the return of Agostini (made possible by Read's departure) was important commercially as Ago brought with him Marlboro sponsorship money – a financial contribution which allowed MV to postpone its plans to abandon racing altogether. In this respect MV had never been the same since Count

Domenico Agusta's untimely death in early 1971. The new regime, with the youngest Agusta brother Corrado as a figurehead, was an entirely different organisation. Now the Italian government, which had in effect taken a controlling interest following Domenico's death on the grounds of 'national interest' due to Agusta's importance in the aerospace industry, was the real power, not the Agusta family. Whether this state of affairs would ever have been allowed to come about under Domenico's rule is open to question; he was a much stronger personality than Corrado.

Ago and Marlboro

The 1976 MV Agusta squad was actually the Agostini and Marlboro team. While the motorcycles and technical assistance came from MV and its mechanics, headed by Arturo Magni, the control came from Agostini and Marlboro. Consequently the motorcycles were clad in Marlboro colours, not those of MV. This meant an elegant red and white paint job, with the Marlboro logo prominent. The famous MV Agusta badge was overshadowed, not only by Marlboro, but by the co-sponsors of the team, including the Api petroleum giant. It was in effect a lease operation, with MV supplying the bikes and technical back-up.

There is no doubt that Giacomo's return to the MV camp recharged a number of batteries within what was by then a group of disillusioned individuals, who had gone, in the short period of some 12 months from the end of the 1974 season, from the high of winning the 500cc World Championship to an all-time low when little had seemed to go right the following year. Of course the lack of a firm hand did not help. First Corrado Agusta's playboy son Rokki had been left in charge of the racing effort (a disaster) and when belatedly Corrado himself had taken 'control' this had been nominal to say the least. One also has to realise that during 1975 the cost accountants in charge of the Agusta Group had questioned whether the company should 'waste money with such poor results?' There is no doubt that without Giacomo Agostini, Marlboro and the other sponsors, the bikes would have been withdrawn at the end of the 1975 season.

Now, with renewed optimism, not just about the five-hundred *Quattro*, but also about its smaller three-fifty four-cylinder brother, the machinery was readied for action. When it appeared in 1976 the latest 349.8cc (53 x 38.2mm) four was equipped with electronic ignition, while a considerable amount of time was spent on the chassis, both the frame and the suspension. It is also worth recalling that very soon after Agostini's departure to Yamaha, MV had retired the smaller four. However, his return had signalled its re-introduction. But the 350 four was an exceptionally highly strung

The view Ago hoped fellow competitors would see of him in 1976 – unfortunately unreliability of his machinery was to blunt his chances most of the time. This is the 350cc MV four.

machine and keeping it in tune was a complex affair. Producing 70bhp at 16,000rpm, and weighing some 115kg (253.5lb), the smaller four was capable, on its day, of beating the best in the world with a rider of Agostini's calibre – but as was to be shown in 1976, it was more likely to break down.

Meanwhile, the 500 four (498.6cc, 58 x 47.2mm) was more reliable, but by 1976 it was under extreme pressure out on the track from the latest breed of high performance multi-cylinder two-strokes from the likes of Suzuki, Kawasaki and Yamaha. As with the 350, the 500 MV received modifications for the 1976 season. However, these were largely limited to the running gear rather than the engine. More frame modifications were carried out; the lateral struts of 1975 having been deleted in favour of a more traditional duplex cradle structure with detachable bottom rails for easy engine removal. The fuel tank was also changed, while the exhaust megaphones were upswept as high as was practical.

The season gets under way

The first outing for the new team came at Modena in early April 1976, and although the 350 four expired after a couple of laps, the 500 model eventually took the chequered flag to get the new venture off to a winning start and send everyone home in a happy mood. Unfortunately, however, the display at Modena turned out to be something of a false dawn, and the 350 four only finished one Grand Prix all season.

On his bigger mount, Agostini got the GP season off to a reliable start: two races, two finishes. At the first round at Le Mans in France Giacomo finished fifth behind winner Barry Sheene (Suzuki), Johnny Cecotto (Yamaha), Marco Lucchinelli (Suzuki) and Tuevo Länsivuori (Suzuki). Next, at the Salzburgring in Austria, the result was:

The four valves-per-cylinder head of the 1976 four-cylinder MV Agusta GP engine.

500cc Austrian GP – Salzburgring

1st	B. Sheene (Suzuki)
2nd	M. Lucchinelli (Suzuki)
3rd	P. Read (Suzuki)
4th	M. Rougerie (Suzuki)
5th	S. Avant (Suzuki)
6th	G. Agostini (MV Agusta 4)

With the first two rounds completed it was clear that the Suzuki was the most competitive of that year's crop of five-hundreds. With this in mind Giacomo Agostini decided to switch to a Suzuki RG500 production bike in an attempt to stand a chance of finishing higher up the order.

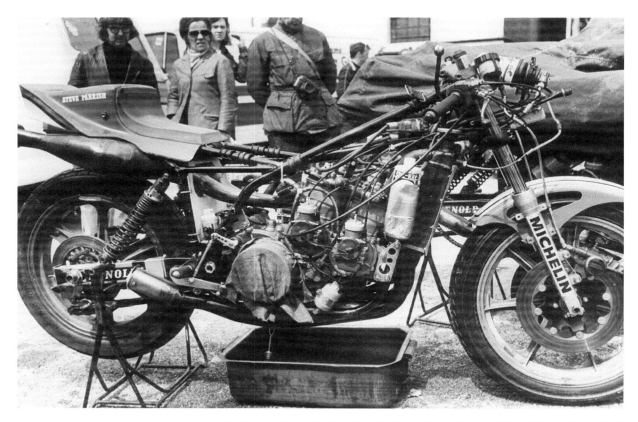

Mid-year 1976 and Ago made a switch to the 500cc class from MV to a Suzuki RG500. However, even though the bike was fast, it was also unreliable in his hands - he didn't finish a GP on the Japanese model.

Suzuki RG500

During 1976, Giacomo Agostini rode a Suzuki RG500 as part of his Marlboro-backed Grand Prix team, alternating this with the works four-cylinder MV Agusta. Ago's experiences with the Suzuki proved something of a disaster, with not a single finish in a GP race that year on one of the Japanese machines. This was in contrast to that year's 500cc World Champion Barry Sheene. But of course Agostini's bike was a privateer effort, Sheene's a works model.

The RG500 (XR14) first appeared in 1974 and had an engine layout which, at least in basic terms, followed the design of the infamous two-fifty square GP design of the mid-1960s. Nicknamed 'Whispering Death' on account of its propensity to seize without warning, this earlier bike had proved fast but notoriously unreliable. However, almost a decade later the technology had allowed the Suzuki engineers to overcome many of the original weaknesses. In place of the earlier one-piece cylinder block the RG500 had four 125cc cylinders and heads sharing a common crankcase and these were, in effect, separate engines coupled by gears. Each cylinder had its own crankshaft running in its own compartment within the crankcase – and each one could be independently stripped down and replaced without disturbing any of the other cylinders.

This was a practical solution, especially since the engine was a racing two-stroke which was likely to pick-up on one cylinder occasionally, particularly during practice when juggling with various jet sizes. With the old 1960s RZ250 the mechanics had to strip the entire engine, disturbing all four cylinders. With the RG500, they simply tackled the one giving the problems.

On the outboard end of each crank sat a thin, steel disc valve. This had a sector cut out of it which controlled the flow of mixture from the 34mm Mikuni carburettor into the crankcase, opening and closing as it spun round. On the inboard side of each crankshaft was a gear, and all four mated with a single wide gear situated in the middle of the cranks. It was this gear-coupling which made the engine so easy to strip and assemble.

Porting of the cylinders followed conventional race practice, with five transfer ports, one mating with a window port in the rear of the piston skirt. The exhaust ports of the front pair of cylinders faced forward so that the exhaust pipes and their respective expansion chambers could be tucked away under the engine. Those of the rear cylinders were in the rear wall so that the pipes went straight out the back with the expansion chambers at high level, tucked away under the rider's thighs.

Ignition was by a Hitachi electronic system on the nearside of the crankcase. Lubrication was taken care of by a pump, which supplied the main bearings and big-ends, and by 3 percent oil in the fuel. Oil for the pump was carried in a tank under the saddle. Bore and stroke of the early RG500 was 56 x 50.5mm, giving a capacity of 497.52cc, but from 1976 (the year Agostini rode an RG), this was changed to 54 x 54mm and 494.69cc. The engine delivered its maximum power of 95.6bhp (up to 100bhp by 1976) at 11,200rpm and would rev to above this figure in the lower gears. Under 9,200rpm, the power dropped off sharply, needing the rider's full use of the 6-speed gearbox (with the square bore and stroke dimensions this was improved). Cooling was by water with a mechanical impeller to ensure a reliable circulation. The early engines were prone to breaking primary drives, seizing cylinders and breaking gearboxes – the last giving the rider a particularly nasty experience.

Besides Sheene's success, Suzuki riders also took the next five positions – Länsivuori, Hennen, Lucchinelli, Newbold and Williams – ensuring a clean sweep of the leaderboard for Suzuki in the 1976 500cc World Championship series. Sheene then won again in 1977, after which Yamaha made a comeback via Kenny Roberts in 1978, 1979 and 1980.

From poor to worse

Actually, it was very much a case of going from poor to worse for Agostini. The Suzuki never finished a Grand Prix in the top 10 – in fact it proved a most unreliable machine for the Marlboro squad. So almost the entire GP season was taken up with machine retirements in the 350cc class on the MV and in the 500cc section on the Suzuki. There is no doubt that with the series of failures – which were frustrating in the extreme – came Giacomo's first serious thoughts of quitting and hanging up his leathers at the end of the season. But towards the end of that year he scored a couple of victories that brought back memories of the great days in earlier years.

The Dutch TT

The Dutch TT at Assen was typical of just how frustrating Ago's rides on

The square four-cylinder layout of the RG500 Suzuki.

the Suzuki were, and shows why he had found it necessary to obtain one of the Japanese square-four two-strokes. During qualifying for the Dutch round, Suzukis filled the top 11 places and had proved so superior that Johnny Cecotto refused to race his works Yamaha four, claiming it was 'too slow', despite the fact that Ago had ridden just such a bike into second place the previous year in Holland, beaten by inches by Barry Sheene in a memorable finish, and of course gone on to win the title.

Both Giacomo and Sheene made poor starts in the 1976 Dutch TT but by lap seven Sheene was leading and Giacomo had moved into second place. Two laps later the Italian had closed the gap separating him from the leader from 10 seconds to 7 seconds. Responding to a pit signal, Sheene then put in the fastest lap of the race. As the race went on Sheene and Ago continued in their respective positions. But there was to be no glory for poor Giacomo; his Suzuki seized on the last lap, the piston disintegrating as the con-rod kept going.

The 15-times world champion had already shown his mettle in the earlier 350cc event, by screaming his four-cylinder MV Agusta into an immediate lead at the beginning of the race. Of course he had done this before – in France and again in Italy. But both times he retired after a few laps with mechanical gremlins. Could he keep his machine ahead of the pursuing pack of Yamahas? He did and after the victory, which also included setting the fastest lap at 94.23mph, Giacomo said: 'It's difficult to ride. The power band is so narrow. It comes in suddenly and then, when you shut off, the engine braking is tremendous. Not like a two-stroke.' Giacomo's win on the 350 MV was the first by a four-stroke in GPs for three years – and was also destined to be the final one before the class was axed at the end of 1982.

A feature of the 1976 Dutch TT and something which was to stick in the memory of every single one of the 130,000 spectators who thronged the circuit was the heat. Worse still, this heat was accompanied by energy-sapping humidity. As the *Motor Cycle* reported in their 3 July 1976 issue: 'Sweat oozed from every pore at the slightest exertion and for riders clad head to foot in leathers and capped by a full face helmet it was the "Hell on wheels" Grand Prix.'

This makes Giacomo's Dutch TT performance even more impressive. Not only was his riding superb, taking the intricate sweeps and curves of the 4.8-mile Assen circuit flat out, with his chin on the petrol tank, but the heat-wave conditions left rivals half his age struggling. For all his film star looks the Italian was a true professional, who took his fitness and performance on race days completely seriously. As proof of this Giacomo had his own gymnasium at his farmhouse home near the town of Bergamo, where he kept himself in peak physical condition, something that helped him win many, many races.

Although he was the heart-throb of countless women, both those with an interest in motorcycle racing and also those with no interest in the sport whatever, Giacomo's usual companion around the race circuits of the world was his girlfriend Lucia Farrello. In a candid moment he once revealed that part of his training regime involved 'no sex within the 3 days before racing!'

After the racing at Assen came another barren spell, where machine troubles ruled out success in Belgium, Finland and Czechoslovakia (Ago didn't ride in Sweden due to poor start money).

A return to winning ways

Right at the end of the season came a return to winning ways. The first success came at the Nürburgring, home of that year's German Grand Prix, the final round of the 500cc World Championships. The date was 29 August 1976 – an important one for both MV Agusta and Giacomo Agostini, because it was to herald the last time either would win a 500cc World Championship race.

Victory at the Nürburgring was in many ways fitting as it had been at this very same venue that Giacomo had first come to the fore in the spring of 1965 (again on an MV). But that day in late summer 1976, over 11 years later, he put on a quite simply brilliant display that deserves to go down in the annals of racing history as a real achievement. It was also to be the last time, until the FIM changed the rules for Grand Prix racing (for the 2002 season), that a four-stroke would win in the blue riband class. For the record here are the top six finishers that day:

1976 German GP - Nürburgring

1st	G. Agostini (MV Agusta)
2nd	M. Lucchinelli (Suzuki)
3rd	P. Hennen (Suzuki)
4th	J. Newbold (Suzuki)
5th	N. Ankoné (Suzuki)
6th	B. Van Dulman (Suzuki)

The other important victory came almost a month later at Mugello in Italy on 26 September 1976. This saw Giacomo, aboard the MV 350 four, put in another superb display to conquer a horde of screeching TZ Yamaha twin-cylinder two-strokes, to give the MV Agusta marque its final victory. Then, except for some demonstration rides (including Brands Hatch in England) that really was that as far as MV Agusta's participation was concerned. The bikes were simply taken off the race circuit and locked away to gather dust at the factory's complex at Casina Costa, Verghera, near the town of Gallarate, a few kilometres from Milan.

At the final round of the 500cc World Championships in 1976, Giacomo Agostini returned to the big MV and scored a famous victory at the Nürburgring. It was also the Italian factory's final Grand Prix win.

Then almost a month later at Mugello in Italy on 26 September 1976, Giacomo, riding the MV 350 four, put in another superb display to conquer a horde of TZ Yamahas, to give MV its final victory.

What might have been

So if MV Agusta had continued to race into 1977, what would have happened? Well, obviously, the engineers knew what a problem the latest crop of two-strokes posed and already had a project on their books which was intended to make the marque more competitive. This was the Boxer Flat Four, as MV (like Honda, with its ill-fated oblong piston technology NR500 project) strove to find a four-stroke formula that would provide the necessary performance.

The Boxer was the work of Ing. Bocchi, formerly with Ferrari (and later with both Laverda and Ducati). Although it was, in many ways, a bold and innovative design, it was destined never to turn a wheel. The main focus of attention was the engine, a liquid-cooled, flat-four four-stroke with double overhead camshafts and four valves per cylinder. This featured cylinders which were placed fore and aft. A six-speed transmission was mounted below the crankshaft and there were straight-cut helical primary drive gears. The quartet of round-slide Dell'Orto carburettors with their integral float chambers were located in pairs almost horizontally above their respective cylinders. There was a complete lack of finning for the heads, cylinder barrels or crankcases. A massive, and again unfinned, oil sump was cast integrally with the crankcases. Ignition was electronic and manufactured by the Varese-based Dansi concern. Bocchi claimed a projected power output of around 110bhp, with maximum engine revolutions of 15,000rpm. If these power figures are correct, then it should have made the MV competitive – but bench horses are not always track horses!

The chassis of the flat four was of the open type, with the engine mounted at three main points. Suspension was taken care of by a pair of hydraulic rear shock absorbers supported by a square section swinging arm; there were 38mm front forks, with 7-spoke magnesium alloy wheels. Although extensively bench-tested and mounted in a chassis the flat four became a victim of MV Agusta's withdrawal from GP racing at the end of the 1976 season.

As for Giacomo Agostini, he found time to take up a big money offer to race a Morbidelli 250 twin at an end of season Italian meeting, which added sparkle to the Italian scene.

He also found time to take up an offer from his old friend Gianfranco Morbidelli to race one of the latter's disc-valve twin-cylinder 250 two-stroke models on home ground.

Johnny Cecotto – America's first champion

Born on 25 January 1956, in Caracas, Venezuela, Johnny Cecotto has the distinction of being America's first World Motorcycle Road Racing Champion. He was also the man who replaced Giacomo Agostini as 350cc world champion in 1975.

Cecotto's first competitive races, on Hondas (including the CB750 four), were

made only after altering his date of birth – he was then only 16 years of age and therefore not old enough to qualify for a racing licence. By the time he joined the European Grand Prix circus in 1975, Johnny Cecotto had become South American champion in both the 350 and 500cc classes, having totalled more than 50 victories in a mere two seasons.

Cecotto's mentor was Andreas Ippolito, the owner of the Venezuelan Yamaha importers Venemotos. In an amazing debut season in Europe, Cecotto simply blasted the opposition to take the 350cc world crown with victories in France, Germany, Italy, and Finland – and in the process became the youngest ever world motorcycling champion up to that time.

But there were problems. No one could doubt his riding skill, but he had little or no engineering knowledge. He thus was unable to provide his team with any feedback (in contrast to Agostini). Some of his mechanics, including Englishman Vince French, were later to comment that

Cecotto on his way to victory in the 1976 Daytona 200 on an OW31 Yamaha; after finishing third in the 1975 American classic.

he was limited to demands for them to change the tyres. They were frustrated because none of them seemed to be able to get across to him the fact that he should be able to assist them in solving other problems, where vital seconds could be lost each lap through lack of feedback to the engineer in the pits.

This failure in communications meant that Cecotto was often forced to ride a less than perfect machine, and he was therefore forced into unnecessary risks in a bid to recoup shortfalls in performance. One can only marvel at his riding skill, which went a long way to compensate for these defects with sheer brilliance. There is no doubt that Cecotto had great talent. But even his great skill could not compensate in the ultra-competitive – and extremely demanding – world of 500cc GP racing to which he transferred for the 1976 season.

However, there was little hint of this in his opening race that year, the Daytona 200, which he won at record speed on an OW31 Yamaha (he had also finished third in 1975, his debut American classic). Cecotto began with what many observers thought was a highly promising runner-up spot behind Barry Sheene in the year's first GP, the French at Le Mans. However, this momentum could not be sustained and mid-season, just before the Dutch TT at Assen, Cecotto's backer Andreas Ippolito withdrew him from the remaining 500 Grand Prix rounds, feeling that his young protégé was putting himself too much at risk, and had crashed his machine far too often.

Even so, Yamaha still had the utmost confidence in the young Venezuelan and he was signed up for the 1977 season for the first time directly from Japan, rather than through their local importer. In this deal he was set to earn $60,000 US dollars – rumoured to be the richest payout up to that time in motorcycle history. The burning question was, could Cecotto knuckle down and become a professional in the Agostini mould? This not only entailed getting back to his winning ways of 1975, but also having the self-control, which meant sidelining the good life, the girls and the fast cars to which he had become accustomed over the previous few months.

Johnny Cecotto's Yamaha 500cc Grand Prix bike and mechanics, circa 1979. He then moved to four wheels at the beginning of the 1980s.

Cecotto had made his European base in Bologna, Italy. He was summoned, together with the other Yamaha works riders, to Japan just prior to Christmas 1976. Their brief was to be fitted out for, and to test, the very latest generation of four-cylinder factory machines, the five-hundred OW20 and seven-fifty OW31 racers.

Much was expected of the South American in the coming season's GP series, but a heavy crash at only the second round of the 1977 500cc title chase at the Salzburgring in Austria effectively sidelined Cecotto for most of the season with injuries that included a badly broken arm. But just to prove his ability and potential Johnny Cecotto made a brilliant comeback to win the 500cc Finnish and Czech GPs at the end of the season, and in the latter event he also won the 350cc race for good measure.

In the final days of 1977 Giacomo Agostini had announced his retirement from the sport, but conversely the coming season was to prove one of the most open ever seen in the 500cc category of the World Championships. Cecotto won the Dutch TT at Assen. Other riders to win that year in the blue riband class of GP racing were: Barry Sheene (2), Wil Hartog (2), Virginio Ferrari (1), Pat Hennen (1) and the new champion, Kenny Roberts (4). But Cecotto did win another world title, that of the 750cc class (the second time it had been held).

After this Cecotto's two-wheel career became something of an anti-climax, as he finished third in the 750cc class in 1979 and fourth in the 350cc category the following year. It was then that the South American made a successful transfer to four wheels, finishing runner-up in the European Formula 2 championships driving a BMW March 822 in 1982, followed by a Formula 1 drive in 1983 and later still saloon car racing in various marques, including BMW. Although he never fulfilled his earlier promise on two wheels, he was one of a select band of former motorcycle racers who have been able to make a truly successful transition to the four-wheel world.

For 1977 Giacomo returned to Yamaha again with backing from Marlboro. He is seen here on the TZR500 four at Misano that year.

Yamaha again

MV Agusta's withdrawal meant that, except for Giacomo's far from satisfactory Suzuki RG500, the Agostini-Marlboro team was bikeless. And so the decision was made to switch back to Yamaha machinery for 1977 – after Giacomo announced he was to continue racing for another year. But this time, as with MV in 1976, it would be funded with sponsors' money, not by Yamaha themselves.

As for machinery, Giacomo went back to bikes he knew, the 500 and 750cc four-cylinder models. What followed could hardly have been called vintage Agostini, but he still did enough to be able to look back with some satisfaction on what was his final season in the sport. In the 500cc GP class Giacomo finished runner-up twice (Le Castellet, France and Brno, Czecho-slovakia), with top 10 finishes at Imola, Italy (fifth); Spa Francorchamps, Belgium (eighth); Anderstorp, Sweden (ninth) and Silverstone, Great Britain (ninth).

But it was on the bigger Yamaha that Giacomo Agostini really excelled in 1977, finishing the season third in the newly instigated 750cc World Champ-ionship. The season got off to a start at Daytona, but without the Marlboro-Yamaha of Giacomo Agostini. The next round was on home soil at Imola, where Ago came home an impressive third to gain a rostrum placing behind American stars Kenny Roberts and Steve Baker.

Giacomo Agostini's 500 GP appear-ances actually worked against the Italian, because he was forced to miss many of the 750cc rounds. The next TZ 750 outing for Ago came at the sixth round of the championship, at the Salzburg-ring in Austria; where he finished

Hockenheim – lap length 4.21 miles.

runner-up behind championship leader Steve Baker. In Holland he was fourth (behind Marco Lucchinelli, Steve Baker and Christian Sarron). Then came rounds across the Atlantic at Lugana Seca, California and Mosport, Canada; both of which were given a miss.

A final victory

The final round of the 750cc series was scheduled for Hockenheim in Germany. And in typical fairytale style Giacomo ended his career at World Championship level by scoring a famous victory. The first six places at Hockenheim were:

750cc German GP – Hockenheim

1st	G. Agostini (Yamaha)
2nd	T. Katayama (Yamaha)
3rd	A. Toracca (Yamaha)
4th	T. Länsivuori (Yamaha)
5th	P. Pons (Yamaha)
6th	V. Palomo (Yamaha)

And so came down the curtain on a truly glittering career, which had seen Giacomo Agostini break virtually every record in motorcycle racing. The statistics of that career are awesome. During his 16 years in the sport he won a record 122 World Championship Grand Prix races – 46 more than his nearest rival, and great friend, Mike Hailwood – and more than double the number of wins scored by any other competitor at that time.

Those 122 victories helped clinch the record number of 15 World

In the 500cc World Championships Barry Sheene was now top man, winning the blue riband crown for Suzuki in both 1976 and 1977.

Barry and his father discuss tactics in 1977.

Championships (eight 500cc and seven 350cc) – six more than joint second placemen Hailwood and Carlo Ubbiali (later Angel Nieto would score 12 – six 50cc; six 125cc).

While he was doing this, Giacomo Agostini still had time to rack up no less than 18 Italian Championship titles and towards the end of his career, to add major 750cc races to his tally, including prestigious events such as the Daytona and Imola 200-mile classics.

Then there were Ago's fantastic Isle of Man TT achievements. During the eight seasons he competed there he won 10 races – equally split between 350 and 500cc classes – and in 1967 he lapped at over 108mph from a standing start on his 500cc MV Agusta triple, to set a new lap record. And among all these statistics were some real highs and lows – but through it all he remained unflustered in a most un-Latin way.

At the age of 35 Giacomo announced his retirement – the official date

Giacomo Agostini not only went out on a winning note with his victory at the final round of the 1977 Formula 750 World Championship at Hockenheim on a TZ750, but also finished the season third overall in the championship. If he hadn't also ridden the 500 Grand Prix bike (shown) he could have done even better.

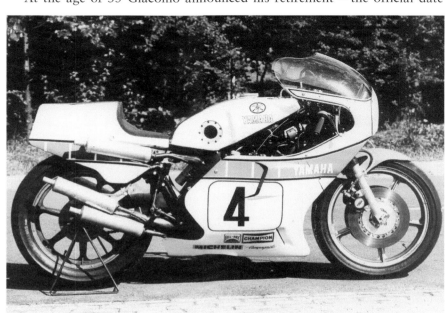

being 22 December 1977. As he had always said he would, he knew the time had come to hang up his leathers. But as is revealed in the following chapter, this was certainly not the end of Giacomo Agostini, in either competitive motorsport or the motorcycle racing world.

Finally, in December 1977, at the age of 35, Giacomo announced his retirement from competitive motorcycle racing. Over the previous 16 years he had broken almost every record there was. This picture, together with Johnny Cecotto (centre) and Phil Read (right) was taken at the F750 Classic at Assen in 1976.

Chapter 9

Team manager

BESIDES his love of motorcycles, from an early age Giacomo Agostini also liked fast cars (even as early as 1966 he owned a Porsche) and he and his three brothers had motor boats and participated in both water and snow skiing near their lakeside home at the foot of the Alps.

Car racing

Like many former motorcycle racing heroes, it was the world of car racing which was something Giacomo felt he needed to try after achieving the ultimate on two wheels. Very few, however, except the legendary John Surtees, have made the switch from two to four wheels a complete success in modern times. And so it was with the man who broke every record in the bike world, Giacomo Agostini. Certainly during the late 1960s and early 1970s he received many offers to drive cars; notably there was interest from Ferrari. However, it wasn't until 1978, after he had quit motorcycles, that he actually took up the challenge. By then he was approaching 36 years of age. And one must remember that Surtees made the switch much earlier, when he was only 26. Agostini's first racing experience came in Formula 2, in the Trivellato team. Then in 1979 he moved to the Formula Aurora, but Giacomo found the going tough. The route he had taken was seen as the best way in Formula 1 – and Giacomo had again set up his own stable in partnership with the Marlboro company.

In 1980 Giacomo continued with Formula Aurora, but to go fast in cars needed time. Ago discovered that not only did people expect miracles because of who he was, but also finding the correct racing line and being careful to avoid putting a wheel in the grass, as he had always done with bikes, did not work on four wheels – where cars regularly 'cut corners'. Ultimately, he says, he 'wasn't given the time to learn'. For the first time he found racing 'became work rather than pleasure'. So at the end of 1980 he finally retired from all forms of competitive racing in motorsport after 20 years.

1981 was a sabbatical year; one in which Ago attended to his business affairs and made plans for his future working life. This was when he hit

Giacomo Agostini has always been a keen sportsman - not just motorcycles - but also both water and snow skiing, and shooting. He is seen here with his friend Gianfranco Morbidelli (far left); circa late 1970s.

on the idea of entering team management – but with two wheels, not four. As others had found before, Giacomo discovered that the car world is a totally different place to the motorcycle one: a less friendly, more serious environment. Through his many years of racing motorcycles he had made so many contacts and friends in the two-wheel world that when it came to it a choice between motorcycles and cars it was easy. Bikes it was.

Team Marlboro

Once again Agostini's friends at the Lausanne offices of the Philip Morris/Marlboro tobacco brand were involved. And so Team Marlboro, managed by Giacomo Agostini from offices in Via Quintino Alto 34, 24100 Bergamo, came into existence. 1982 was the team's first year and two riders, both with works Yamahas, were signed: New Zealander Graeme Crosby (known to his many fans simply as 'Croz') and Graziano Rossi (father of today's Moto GP star Valentino).

In a strange quirk of fate Crosby was to give the newly formed équipe its first victory, and it came in the very first race Croz participated in for the Team Marlboro Agostini Yamaha set-up – no less an event than the Daytona 200. It was just as Giacomo himself had experienced during his first ride for Yamaha eight years before.

In a record-breaking ride, in which he set a new average speed of 109.10mph, Croz won in a time of 1 hour, 50 minutes, 45.68 seconds. The first six places were:

Ago's first success as a team manager came in 1982 when his Team Agostini Marlboro rider Graeme Crosby won the Daytona 200 on a Yamaha 750.

Daytona 200 Miler

1st	G. Crosby	(Yamaha)
2nd	F. Spencer	(Honda)
3rd	R. Pietri	(Honda)
4th	M. Baldwin	(Honda)
5th	D. Singleton	(Yamaha)
6th	S. Gervais	(Yamaha)

What better start could one have wished for, at the beginning of a new career?

On the Grand Prix trail

Both Crosby and Rossi already had Grand Prix experience at 500cc level; their respective positions being Crosby (Suzuki) fifth in 1981, and Rossi

1983 marked the arrival of Kenny Roberts (shown here) and Eddie Lawson in the Marlboro team.

(Suzuki) fifth in 1980. Rossi had also been third in the 1979 250cc championship riding a Morbidelli. There were 12 rounds in the 1982 500cc championship. And although Crosby didn't win a GP, he nonetheless put in a reliable performance throughout the year – and as the season went on he improved. With riders of the calibre of Kenny Roberts, Barry Sheene, Freddie Spencer, Marco Lucchinelli, Takazumi Katayama, Kork Ballington, Loris Reggiani, Franco Uncini, Randy Mamola, Raymond Roche and Virginio Ferrari on the scene it was certainly a competitive year.

Crosby scored points in 8 of the 12 rounds to finish the year runner-up in the championship behind Suzuki rider Franco Uncini. Actually he got on the rostrum no less than five times: third at Misano (Italy); second at Rijeka (Yugoslavia); third at Silverstone (Great Britain); third at Anderstorp (Sweden) and third at Mugello (San Marino).

Up a gear

1983 brought Kel Carruthers, Kenny Roberts and Eddie Lawson to the Marlboro team. Ago was in charge, while Kel looked after the technical preparation of the machines. There is no doubt this was a really strong squad. However, the ultimate prize, the 500cc championship, eluded them; this was the year that Freddie Spencer won the title on the new three-cylinder Honda.

Roberts finished the 1983 season a mere two points adrift of Spencer – 142 compared to the Honda man's 144. He then announced his retirement as a competitive rider – going on to form his own Marlboro-backed Team

Roberts (but still with Yamaha machinery). New boy Lawson was fourth on another of Yamaha's disc-valve V-four two-strokes.

Lawson becomes number one

With Roberts now retired (except for a one-off winning ride at Daytona where he beat Spencer in the 200-miler), Eddie Lawson had been promoted by Giacomo Agostini to number one rider in the Agostini Marlboro Yamaha

Eddie Lawson celebrates his 1986 World Championship title. Giacomo Agostini was his team manager for the majority of his career, first with Yamaha and later with the Italian Cagiva marque.

'Steady' Eddie Lawson

'Steady' Eddie Lawson was born in Los Angeles, California, on 3 November 1958 and was, like Kenny Roberts Senior, an American graduate of the dirt-track-dominated AMA (American Motorcycle Association) National Championship series. Eddie began competitive motorcycling at an early age, but first sprung to the public's attention after winning on a Yamaha two-fifty in 1979.

Then came a spell as a works rider for the American Kawasaki team, riding in the US Superbike Championship in 1981 and 1982. Kawasaki saw fit to commemorate this achievement with the limited edition Eddie Lawson Z1100R Replica street bike. At this time in his career he got to ride a four-cylinder five-hundred Grand Prix bike in the shape of the Kawasaki KR500 square four disc-valve two-stroke.

With Kawasaki pulling the plug on its Grand Prix effort, Eddie Lawson was drafted into the Team Marlboro Yamaha squad managed by Giacomo Agostini. Following Kenny Roberts was probably the hardest act in racing, but Lawson's great drive and natural talent – combined with the experience of Agostini – saw him pass this demanding test with flying colours. Actually, Lawson and Agostini were an excellent pairing. Both were meticulous in their preparation. It was not just the machinery (which in any case was entrusted to others) but their personal behaviour, their professional mannerisms, how they dealt with the media and a whole host of other areas where the two men complimented each other's abilities.

Lawson's record stands for itself, and he won the all-important 500cc (the 350cc class had been axed at the end of 1982) in 1984, 1986 and 1988. His fourth title came in 1989 after he had left Agostini and Yamaha to join the Rothman Honda squad – making Eddie the only rider to win the 500cc crown in consecutive seasons on different makes of motorcycles; something even his mentor had been unable to achieve.

At the end of 1990 he signed for the Italian Cagiva team for one of the biggest fees ever seen in motorcycle sport at that time. And it was at Cagiva where he was reunited with Giacomo Agostini, who had become team manager at the Varese factory. Agostini was largely responsible for brokering the deal that brought Lawson to the team.

Lawson's victory for the Italian marque (after a decade of trying) at the Hungarian Grand Prix in 1991 was a considerable achievement. Cagiva supremo Claudio Castiglioni was so overjoyed that he promptly presented Lawson with a brand new Ferrari Testarossa!

Eddie Lawson, having put Cagiva on the Grand Prix map, hung up his racing leathers at the end of 1992, to pursue a new career on four wheels, driving American Indy Lights cars.

squad for the 1984 season.

After winning the title in 1983, Spencer began as favourite, with other contenders including Randy Mamola and Frenchman Raymond Roche. Lawson (and his new teammate Virginio Ferrari) were equipped with Yamaha's brand new reed-valve OW76 engine mounted in an Antonio Cobas inspired twin-spar aluminium frame. Lawson set the early pace, winning three of the first quartet of rounds counting towards the 500cc World Championship (South Africa, Spain and Austria); the remaining one (at Misano in Italy) went to Spencer (riding a V4 Honda NSR 500 instead of the previous year's triple). Lawson went on to win the title by gaining 142 points, compared to runner-up Randy Mamola's 111. However, Lawson's teammate Ferrari scored a mere 22 points and finished ninth in the champi-

onship table.

In 1985 Eddie Lawson lost the title to Spencer (who, riding Honda machines, became the first man in history to win both the 500cc and 250cc championships in a single season). In 1986 Lawson recaptured the 500cc title. His teammate, British rider Bob McElnea, finished in fifth place. That same year saw a 250cc team added, and the two riders, German Martin Wimmer and Japanese Tadahiko Taira, finished sixth and ninth respectively in the championship standings.

In 1987 Eddie Lawson finished third in the 500cc class, with McElnea tenth. In the 250cc class Luca Cadalora, who had joined the team, finished seventh, with Wimmer eighth.

Then came 1988 and 1989, when 'Steady Eddie' won two more 500cc

The 1983 Team Agostini Marlboro duo of Eddie Lawson (4) and Kenny Roberts (2).

After Roberts retired the Belgian Didier de Radigues became a member of the team.

It was Eddie Lawson who really shone; winning his first 500cc World Championship for the Marlboro Agostini squad in 1984.

The 1988 Marlboro Yamaha Team Agostini squad. Left to right: Tadahiko Taira (250); Martin Wimmer (250); Giacomo Agostini; Eddie Lawson (500) and Rob McElnea (500).

titles – but the 1989 one was aboard a Honda. Giacomo Agostini had signed former Honda champion Freddie Spencer as a replacement – but it was a bad choice, with Spencer making little impression. But in 1990 John Kocinski gave Yamaha and Agostini the 250cc title.

A switch to Cagiva

Then came a surprise, a switch by both Agostini and Lawson to the Italian Cagiva marque as team manager and number one rider respectively.

By the time Lawson and Agostini joined Cagiva, the Varese company had spent almost a decade trying to get on terms with the Japanese. In fact, had the two former Yamaha men not agreed to join them, Cagiva's owners, the Castiglioni brothers, would have quit. But the basis of a good bike already existed and the motorcycle, the first 500 GP model to sport a carbon-fibre

chassis, which had been developed in conjunction with Ferrari, was now just waiting for a top-line rider.

That rider was four-times 500cc world champion Lawson, and his mentor 15-times world champion Giacomo Agostini. After a comprehensive test, Lawson signed to race the red Italian machine for two years (1991 and 1992), with the up-and-coming Alex Barros as his understudy. At last Cagiva had the combination it needed to succeed in the blue riband class of motor-cycle racing.

Together with Agostini, Lawson soon put Cagiva in the position the Castiglionis had always dreamed of, qualifying on the front row of a 500 Grand Prix, leading a race and earning a rostrum placing for the factory for the first time in the dry.

Coded V591, the 1991 Cagiva was putting out a claimed 169bhp at 12,000rpm and with further development over the following winter looked to at last have

Eddie Lawson celebrating yet another victory on the rostrum in the traditional manner.

the Japanese works bikes in its sights. In 1992, the marque's hopes were finally to be fulfilled. And after waiting for a new engine, which arrived in time for the Dutch TT in late June, Lawson immediately achieved another Cagiva first, by setting pole in qualifying. This performance was no flash in the pan, as at the very next Grand Prix in Hungary the new V592 Cagiva was not only fastest in practice, but also went on to gain that long-awaited GP race victory.

By now Cagiva were actually forging ahead of their Japanese rivals in many areas (helped no doubt by input from both Lawson and Agostini), and the 80-degree V592 *Bombardone* (Big Bang) machine had, for example, the first electronic speed-shifter to be found on a 500cc GP bike. There were also experiments with semi-active suspension in collaboration with Showa; various engine firing angles to suit individual circuits and work on a form of traction control. Finally a state-of-the-art electronic fuel injection system was developed jointly with TAG-McLaren.

After Lawson retired at the end of 1992, Giacomo Agostini stayed with Cagiva and was instrumental in signing both Lawson's replacement for 1993, Doug Chandler, and, finally, John Kocinski, after Chandler was injured. As previously mentioned, Kocinski had already won the 250cc title on a Marlboro Yamaha in 1990, before Agostini quit and joined Cagiva.

After two fourth places in his first two rides for Cagiva, Kocinski took victory at the third GP – the United States round at Luguna Seca – and

Cagiva

Cagiva was established in 1978 and grew rapidly in the first decade of its existence to become a major force in the European motorcycle industry, although not without problems. At various times the company owned Husqvarna, Moto Morini, CZ, and Ducati: it was responsible for the rebirth of the legendary MV Agusta marque.

It all began when the Castiglioni family purchased the old lakeside Varese factory, the former home of Aermacchi and later the Italian arm of the American Harley-Davidson company. Cagiva is an amalgam of CA from Castiglioni, GI from Giovanni, the father of the brothers Claudio and Gianfranco who controlled the organisation, and VA from Varese.

When asked why the family had acquired the plant, Gianfranco Castiglioni gave this simple reply: 'Because we love motorcycles of course!' And certainly no one could have accused the Castiglionis of a lack of interest in bikes, because the Cagiva name had already been seen on the heavily modified RG500 Suzuki square-four that future World Champion Marco Lucchinelli rode for the brothers before they became motorcycle manufacturers in their own right. In fact racing was to soak up a vast amount of cash as Cagiva struggled in the blue riband class of GP racing from its entry in 1980 until its ultimate exit at the end of 1994. In 1981 came the first Cagiva-made engine, which was housed in a Dutch Nico Bakker chassis; in 1983 Cagiva followed Suzuki's example and built a square-four engine (previously the motor had been an across-the-frame four); in 1985 the C10/V was the Italians' first V4 500, a configuration which the company kept to the very end; in 1988 the signing of American superstar Randy Mamola was intended to take Cagiva to the top, but a tyre deal with Pirelli restricted progress and after following the Japanese for almost a decade, Cagiva took the initiative and introduced the first 500 with a carbon-fibre chassis and in 1992 in the hands of Eddie Lawson (and now under the management of Giacomo Agostini) the new V592 was the first GP-winning Cagiva and marked the Varese factory's arrival as a major force in the 500 Grand Prix class. But ultimately, for all their billions of lira spent, and the partnership of Lawson and Agostini, Cagiva didn't win a world championship in GP racing.

However, Cagiva did have the satisfaction of winning the world 125cc motocross title on more than one occasion. And in fact it was dirt bikes that received the first attention of the company's engineers right from the off in the autumn of 1978, with the authorisation of a brand new 124.6cc (56 x 50.6mm) reed-valve two-stroke single with liquid-cooling, 6-speeds and magnesium engine covers.

The bread-and-butter Cagiva street bike range for the company's first two years of trading centred around updated versions of the bikes previously marketed as Harley-Davidsons. All were two-stroke singles, including air-cooled 250cc motocross and enduro mounts. During these early years, there is no doubt that Cagiva took full advantage of the former stock of spares and motorcycles inherited in the Harley-Davidson buyout. And one of these, the SST 125, became the top-selling bike on the Italian market in the all-important 125cc sector between 1979 and 1982.

But Cagiva didn't simply sit still. Unlike much of the Italian industry during the early 1980s, which seemed locked in a time warp, the Varese factory brought out a succession of new models from the end of 1981 onwards, both two and four-stroke. To illustrate the marque's early progress is to reveal that Cagiva built 6,000 bikes in 1979 (its first full year of trading), 13,000 in 1980 and

Virginio Ferrari with Cagiva's own Grand Prix 500 in 1981. The Castiglioni brothers, who owned Cagiva, spent a king's ransom attempting to beat the Japanese in the blue riband class of motorcycle racing. Eventually, on the brink of winning the world title they quit in the mid-1990s.

by 1982 production had tripled to 40,000. This was also evident in the work-force: 130 in 1978 increased to 300, 50 of whom were working on research and development, by the beginning of 1982. In 1981 the first foreign factory opened in Venezuela, which began producing Cagiva machines for the South American market from kits built in Varese.

At the Milan Show in November 1981 the company displayed its first four-stroke (an ohc single displacing 350cc), but the Castiglionis had even grander plans. They dreamed of a product line stretching from the smallest scooter to the most powerful superbike. To achieve this relatively quickly – particularly the larger capacity, multi-cylinder models – they reasoned it would be best to form a partnership with another manufacturer. But who? Eventually, at a press conference held in June 1983, it was announced that the famous Ducati company and Cagiva had reached an agreement whereby Ducati would supply Cagiva with engines for a period of seven years. In fact, the state-owned Ducati firm was acquired lock, stock and barrel less than two years later!

The next target was North America, but here Cagiva, and even Ducati, had problems. This was solved by buying out the Swedish Husqvarna marque, with production being transferred to Italy. With Husqvarna's dealer network in the States, Cagiva had a ready-made set-up.

The following year, 1987, Cagiva purchased yet another marque to add to their growing portfolio: Moto Morini, and as the 1990s dawned Cagiva acquired the famous Czech brand CZ.

Although by now Ducati had been rebuilt into a major success story, huge losses were being recorded within the rest of the Cagiva group. By the mid-1990s Cagiva were in dire straights. This led to Moto Morini production being discontinued, followed later by the closing of the CZ works. In 1997 51 percent of Ducati was sold to an American investment corporation; followed by the remaining 49 percent in 1999.

The sale of Ducati allowed Cagiva's long-running four-cylinder superbike, the MV Agusta F4, to finally enter production in 1998. This latter project was closely linked with Giacomo Agostini himself – the great man doing a consid-erable amount of test riding and publicity for the newly formed MV marque.

The young Italian Luca
Cadalora rode for Agostini
in the 250cc class during
1988 – a star in the
making.

almost repeated this success in the final round of the 1993 series at Jarama, Spain, until another rider took him out while being lapped.

The 1994 season began with an all-new composite chassis combining carbon spars with an aluminium steering head and swinging arm – this providing an exceptionally taut and light assembly. In addition the engine was further developed so that the V594 was fast enough to give Kocinski victory at the first round of that year's championship series in Australia.

However, from then on things didn't go so well, and Cagiva had serious financial problems to deal with, so at the end of the season the team announced its withdrawal from the sport. Factory boss Claudio Castiglioni said 'We are tired of racing GPs.'

The superbike project

Another reason for Cagiva's withdrawal was its superbike project, which in the shape of the stunning MV Agusta F4 was to make its public debut in 1998, going on sale the following spring. Giacomo Agostini has played a key role in the evolution of this superb bike, being an advisor, tester and ultimately publicity man for the project.

The MV Agusta F4 has seen the rebirth of one of the most famous and certainly glamorous names in motorcycling. But it could just as well have been marketed as a Cagiva, a Ducati or even a Ferrari. The fact that it is an MV represents a fitting end to one of the strangest projects that the industry has ever witnessed. The F4 project really began as the result of dinner-time discussions between two men – Claudio Castiglioni and Massimo Tamburini – with the added intervention of Piero Ferrari, son of the legendary Enzo, and Ferrari's owners, Fiat.

The rumours begin

The first rumours of a brand new Cagiva-masterminded superbike came at the beginning of 1991. Photographs of a new engine, an across-the-frame four, were released – by mistake – at a Ferrari press conference in 1993. The Cagiva company had kept the engine behind closed doors, even keeping it out of sight when a fully finished prototype was pictured on the road in Italy. However, when Ferrari featured a colour photograph of the power unit at the launch of its new 465 GT car, Cagiva boss Claudio Castiglioni and Piero Ferrari were forced into admitting that they had test-ridden a motorcycle with this engine.

Castiglioni said at the 1993 press conference that producing target power was 'no problem'. The photograph revealed that the straight four, topped by a bank of fuel injectors, was similar to half a Ferrari V8. It featured several

interesting innovations, including a radial valve cylinder head and a cassette-type six-speed gearbox. There is no doubt that Cagiva's much-publicised financial woes of the mid-1990s held up development of the F4 project, just as with production of the new Ducati 916 V-twin. However, the subsequent monies raised from the sale of Ducati resolved both issues.

When the liquid-cooled 749.4cc (73.8 x 43.8mm) beauty finally went on sale, everyone agreed the long wait had been worthwhile. And this is what Giacomo Agostini himself said of the rebirth of the magical name at its launch in 1998:

MV Agusta is part of my life. It represents for me a real symbol of many joys, hopes and great triumphs. I have to share my victories with this mythical make: as a matter of fact, thirteen of my fifteen World Championship titles were won with the MV Agusta motorcycle. During the years, MV Agusta has become popular all over the world among sportsmen and sporting enthusiasts and has been able to incite admiration and great passion in conjunction with its name. A real enthusiasm and an immeasurable competitive passion sustained the activity of the Agusta family, through a personal involvement. The same interest and passion explains Cagiva's choice of giving new life to the mythical MV, the trademark which has influenced most of world motorcycling history. The MV Agusta F4, besides a name famous and known worldwide, can boast advanced technological research and high-

McElnea leading his Agostini teammate Tadahiko Taira in the 1987 Dutch TT at Assen.

The 1988 works Yamaha YZR500 GP machine as used by the Marlboro-backed Agostini team.

quality mechanical innovations. I will be really moved and proud seeing again on the race tracks and roads the Italian motorcycle with its characteristic logo: the one of the inimitable MV Agusta.

And for a more personal view of things, after testing the new F4 at the Agusta Aerospace company test strip at Vergiate, the then 56-year-old had this to say in May 1998:

I'm glad to dispel once and for all those who said this bike would remain an unfulfilled dream. The MV F4 is now working and it is a very beautiful bike. The engine has such pull in the lower gears and great flexibility. At first I thought that the ratios were a bit short but now I think they are fine. The revs rise progressively and the limiter comes in at 13,000rpm. When the limiter does come in it's quite gentle without the feeling of the engine suddenly pulling back, as happens with other bikes. Frankly I didn't expect to find this 750 at such an advanced stage in its development. I believe the F4 will set a new standard for sports bikes. No other bike has such a mix of styling, technology and tradition.

I found the above comments to be true when I became the first person to test one of the new F4s in the UK during spring 1999, for British importers Three Cross. Because of my close contacts with Cagiva (as their first British importer) I have been fortunate to follow closely the devel-

1989 Marlboro Yamaha Team Agostini 500cc rider Niall Mackenzie and his girlfriend Jane.

In 1989 Giacomo Agostini made his only really major mistake as a team manager when he signed the former 250 and 500cc World Champion Freddie Spencer. Sadly the American was unable to recapture the form of earlier years and had a disappointing year before announcing his retirement from the sport.

The 1990 Marlboro Yamaha Team Agostini 250cc pairing of Alex Criville (left) and Luca Cadalora.

Cagiva tried for over a decade to win a 500cc Grand Prix (a 1988 model is shown), before Eddie Lawson and Giacomo Agostini arrived to resolve the problem in 1991.

In 1993 John Kocinski replaced Lawson (and the injured Doug Chandler) to give the Agostini-managed Cagiva team more success.

opment of this, the most glamorous of all modern motorcycles. And, to my mind, having Giacomo Agostini involved was a fitting tribute to both man and machine. But perhaps, for me, the crowning moment came at Mallory Park in June 1999, when both Ago and his old rival Phil Read did a number of demonstration laps aboard a pair of F4s at the Post TT Bike Fest race meeting. Somehow this finally brought to an end the disagreements these two great riders had traded a quarter of a century earlier.

Retaining an interest

At the time of writing (summer 2003), besides his various business interests, Giacomo Agostini spends a considerable amount of time during the summer months of each year attending historic motorcycle functions all over the world. This includes riding motorcycles – MV Agustas in particular – thus allowing both his original fans, and the many new ones who were too young to see him in action first time round, to appreciate his skill. There is little doubt that not only are his riding skills still there, but his genuine love of two wheels also remains as strong as ever.

Long may this continue.

Chapter 10

A place in history

ONLY a few individuals in any sport can truly be labelled 'super-stars'. One such man is Giacomo Agostini. In motorcycle racing he is truly the 'Champion of Champions'.

His record speaks for itself. Most records are there to be bettered. But in Giacomo Agostini's case it is unlikely that his figures of 15 World Championships, 122 Grand Prix victories and 14 Italian titles will ever be improved upon.

John Surtees (right) and Giacomo Agostini with a pair of MV Agusta Grand Prix racers. This photograph was taken in 1981.

Giacomo regularly has outings on the bikes he rode during his career. This photograph dates from the 1980s.

The facts are proof of Giacomo Agostini's greatness. Some so-called experts have said he was lucky, some that he had little opposition, and others that he simply had the best bikes. But if one really studies his career, he still consistently beat the best there was. And when there was no one to give him a serious race he set out to break race and lap records – as John Surtees had done in an earlier era.

Giacomo Agostini – Mino to his friends and Ago to his countless fans –

With its fairing signed 'Milan '91 G. Agostini' this three-cylinder works MV dates from around 1970 and was on display at the International Milan Motorcycle Show in November 1991.

The fabulous MV Agusta F4 Superbike with which Giacomo Agostini was closely associated, at the National Exhibition Centre, Birmingham, November 1998.

began his competitive career in the summer of 1961, aged 19. Not in road racing, but in hill climbs. Then in 1962 he switched to road racing, before being spotted and signed up by Alfonso Morini. And it was with the Bologna marque that Giacomo Agostini first made his mark – winning the Italian Junior hill climb and road racing championship titles. Amazingly, little more than a few months after beginning road racing, the youthful Agostini found himself taking part in the Italian Grand Prix at Monza in September 1963. And what an international debut it was, as he led the best riders in the world for three laps before being slowed by vibration and a broken footrest. But already he had shown that here, truly, was a future star.

At the end of 1963 Giacomo was signed as Morini's number one rider, replacing the legendary Tarquinio Provini, who had quit to race the four-cylinder Benelli. The following year, 1964, Giacomo Agostini won the Italian Senior championship title, beating Provini. He also rode in the West German and Italian GPs, finishing fourth in both.

Then, hungry to take part at Grand Prix level in 1965, he let his ambitions be known. This resulted in an offer from Count Domenico Agusta to ride 350 and 500cc MVs; his teammate no less a man than the great Mike Hailwood. And Giacomo has always been at considerable pains to say how much he admired – and learned from – this legendary star.

Although Giacomo Agostini raced the old heavyweight fours, his

The author became the first man in Britain to test the new MV in spring 1999.

favoured mount was the *Tre Cilindri* and it was the young Italian who rode this machine to a fantastic debut victory at no lesser circuit than the Nürburgring in its first outing during May 1965, in the process beating world champion Jim Redman. Then at the final round, in Japan, with the world title within his grasp, a broken contact breaker spring saw the championship snatched away from him.

When Hailwood quit MV to join Honda for 1966, Giacomo was left alone to defend the MV colours. This was to signal a fabulous period in racing history with the now legendary duels between Mike and Giacomo mounted on Honda and MV respectively. Probably the greatest of these battles was the 1967 Senior TT, which Giacomo Agostini ultimately lost after some two hours of intense action, when his chain snapped on the final lap while he was in the lead.

After Honda departed the GP scene at the end of 1967 there came what are now referred to as the 'easy years' (*MV Agusta*, Mario Columbo and Roberto Patrignani). However, the job of winning races still had to be achieved. In addition many race and lap records were broken and individual battles took place – for example the formidable combination of Renzo Pasolini and the 350 and 500cc Benelli fours was a difficult one to overcome, at least in Italy.

Giacomo Agostini, pictured at Goodwood in summer 1998, together with his much-loved MV Grand Prix 500 machine.

There were a plethora of other achievements including equalling Mike Hailwood's record (achieved in 1966) of 19 GP victories in a single season during 1970. Riding the then fastest road race in the world during the 500cc Belgian GP (12 laps – 107 miles) at an average speed of 128.506mph, on 1 July 1973, was yet another achievement. Ago also became the only man to be double world champion in five consecutive years (350 and 500cc): 1968, 1969, 1970, 1971, and 1972.

In 1970 Giacomo Agostini became the first rider in Isle of Man TT history to win the Junior and Senior races three years in succession. Then, in October 1972, by winning his 13th Italian Senior Championship title, he beat the previous record of 12 titles held by Tarquinio Provini.

After 1971 things became much more difficult with challenges from the likes of Jarno Saarinen and Renzo Pasolini on Yamaha and Aermacchi two-strokes respectively, as well as from within the MV camp with the arrival of Phil Read. 1973 was a year which promised fans true competition, of the like not witnessed since the Hailwood-Agostini battles of 1966–7, with Jarno Saarinen and the new four-cylinder Yamaha 500 in GPs blue riband class. However, the tragic crash at Monza in May 1973 in which both Jarno and Renzo Pasolini lost their lives left the field once more open to MV. But without team orders Read and Agostini fought a bitter battle both on and off the track.

Quite simply these two great riders could not exist together in the same team. And in a move which stunned the racing world, Ago eventually signed for Yamaha. Read openly voiced doubts about whether the Italian would be able to make the transition from four-strokes to two-strokes. However, in typical fashion Giacomo Agostini achieved what everyone had thought impossible by winning his first race on a Yamaha – in no less an event than the American Daytona 200!

At MV Giacomo had gained a record breaking 13 championship titles. With Yamaha he proceeded to add another two, taking the 350cc in 1974 and the 500cc the following year. But at the beginning of 1976 he again surprised racegoers by returning to MV (Read having departed) and scoring the Italian marque's final victories in world championship 350cc and 500cc competition, at Assen (Dutch TT) and the Nürburgring (German GP).

In Giacomo Agostini's final year of racing, 1977, he still managed to finish third overall in the newly formed 750cc World Championship on a Yamaha TZ four and in the process went out in winning style with a great victory in the last round of the series at Hockenheim, Germany.

In later years Giacomo was to display a new talent when he became team manager for first the Marlboro Yamaha squad and later Cagiva; guiding riders such as Eddie Lawson, Luca Cadalora, John Kocinski, Alex Barros and Alex Criville. Later still he played a major role in the development and publicity of the fabulous MV Agusta F4 superbike project.

With his natural riding abilities, cool professional approach to both racing and management and, above all, the determination to succeed, Giacomo Agostini has not only been a great champion, but also a great ambassador for the sport.

I would like to finish by including the following quotation from my old friend and fellow author Mick Woollett's 1990 book *The Grand Prix Riders*: 'always helpful and speaking better and better English as the years go by, Giacomo will be remembered as a gentleman on and off the track.'

Gentleman is a word which really sums up Giacomo Agostini perfectly: motorcycling's Champion of Champions.

Appendices

Giacomo Agostini Motorcycle Grand Prix Results

1963

Position	Class	Machine	Circuit	Event
Retired	250cc	Moto Morini	Monza	Italian GP

1964

Position	Class	Machine	Circuit	Event
4	250cc	Moto Morini	Solitude	West German GP
4	250cc	Moto Morini	Monza	Italian GP

1965

Position	Class	Machine	Circuit	Event
1	350cc	MV Agusta	Nürburgring	West German GP *
2	500cc	MV Agusta	Nürburgring	West German GP
3	350cc	MV Agusta	Isle of Man	Junior TT
Retired	500cc	MV Agusta	Isle of Man	Senior TT
3	350cc	MV Agusta	Assen	Dutch TT
2	500cc	MV Agusta	Assen	Dutch TT
2	500cc	MV Agusta	Spa Francorchamps	Belgian GP
Retired	350cc	MV Agusta	Sachsenring	East German GP
2	500cc	MV Agusta	Sachsenring	East German GP
Retired	350cc	MV Agusta	Brno	Czech GP
2	500cc	MV Agusta	Brno	Czech GP
1	350cc	MV Agusta	Imatra	Finnish GP
1	500cc	MV Agusta	Imatra	Finnish GP
1	350cc	MV Agusta	Monza	Italian GP
2	500cc	MV Agusta	Monza	Italian GP
5	350cc	MV Agusta	Suzuka	Japanese GP

* First GP victory.
350cc - Runner-up
500cc - Runner-up

1966

Position	Class	Machine	Circuit	Event
Retired	350cc	MV Agusta	Hockenheim	West German GP
2	500cc	MV Agusta	Hockenheim	West German GP
2	350cc	MV Agusta	Clermont-Ferrand	French GP
2	350cc	MV Agusta	Assen	Dutch TT
2	500cc	MV Agusta	Assen	Dutch TT
1	500cc	MV Agusta	Spa Francorchamps	Belgian GP
1	350cc	MV Agusta	Sachsenring	East German GP
Retired	500cc	MV Agusta	Sachsenring	East German GP
2	350cc	MV Agusta	Brno	Czech GP
2	500cc	MV Agusta	Brno	Czech GP
Retired	350cc	MV Agusta	Imatra	Finnish GP
1	500cc	MV Agusta	Imatra	Finnish GP

2	350cc	MV Agusta	Dundrod	Ulster GP
2	500cc	MV Agusta	Dundrod	Ulster GP
1	350cc	MV Agusta	Isle of Man	Junior TT *
2	500cc	MV Agusta	Isle of Man	Senior TT
1	350cc	MV Agusta	Monza	Italian GP
1	500cc	MV Agusta	Monza	Italian GP

* First TT victory
350cc - Runner-up
500cc - World Champion

1967

Position	Class	Machine	Circuit	Event
2	350cc	MV Agusta	Hockenheim	West German GP
1	500cc	MV Agusta	Hockenheim	West German GP
2	350cc	MV Agusta	Isle of Man	Junior TT
Retired	500cc	MV Agusta	Isle of Man	Senior TT
2	350cc	MV Agusta	Assen	Dutch TT
2	500cc	MV Agusta	Assen	Dutch TT
1	500cc	MV Agusta	Spa Francorchamps	Belgian GP
2	350cc	MV Agusta	Sachsenring	East German GP
1	500cc	MV Agusta	Sachsenring	East German GP
7	350cc	MV Agusta	Brno	Czech GP
2	500cc	MV Agusta	Brno	Czech GP
1	500cc	MV Agusta	Imatra	Finnish GP
1	350cc	MV Agusta	Dundrod	Ulster GP
20	500cc	MV Agusta	Dundrod	Ulster GP
Retired	350cc	MV Agusta	Monza	Italian GP
1	500cc	MV Agusta	Monza	Italian GP
2	500cc	MV Agusta	Mosport	Canadian GP

350cc - Runner-up
500cc - World Champion

1968

Position	Class	Machine	Circuit	Event
1	350cc	MV Agusta	Nürburgring	West German GP
1	500cc	MV Agusta	Nürburgring	West German GP
1	500cc	MV Agusta	Barcelona	Spanish GP
1	350cc	MV Agusta	Isle of Man	Junior TT
1	500cc	MV Agusta	Isle of Man	Senior TT
1	350cc	MV Agusta	Assen	Dutch TT
1	500cc	MV Agusta	Assen	Dutch TT
1	500cc	MV Agusta	Spa Francorchamps	Belgian GP
1	350cc	MV Agusta	Sachsenring	East German GP
1	500cc	MV Agusta	Sachsenring	East German GP
1	350cc	MV Agusta	Brno	Czech GP
1	500cc	MV Agusta	Brno	Czech GP
1	500cc	MV Agusta	Imatra	Finnish GP
1	350cc	MV Agusta	Dundrod	Ulster GP
1	500cc	MV Agusta	Dundrod	Ulster GP
1	350cc	MV Agusta	Monza	Italian GP
1	500cc	MV Agusta	Monza	Italian GP

350cc - World Champion
500cc - World Champion

1969

Position	Class	Machine	Circuit	Event
1	350cc	MV Agusta	Jarama	Spanish GP
1	500cc	MV Agusta	Jarama	Spanish GP
1	350cc	MV Agusta	Hockenheim	West German GP
1	500cc	MV Agusta	Hockenheim	West German GP
1	500cc	MV Agusta	Le Mans	French GP
1	350cc	MV Agusta	Isle of Man	Junior TT
1	500cc	MV Agusta	Isle of Man	Senior TT
1	350cc	MV Agusta	Assen	Dutch TT
1	500cc	MV Agusta	Assen	Dutch TT
1	500cc	MV Agusta	Spa Francorchamps	Belgian GP
1	350cc	MV Agusta	Sachsenring	East German GP
1	500cc	MV Agusta	Sachsenring	East German GP
1	350cc	MV Agusta	Brno	Czech GP
1	500cc	MV Agusta	Brno	Czech GP
1	350cc	MV Agusta	Imatra	Finnish GP
1	500cc	MV Agusta	Imatra	Finnish GP
1	350cc	MV Agusta	Dundrod	Ulster GP
1	500cc	MV Agusta	Dundrod	Ulster GP

350cc - World Champion
500cc - World Champion
Note: Did not contest the final two rounds (Imola, Italy and Opatija, Yugoslavia).

1970

Position	Class	Machine	Circuit	Event
1	350cc	MV Agusta	Nürburgring	West German GP
1	500cc	MV Agusta	Nürburgring	West German GP
1	500cc	MV Agusta	Le Mans	French GP
1	350cc	MV Agusta	Opatija	Yugoslav GP
1	500cc	MV Agusta	Opatija	Yugoslav GP
1	350cc	MV Agusta	Isle of Man	Junior TT
1	500cc	MV Agusta	Isle of Man	Senior TT
1	350cc	MV Agusta	Assen	Dutch TT
1	500cc	MV Agusta	Assen	Dutch TT
1	500cc	MV Agusta	Spa Francorchamps	Belgian GP
1	350cc	MV Agusta	Sachsenring	East German GP
1	500cc	MV Agusta	Sachsenring	East German GP
1	350cc	MV Agusta	Brno	Czech GP
1	350cc	MV Agusta	Imatra	Finnish GP
1	500cc	MV Agusta	Imatra	Finnish GP
1	350cc	MV Agusta	Dundrod	Ulster GP
1	500cc	MV Agusta	Dundrod	Ulster GP
1	350cc	MV Agusta	Monza	Italian GP
1	500cc	MV Agusta	Monza	Italian GP

350cc - World Champion
500cc - World Champion
Note: Did not contest final round (Barcelona, Spain).

1971

Position	Class	Machine	Circuit	Event
1	350cc	MV Agusta	Salzburg	Austrian GP
1	500cc	MV Agusta	Salzburg	Austrian GP
1	350cc	MV Agusta	Hockenheim	West German GP
1	500cc	MV Agusta	Hockenheim	West German GP

Retired	350cc	MV Agusta	Isle of Man	Junior TT
1	500cc	MV Agusta	Isle of Man	Senior TT
1	350cc	MV Agusta	Assen	Dutch TT
1	500cc	MV Agusta	Assen	Dutch TT
1	500cc	MV Agusta	Spa Francorchamps	Belgian GP
1	350cc	MV Agusta	Sachsenring	East German GP
1	500cc	MV Agusta	Sachsenring	East German GP
Retired	350cc	MV Agusta	Brno	Czech GP
1	350cc	MV Agusta	Anderstorp	Swedish GP
1	500cc	MV Agusta	Anderstorp	Swedish GP
1	350cc	MV Agusta	Imatra	Finnish GP
1	500cc	MV Agusta	Imatra	Finnish GP
Retired	350cc	MV Agusta	Monza	Italian GP
Retired	500cc	MV Agusta	Monza	Italian GP

350cc - World Champion
500cc - World Champion

Note: Did not contest Dundrod, Ulster and Jarama, Spain.

1972

Position	Class	Machine	Circuit	Event
2	350cc	MV Agusta	Nürburgring	West German GP
1	500cc	MV Agusta	Nürburgring	West German GP
4	350cc	MV Agusta	Clermont-Ferrand	French GP
1	500cc	MV Agusta	Clermont-Ferrand	French GP
1	350cc	MV Agusta	Salzburg	Austrian GP
1	500cc	MV Agusta	Salzburg	Austrian GP
1	350cc	MV Agusta	Imola	Italian GP
1	500cc	MV Agusta	Imola	Italian GP
1	350cc	MV Agusta	Isle of Man	Junior TT
1	500cc	MV Agusta	Isle of Man	Senior TT
Retired	350cc	MV Agusta	Opatija	Yugoslav GP
Retired	500cc	MV Agusta	Opatija	Yugoslav GP
1	350cc	MV Agusta	Assen	Dutch TT
1	500cc	MV Agusta	Assen	Dutch TT
1	500cc	MV Agusta	Spa Francorchamps	Belgian GP
Retired	350cc	MV Agusta	Sachsenring	East German GP
1	500cc	MV Agusta	Sachsenring	East German GP
Retired	350cc	MV Agusta	Brno	Czech GP
1	500cc	MV Agusta	Brno	Czech GP
1	350cc	MV Agusta	Anderstorp	Swedish GP
1	500cc	MV Agusta	Anderstorp	Swedish GP
1	350cc	MV Agusta	Imatra	Finnish GP
1	500cc	MV Agusta	Imatra	Finnish GP

350cc - World Champion
500cc - World Champion

Note: Did not contest final round (Barcelona, Spain).

1973

Position	Class	Machine	Circuit	Event
1	350cc	MV Agusta	Paul Ricard	French GP
Retired	500cc	MV Agusta	Paul Ricard	French GP
Retired	350cc	MV Agusta	Salzburg	Austrian GP
Retired	500cc	MV Agusta	Salzburg	Austrian GP
Retired	350cc	MV Agusta	Hockenheim	West German GP
Retired	500cc	MV Agusta	Hockenheim	West German GP

1	350cc	MV Agusta	Monza	Italian GP
1	350cc	MV Agusta	Assen	Dutch TT
Retired	500cc	MV Agusta	Assen	Dutch TT
1	500cc	MV Agusta	Spa Francorchamps	Belgian GP
2	350cc	MV Agusta	Brno	Czech GP
1	500cc	MV Agusta	Brno	Czech GP
2	350cc	MV Agusta	Anderstorp	Swedish GP
2	500cc	MV Agusta	Anderstorp	Swedish GP
1	350cc	MV Agusta	Imatra	Finnish GP
1	500cc	MV Agusta	Imatra	Finnish GP

350cc - World Champion
500cc - 3rd

Note: 500cc Italian GP at Monza abandoned after fatal accident in 250cc event involving Jarno Saarinen and Renzo Pasolini. Also did not contest Isle of Man TT.

1974

Position	Class	Machine	Circuit	Event
1	350cc	Yamaha	Clermont-Ferrand	French GP
Retired	500cc	Yamaha	Clermont-Ferrand	French GP
1	350cc	Yamaha	Salzburg	Austrian GP
1	500cc	Yamaha	Salzburg	Austrian GP
1	350cc	Yamaha	Imola	Italian GP
Retired	500cc	Yamaha	Imola	Italian GP
1	350cc	Yamaha	Assen	Dutch TT
1	500cc	Yamaha	Assen	Dutch TT
2	500cc	Yamaha	Spa Francorchamps	Belgian GP
No start	350cc	Yamaha	Anderstorp	Swedish GP
Retired	500cc	Yamaha	Anderstorp	Swedish GP
6	500cc	Yamaha	Brno	Czech GP
1	350cc	Yamaha	Opatija	Yugoslav GP

350cc - World Champion
500cc - 4th

Note: Did not contest Nürburgring, Germany; Isle of Man TT; Imatra, Finland and Barcelona, Spain.

1975

Position	Class	Machine	Circuit	Event
2	350cc	Yamaha	Le Castellet	French GP
1	500cc	Yamaha	Le Castellet	French GP
1	350cc	Yamaha	Jarama	Spanish GP
Retired	350cc	Yamaha	Salzburgring	Austrian GP
Retired	500cc	Yamaha	Salzburgring	Austrian GP
Retired	350cc	Yamaha	Hockenheim	German GP
1	500cc	Yamaha	Hockenheim	German GP
2	350cc	Yamaha	Imola	Italian GP
1	500cc	Yamaha	Imola	Italian GP
4	350cc	Yamaha	Assen	Dutch TT
2	500cc	Yamaha	Assen	Dutch TT
Retired	500cc	Yamaha	Spa Francorchamps	Belgian GP
Retired	500cc	Yamaha	Anderstorp	Swedish GP
2	350cc	Yamaha	Imatra	Finnish GP
1	500cc	Yamaha	Imatra	Finnish GP
Retired	350cc	Yamaha	Brno	Czech GP
2	500cc	Yamaha	Brno	Czech GP

350cc – Runner-up
500cc – World Champion

Note: Did not contest Isle of Man TT and Opatija, Yugoslavia.

1976

Position	Class	Machine	Circuit	Event
Retired	350cc	MV Agusta	Le Mans	French GP
5	500cc	MV Agusta	Le Mans	French GP
Retired	350cc	MV Agusta	Salzburgring	Austrian GP
6	500cc	MV Agusta	Salzburgring	Austrian GP
Retired	350cc	MV Agusta	Mugello	Italian GP
Retired	500cc	Suzuki	Mugello	Italian GP
Retired	350cc	MV Agusta	Opatija	Yugoslav GP
1	350cc	MV Agusta	Assen	Dutch TT
Retired	500cc	Suzuki	Assen	Dutch TT
Retired	500cc	Suzuki	Spa Francorchamps	Belgian GP
Retired	350cc	MV Agusta	Imatra	Finnish GP
Retired	500cc	Suzuki	Imatra	Finnish GP
Retired	350cc	MV Agusta	Brno	Czech GP
Retired	500cc	Suzuki	Brno	Czech GP
Retired	350cc	MV Agusta	Nürburgring	German GP
1	500cc	MV Agusta	Nürburgring	German GP

1977

Position	Class	Machine	Circuit	Event
5	500cc	Yamaha	Imola	Italian GP
2	500cc	Yamaha	Le Castellet	French GP
Retired	500cc	Yamaha	Assen	Dutch TT
8	500cc	Yamaha	Spa Francorchamps	Belgian GP
9	500cc	Yamaha	Anderstorp	Swedish GP
Retired	500cc	Yamaha	Imatra	Finnish GP
2	500cc	Yamaha	Brno	Czech GP
9	500cc	Yamaha	Silverstone	British GP
3	750cc	Yamaha	Imola	Italian GP
2	750cc	Yamaha	Salzburgring	Austrian GP
4	750cc	Yamaha	Assen	Dutch TT
1	750cc	Yamaha	Hockenheim	German GP

750cc – 3rd

Note: 500cc and 750cc championships held at different dates; hence 500cc listing first, followed by 750cc.

Index

ND - #0353 - 270225 - C0 - 260/195/16 - PB - 9781780912172 - Gloss Lamination